Pararasan
and
Sagithini

THE MINI ENCYCLOPAEDIA OF

MAGIC

THE MINI ENCYCLOPAEDIA OF MAGIC

Bruce Smith

ARCTURUS

Published by Arcturus Publishing Limited
For Bookmart Limited
Registered Number 2372865
Trading as Bookmart Limited
Desford Road
Enderby
Leicester
LE9 5AD

This edition published 1995

Printed and bound in Great Britain

ISBN 1 900032 20 1

Editor: Shona Grimbly
Consultant Magicians: Anthony Owen and Marc Paul
Design: wilson design associates
Illustrator: Colin Woodman

CONTENTS

CARD TRICKS

♥

ROPE & RING TRICKS

♦

HANDKERCHIEF TRICKS

♠

COIN & BANKNOTE TRICKS

♣

INTRODUCTION

The art of the magician is to deceive and, paradoxically, the better a magician's audience is deceived, the better it is pleased. If the magician can successfully "bewitch, bother and bewilder" those who watch his act, they will go away with plenty to wonder at and talk about.

The Mini Encyclopaedia of Magic gives the apprentice magician an excellent grounding in the art of deception. From straightforward self-working card tricks like "Odd One Out" and "Clock Tower Card" to the truly startling effect of the "Buttonhole Release" rope trick and the mysterious vanishing and reappearance of the "Coin in a Ball of Wool", the budding magician is introduced to a wide variety of achievable illusions using playing cards, rope, rings, handkerchiefs, coins and banknotes.

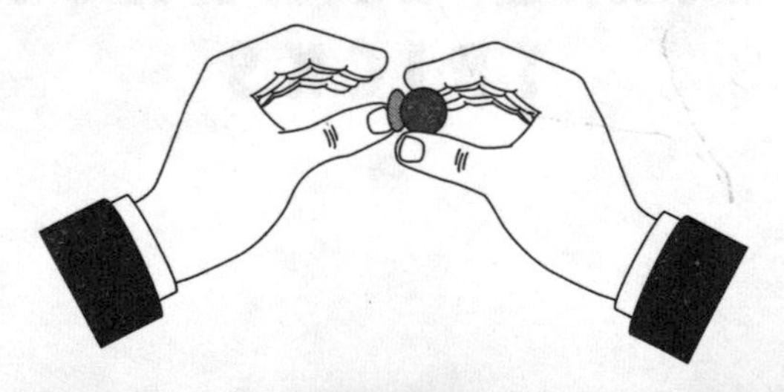

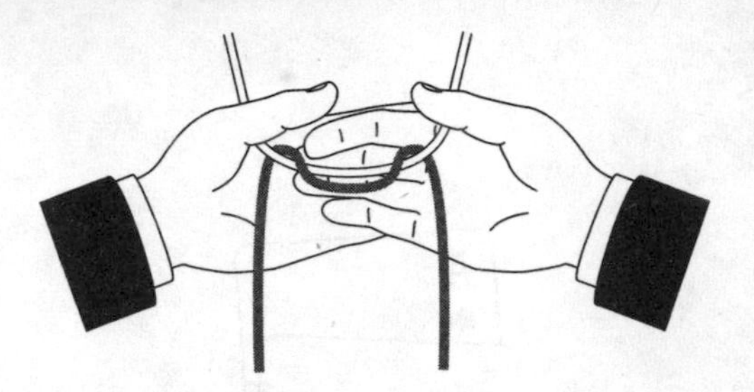

Written by a member of the Magic Circle, the book takes the reader through easy-to-follow illustrated step-by-step instructions to learn how to perform 80 astonishing illusions, while also imparting the secrets of classic magic skills such as forcing a card, palming, and sleight-of-hand vanishes. Woven in with the tricks is a wealth of amusing "patter" and "business" that help the magician put together an effective stage performance.

Packed with essential tips on equipment plus fascinating anecdotes about famous magicians, magic history and magic lore, *The Mini Encyclopaedia of Magic* is a "must" for every budding magician.

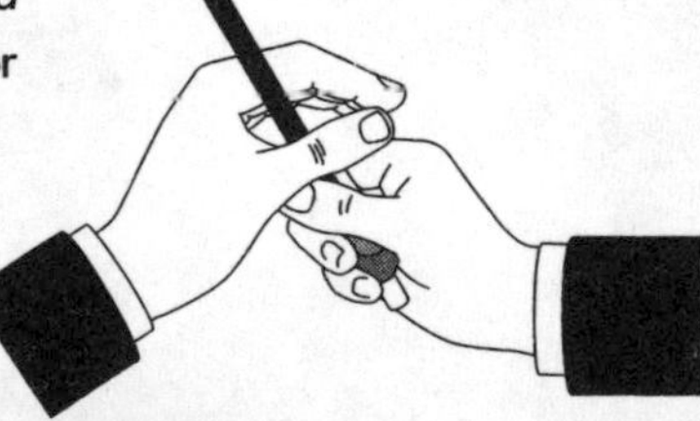

CARD TRICKS

GLOSSARY OF TERMS

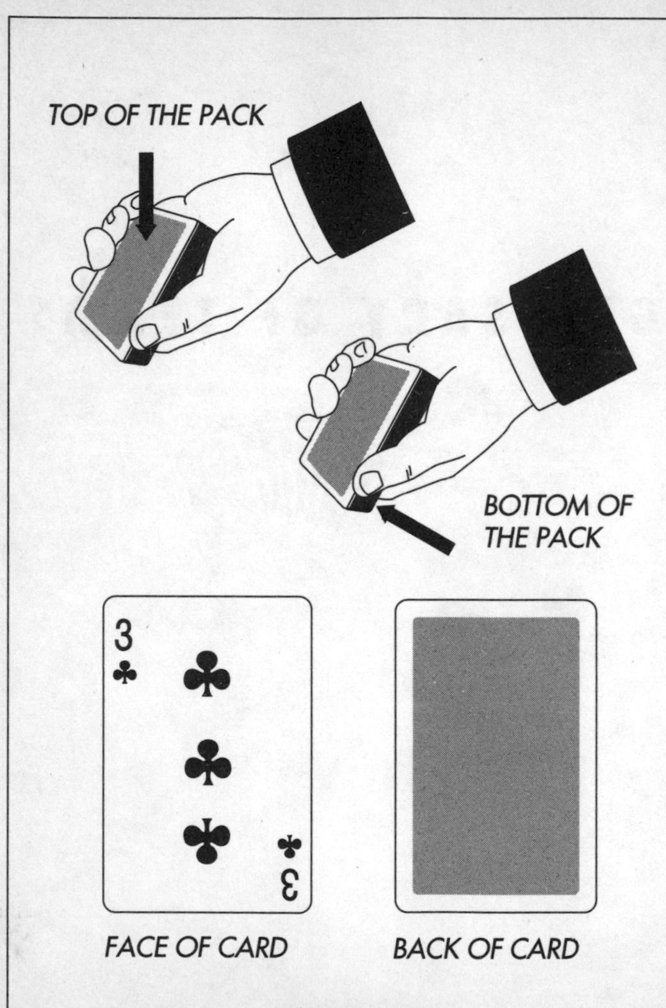
TOP OF THE PACK
BOTTOM OF THE PACK
3
3
FACE OF CARD
BACK OF CARD

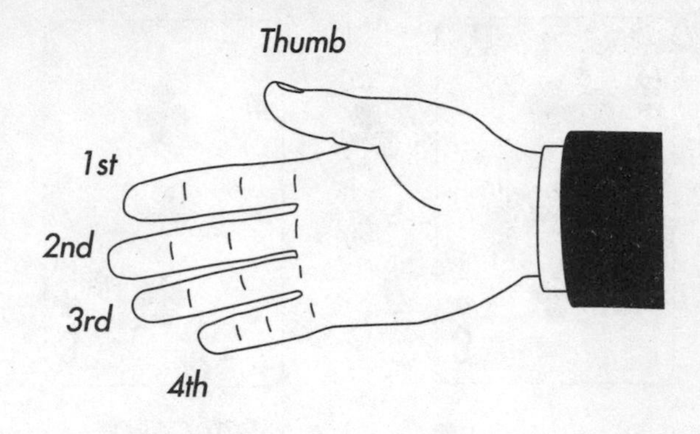

ONE WAY BACK DESIGN (NOT SYMMETRICAL)

MAJORITY OF PIPS POINTING DOWNWARDS

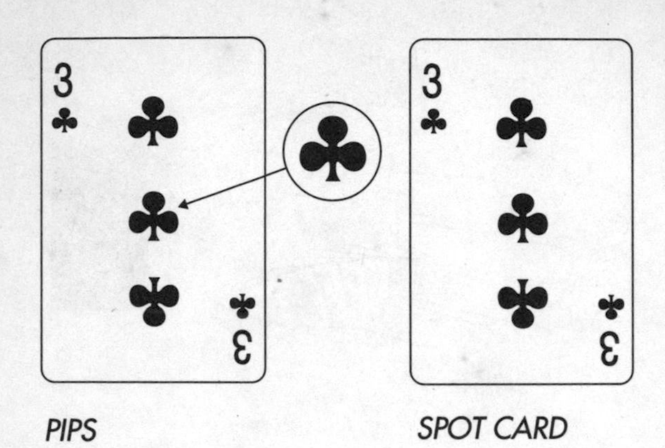
PIPS
SPOT CARD

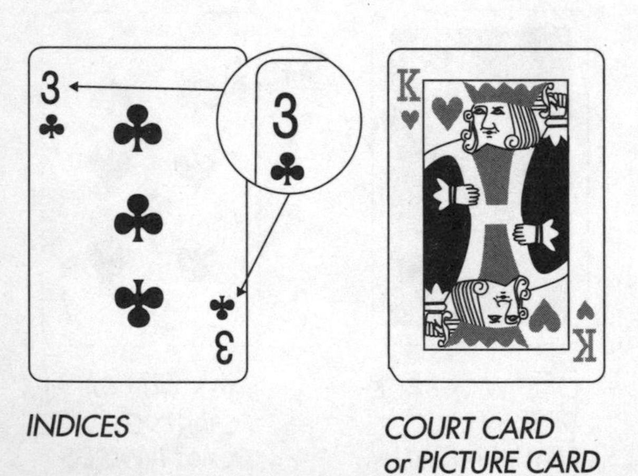
INDICES
COURT CARD
or PICTURE CARD

DEALING
POSITION
FAN OF
CARDS
CUTTING
THE PACK
COMPLETING
THE CUT

SELF-WORKING CARD TRICKS

♥ THE SEVEN CARD POKER HAND ♦

Effect *A spectator chooses any card from three poker hands by just thinking of it. The magician correctly identifies the chosen card.*

Preparation *No preparation is needed for this effect.*

• • • • • • • • • • • • • • •

1 Have the cards shuffled by the spectator while you explain that when gambling a poker player must always have an expressionless face – hence the term "poker face". Deal three hands of seven cards each, face up.

2 As you deal out the three hands, explain that you can find a spectator's chosen card by studying their facial expressions. Concentrate on the hands for a moment. Then ask a spectator to JUST THINK of any one card in any of the hands. Ask which hand the chosen card is in.

Sandwich the chosen pile between the other two.

3 Collect up the three hands and sandwich the pile containing the chosen card between the other two.

4 Deal out the same 21 cards into three face-up hands of seven cards, and again ask which pile contains the chosen card. Collect up the cards as before, sandwiching the indicated hand between the others. Explain to your audience once more how you should be able to tell which is the chosen card by looking at the spectator's face. Just a flicker of an eyelid or a twitch of an ear can give them away.

TOP TIPS FOR TRICKSTERS

Never repeat a trick for the same audience. The surprise is lost the second time and they will watch you more closely!

5 Repeat this dealing, questioning and sandwiching once more. The selected card will now automatically be the 11th card from the top.

6 Deal the cards one at a time on to the table face up, looking at the spectator. When you get to the 11th card, hesitate. Then dramatically show the audience the card that is the chosen card.

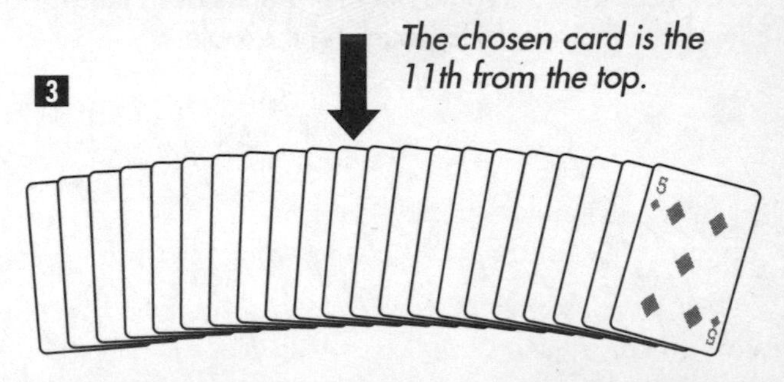

The chosen card is the 11th from the top.

THE HOOKER RISING CARDS

Many magicians used to believe that this effect, like the Indian Rope Trick, was a myth. The story was that in 1918 an amateur magician, Dr Hooker, put on a show during which he made selected cards rise out of a pack and float up in the air. Although the secret of this effect was lost for nearly 80 years, in November 1993 a Californian magician and illusion builder performed the Hooker Rising Cards at the 3rd Los Angeles Conference of Magic History.

♠ ODD ONE OUT ♣

Effect *A card flies invisibly from one pile to another.*

This trick works automatically. Try it out on a friend, following the instructions carefully.

• • • • • • • • • • • • • • •

1 Ask your friend to hold out their hands as in illustration 1 with their knuckles touching the table.

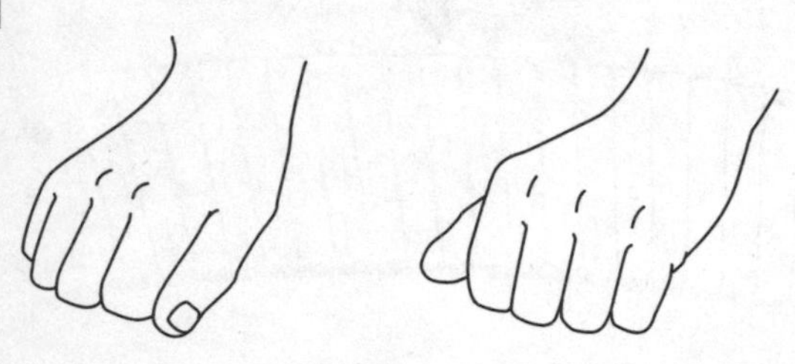

2 From your pack of cards put two cards into each gap between the fingers, except for the last gap, into which you put only ONE card – THE ODD CARD.

3 Starting from the left, remove each pair of cards and split them. Place them separately on the table making two piles (illustration 3).

4 Repeat this with all the pairs – splitting them and adding one card to each pile. Point out that two is an even number.

2 *Put two cards in each gap, except for the last gap.*

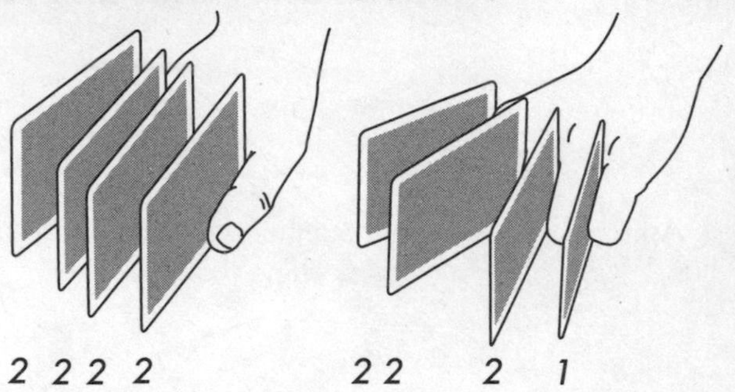

5 Ask your friend to choose one pile. Explain that you will add the odd card to the pile they choose. When they have selected a pile, bury the odd card somewhere in the middle. Point out that this pile is now odd and the other is even.

6 Replace the cards from the "odd" pile in pairs between the fingers of one hand, as you did originally – amazingly all the cards will be paired up and the odd card has vanished.

TOP TIPS FOR TRICKSTERS

Always practise what you are going to say with your tricks. This is known as the magician's "patter" and should be rehearsed just as carefully as the working and method of the trick.

3 *Deal the cards into two equal piles.*

7 Point out that there were an even number of cards. Your friend has two hands, ten fingers, eight gaps between them – all even numbers. The only odd thing in the trick is the one card which seems to have vanished.

8 Replace the "even" pile in pairs between the fingers of the other hand. You will be left with one odd card. It appears as though it has magically jumped across.

HARRY HOUDINI (1874-1926)

Although he later became famous for his daring death-defying escapes, in his early days in show business Houdini was billed as the "King of Kards" (sic). He would perform sleight-of-hand card tricks similar to the ones described in this book. Even when he was a world famous "escapologist" he would still feature card tricks in his stage performances.

♥ THE INVISIBLE DICE ♦

Effect *The magician spreads six cards out across the table and a spectator is given a sealed prediction. The magician gives a second spectator an invisible dice and asks them to roll it across the table top and call out the number it shows! Whatever the number they call the magician's prediction is correct!*

Requirements *You need five blue-backed cards – the Ace, Three, Four and Six of Clubs and the Five of Hearts. You will also need one red-backed card – the Two of Clubs. In addition, write a prediction which reads "You will choose the red card."*

Preparation *Put the cards into a pile which runs from top to bottom as follows – the face-down Three of Clubs, the face-up Ace of Clubs, the face-down Five of Hearts, the face-up Four of Clubs, the face-down Six of Clubs and the face-up Two of Clubs.*

• • • • • • • • • • • • • • • •

1 Deal out the cards from the pile from left to right. Explain to the audience that you have six cards – one to

2 *The cards turned the other way up.*

six – three face up and three face down. Tell them they will see why in just a moment (illustration 1).

2 Ask a member of your audience to act as safekeeper for your prediction envelope.

3 Reach into your pocket and mime removing your invisible dice. Tell your audience that this is the world famous invisible dice. "It is the only one in the world. Well, if there is another one, I've never seen it!"

4 Hand it to a member of the audience. Choose someone who you think will go along with the act and join in. It's no fun if they just stare at you and say "There's nothing there," so choose carefully.

5 Ask them to roll the dice across the table top. Tell them not to throw it too hard, or it might fall on the floor and take ages to find! When they have rolled the dice ask them what number they have on top. "Are you happy with that number or do you want to roll it again to make sure it's not loaded?" When they have decided on a number ask someone to read out the prediction, and continue for your big finish as in step 6.

6 i) If they choose number one, point to the Two of Clubs at the far right of the row. Tell them this is number one. Turn all the cards face down to show that it is the only red backed card!

ii) If they choose number two, point to the Two of Clubs. Again, turn all the cards face down to show that the two is red backed!

iii) If three is chosen count from left to right and show the third card is the Five of Hearts. Turn all the other cards face up to show it is the only red one out of the six!

iv) As for three, but count from right to left!

v) If five is chosen turn all the cards face up to show the Five of Hearts is the only red one!

vi) If six is chosen count from left to right and show the "sixth" card is the only one with a red back!

YOU WILL CHOOSE THE RED CARD

TOP TIPS FOR TRICKSTERS

When you perform try to relax and stand naturally. Don't fidget or shuffle your feet.

Effect *A pile of cards are mixed to a spectator's instructions, but end up in their original order.*

Requirements *For this you will require all 13 cards from one suit.*

Preparation *Set the cards in order Ace through to King as in illustration 1.*

•••••••••••••••

1 Spread the cards out face up on the table, as in illustration 1, to display the cards in suit order. Now explain to the audience that any casino will tell you that most of the traditional ways that cards are handled aren't particularly secure! Cutting cards does not change the order of the cards and there are many false shuffles to enable you to control the order of the cards while

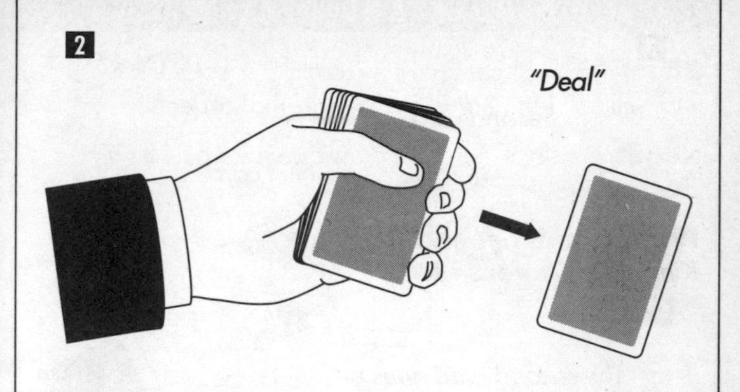

shuffling them. However, there is a method of really mixing cards which you will demonstrate that is called the *Duck and Deal*.

2 Gather up the pile face down in the dealing position and ask the spectator if they want you to deal or duck the first card. If they say "Deal", simply deal the card face down on the table (illustration 2). If they say "Duck", slide the first card under the second card (illustration 3) and place them both face down on the table (illustration 4).

TOP TIPS FOR TRICKSTERS

Always practise in front of a mirror or a video camera so that you can see exactly how your tricks will look to your audience.

The second card goes on top of the first – then both cards go on the table.

3 Ask the spectator if they want to deal or duck the new top card of the pile, and continue – following their instructions at every step – right through the pile. As far as the audience is concerned it now seems as if the cards have been mixed in a haphazard way, and you should emphasise that at each step it is the spectator's choice whether they wish to duck or deal. If you try this yourself you will be convinced that you have thoroughly shuffled

TOP TIPS FOR TRICKSTERS

Try to use a pack of cards which have a "linen" finish (this is usually marked on the box), as these are the easiest cards to handle.

the cards, but if you go through the pile you will be surprised to discover that in fact the cards are now in reverse order.

4 Collect up the cards from the table, keeping them face down, and repeat the process, going through the pile asking "Duck" or "Deal" with each card. Repeating the action adds to the effect and gives the impression that the cards are thoroughly shuffled. In fact what this

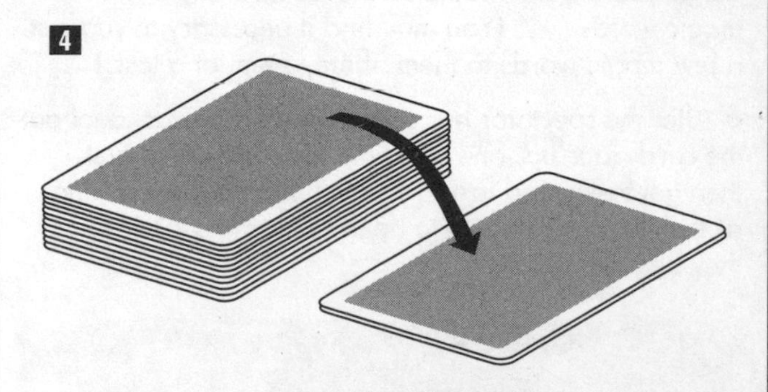

Both top cards go on the table.

TOP TIPS FOR TRICKSTERS

Never reveal the secret behind your tricks. If you can do the tricks people will think you are special and have magical powers – if they know that anybody can do them they will be less impressed.

second process does is to return the cards to the order they were in at the start of the trick.

5 At the end, after following all the spectator's instructions as to whether they want each card ducked or dealt on to the table, you should recap by saying, "The choice throughout has been yours. You have been the magician – I have only been the spectator following your instructions. You would expect the cards to be really mixed up, but as you are the magician please now say a few magic words . . ." (You may find it necessary to suggest a few magic words to them, if they seem at a loss.)

6 After the spectator has said the magic words, deal out the cards face up, one at a time. Deal slowly at first, then get faster and faster. This will increase the drama as the cards are shown to be in the same suit order as they began!

CARDINI (1899-1973)

Cardini was the stage name of the Welsh born magician Richard Pitchford. He found fame after he moved to America where he toured the theatres performing an act of flawless card manipulations, apparently plucking fans of cards from thin air. At the height of his fame he returned to London (where he had once been the manager of the magic department in the famous shop Gamages) to star in a Royal Variety Command Performance.

♥ ONE WAY CARDS ♦

Effect *A card is chosen from a pile and the magician successfully identifies it.*

Requirements *For this effect you can only use the cards shown in illustration 2. You are able to tell whether these cards have been turned around because the majority of the pips point one way – either up or down. This explains why they are called One Way Cards.*

Preparation *Arrange the cards beforehand so the majority of the pips on the cards all point the same way.*

•••••••••••••••

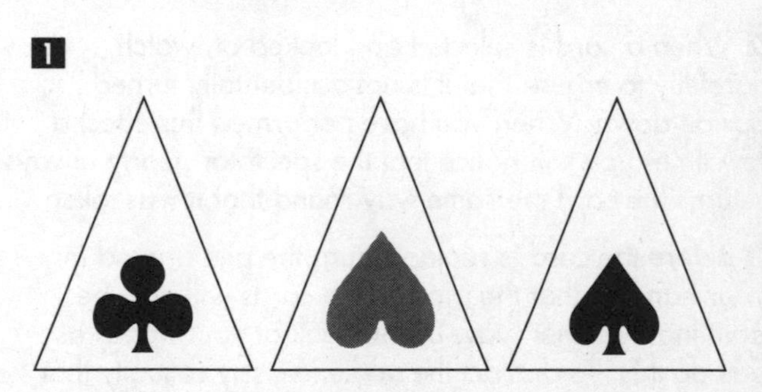

All these suits point up.

1 Start by having the cards thoroughly shuffled. Show the audience that the cards are all different and then fan them face down for one to be freely selected.

2

2 When a card is selected and looked at, watch carefully to ensure that it is not accidentally turned upside down. When you have performed this effect a few times you will notice that the spectator nearly always returns the card the same way round that it was taken.

3 Before the card is replaced turn the pile around in your hand so that the pips on the cards will now be pointing the other way. Do not look at your hands as you do this. To distract the audience, say casually that the spectator could have chosen any one of the cards, and fan the cards again so the audience can see they are all different. Do not look at the cards, or the audience will accuse you of cheating! Ask the audience to remember the card chosen, and make sure everyone has seen it. This is a good time to turn the pile around as the audience is now more interested in the chosen card than in what you are doing. This is a basic form of magician's misdirection.

4 Ask the spectator to replace the selected card anywhere in the pile. It is now simple for you to find this card by dealing the cards face up and looking for the one with the pips pointing in a different direction (see illustration 3).

♠ THE SEVEN PILE TRICK ♣

Effect *A spectator has a free choice of four piles of cards. The magician has accurately predicted which pile would be selected.*

Requirements *Write a prediction, as in illustration 2, reading "YOU WILL CHOOSE THE SEVEN PILE". You also need four face-down piles of cards containing i) the four Sevens; ii) any seven odd value cards; iii) two Threes and an Ace; and iv) an Eight, Six, Four and Two.*

•••••••••••••••••

1

2

YOU WILL CHOOSE THE SEVEN PILE

1 Ask a spectator to select any one of the four-face down piles. Assure them they can change their mind until they finally settle on one chosen pile.

2 If they choose i), ii), or iii) ask them to read the prediction. You now have an "out" for each pile. If they chose i) show they picked the only pile with the four sevens. If they chose ii) count the cards face down to show it is the only pile containing seven cards. And if they chose iii) show that it is the only pile in which the values add up to seven.

3

YOU WILL CHOOSE THE EVEN PILE

3 If they chose iv) you pick up the prediction and display it – as in illustration 3 – keeping your thumb over the "S" so that it appears to read: "YOU WILL CHOOSE THE EVEN PILE". Show that their selected pile is the only one which contains even cards. Whichever pile they choose it seems as though you knew all along!

TOP TIPS FOR TRICKSTERS

Your tricks will always have more impact if you "routine" three or four of them together to make a short show.

♥ CLOCK TOWER CARD ♦

Effect *A spectator freely selects the only red card in the pack – and proves your prediction correct.*

Requirements *Remove all the black cards and one single red card from the pack (the value of the red card does not matter). Discard the rest of the pack.*

Preparation *Prepare a prediction (as in illustration 3) which reads "YOU WILL NOT CHOOSE A BLACK CARD". Put the red card in the 13th position from the top of the pile.*

•••••••••••••••

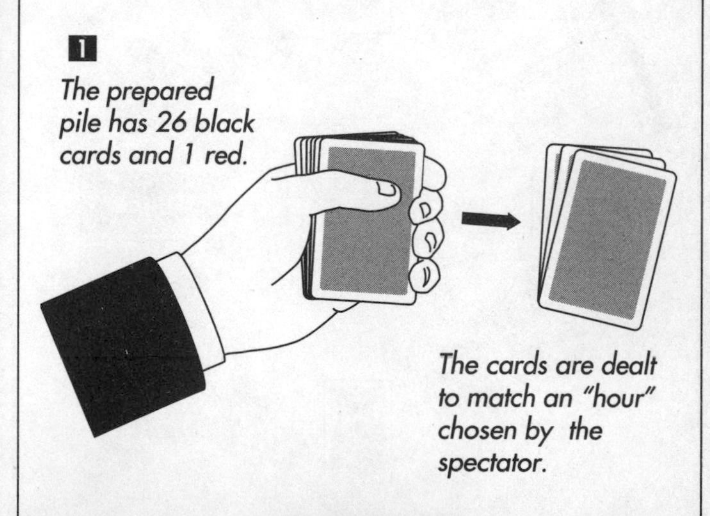

1

The prepared pile has 26 black cards and 1 red.

The cards are dealt to match an "hour" chosen by the spectator.

1 Put the prediction face down on the table. In this effect do not let the audience see the face of the cards.

2 Ask someone to picture a clock tower and imagine it chiming any hour. Ask them to take the pile of cards where you can't see them and count off the number of cards that matches their chosen hour (i.e. between one and twelve). They keep the cards they have dealt off and hand you back the rest of the pile.

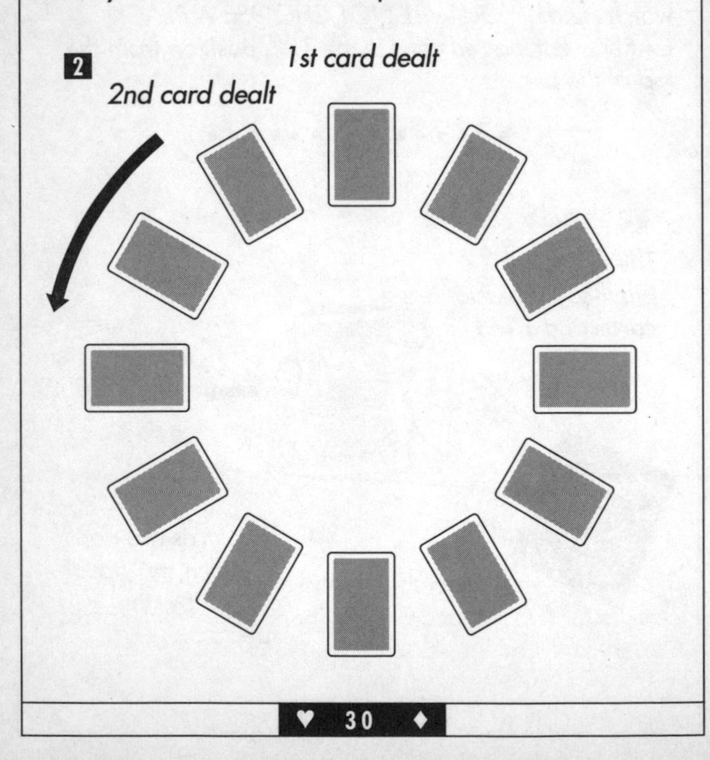

3 Deal cards off the top of the pile around the table to make a clockface (illustration 2). Start at the 12 o'clock position and deal the next 11 cards round anti-clockwise to make the face.

4 Ask the spectator what time they chose, and turn over the card in that position. It will be the red card. Ask them to read out the prediction. The chances are they will not be impressed as this is just a 50/50 chance.

3

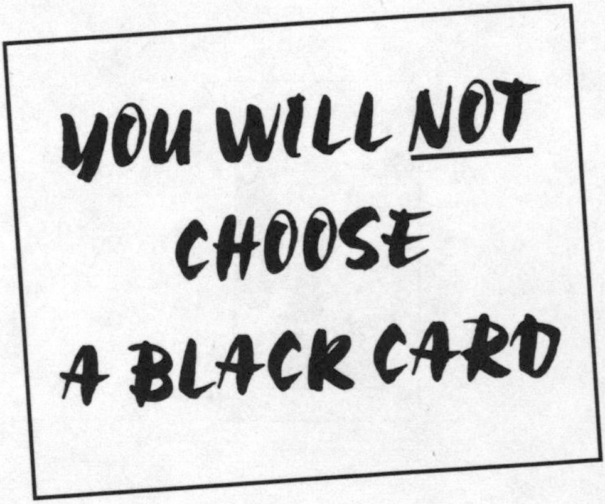

YOU WILL NOT
CHOOSE
A BLACK CARD

5 But when you reveal that all the other cards in the clockface, in their hand and in the pile are black cards, then they will be impressed!

FAKE CARDS

All the tricks in this section are accomplished using fake cards which can be easily made at home.

♥ QUEENS TO FOURS ♦

Effect *The four Queens are shown singly. They each magically transform into the corresponding Four. Everything can then be examined.*

Requirements *You will need to make a fake card by carefully cutting out the two shaded areas marked in illustration 1 from a Queen of Hearts. In addition to this fake card you will need the four Fours.*

Preparation *Arrange the five cards in a pile face up with the Four of Hearts on top and the fake Queen on top of that, giving the illusion that this is a complete Queen of Hearts. The cut-out areas in the Queen will not be noticed by the spectator. The heart in the Four of Hearts is in the right position to complete this deception.*

● ● ● ● ● ● ● ● ● ● ● ● ● ● ● ● ●

1

1 Hold the pile squared in the left hand and display to the audience the face card, apparently a regular Queen of Hearts.

2 Turn the left hand over so that the backs of the cards are uppermost, and with your right hand reach under the pile. Apparently you are going to slide out

2

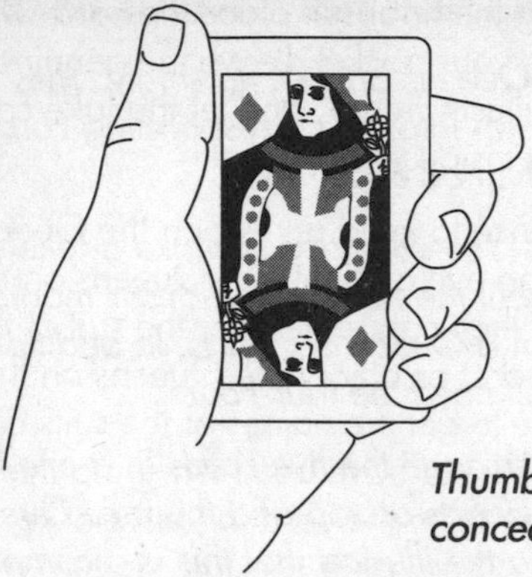

Thumb and little finger conceal corners.

the Queen of Hearts face down. In reality your right fingers contact the Four of Hearts through the hole in the Queen and push the Four out of the pile. Grab the card with the right hand and, keeping it face down, place it on the table.

3 Turn the pile in the left hand back face up. You now appear to show a Queen of a different suit. Illustration 2 shows how your left thumb and fingers can cover the unmatching corner indices.

4 Repeat the process of reversing your left hand and pulling out the next Four, and placing it face down on the table. Do the same with the next Four. As you place each card on the table dramatically name it. Do not rush this. Make sure the audience can see your hands are empty and not holding any extra cards.

5 After displaying the final suit place the card, with the back outwards, in your pocket. Leave the genuine card sticking out as in illustration 3, and let the fake card secretly slip down inside your pocket.

6 Ask your audience to keep an eye on the Queen in your pocket and an eye on the three Queens on the table. Ask them if they can remember the suit of the Queen in your pocket or any of the Queens on the table. They may manage to get the names of the suits correct – but tell them they should have been watching the values more closely. Show them the card in your pocket has turned into a Four. Then ask a spectator to turn over the three cards on the table. To the amazement of the audience these have turned into Fours as well.

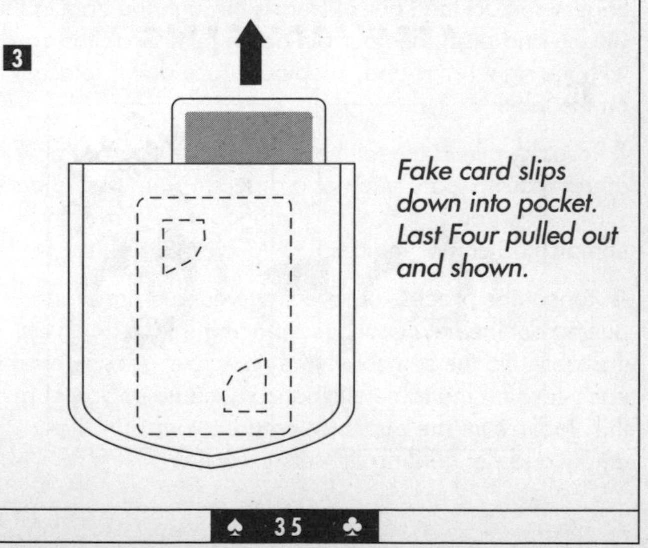

Fake card slips down into pocket. Last Four pulled out and shown.

♠ JOKER'S WILD ♣

Effect *A message appears magically on the face of the Joker under impossible conditions.*

Requirements *For this you require two identical Jokers, a few extra cards and an elastic band.*

Preparation *Prepare one of the Jokers by writing a suitable message on it as in illustration 1. Add this Joker to the face of the pile and put the elastic band around the whole pile.*

Cut the other Joker in half and discard the bottom half. The elastic band holds the half Joker in position covering the secret message, so the card appears to the audience as a single complete joker.

●●●●●●●●●●●●●●●

1

JOKER JOKER

JOKER HAPPY BIRTHDAY! JOKER

2

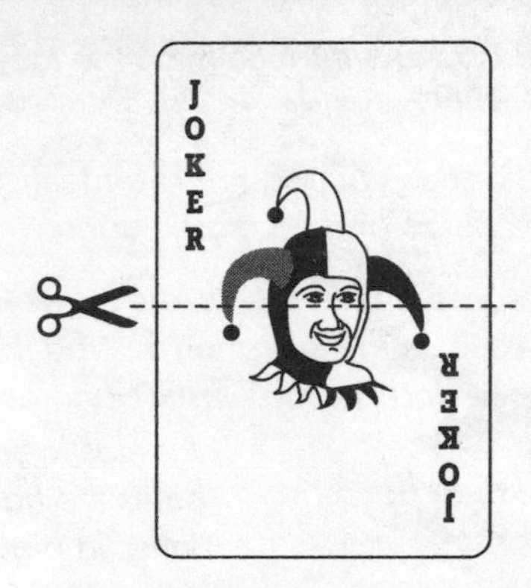

Cut the second Joker in half.

1 Show the Joker on the face of the pile. Tell the audience that the Joker is very clever. In fact, the Joker is actually the most intelligent card in the pack. He has a degree in spelling . . .

2 Turn the pile over and pull the genuine Joker out from under the elastic band (illustration 4). Ensure that you keep the Joker face down. Ask a spectator to keep their hand on top of the Joker. Take the same pen or pencil you used to write on the card and place it under their hand next to the Joker.

TOP TIPS FOR TRICKSTERS

Never turn your back on an audience – that's when they might sneak out!

3 Discard the rest of the pile. Take care that the audience do not see the half Joker on the face of the pile as you place it to one side.

An elastic band holds the half Joker in place.

4 Now turn the Joker face up to show that a message has magically appeared! . . . proving that this really is the world's most intelligent Joker.

5 You can make any suitable message appear on the card. For example, you could have "Happy Birthday", "Congratulations", or the name of your client or your company!

6 An even more impressive effect is obtained by combining this effect with the Clock Tower trick, so that you can apparently make the name of a freely chosen card appear on the face of the Joker. You can have fun by pretending that the Joker is also a magician. Explain that he is going to do the trick by reading the minds of your friends.

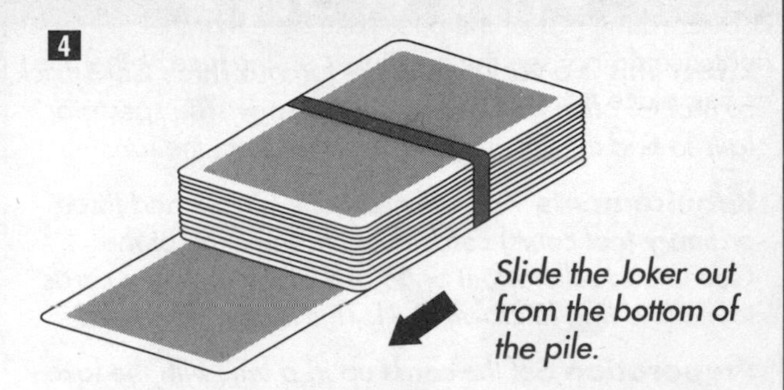

Slide the Joker out from the bottom of the pile.

DAI VERNON (1894-1993)

Dai Vernon is still affectionately remembered by magicians as "The Professor" because of his apparently endless fountain of magical knowledge. Born in Canada, by the age of 12 Vernon had mastered all the sleight-of-hand tricks in the classic book on card handling – The Expert at the Card Table. *Vernon fell in love with magic and spent the rest of his life baffling everyone with his ability. At top nightspots in New York he performed his elegant Harlequin Act, which concluded with him filling the stage with live butterflies! He turned down the opportunity to become a famous stage magician and became a lecturer and author on his true love – close-up sleight-of-hand and card magic. He spent the last 30 years of his life in Hollywood, as a mentor for many great close-up magicians. He died aged 98.*

♠ FIND THE LADY ♣

Effect *This is a variation of the famous Three Card Trick or Monte, often known as Find the Lady. The spectator fails to find the Queen as it vanishes from the fan.*

Requirements *You will need one Queen and three ordinary (not court) cards. Cut off one edge of the Queen and sellotape it on to one of the ordinary cards to make a flap (illustration 1). This is your fake card.*

Preparation *Set the cards up in a fan, with the fake card with the Queen flap at the bottom. Insert one of the ordinary cards under the flap (as in illustration 2) and the other card goes on top to cover everything. It should appear that the Queen is in the centre of the fan (see illustration 3).*

• • • • • • • • • • • • • • • • • • • •

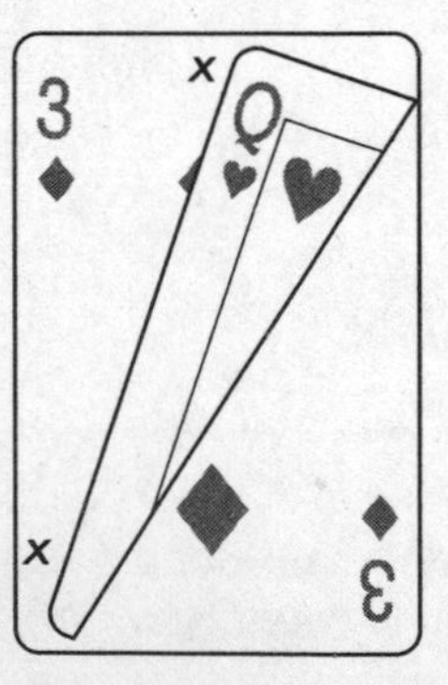

Stick Queen flap to the other card with a hinge of sellotape between the Xs.

2

1 Display the fan face up to your audience. Point out the Queen in the centre. Explain that the Three Card Trick or Find the Lady has been used to win money for many years. You can see it performed all over the world, in Times Square in New York, at racecourses, in bars – anywhere that card sharpers and conmen think that they can win some money.

TOP TIPS FOR TRICKSTERS

Never force your tricks on your friends. Wait until they ask to see them.

2 Turn the fan face down and ask a spectator to remove the card they think is the Queen. They will remove the centre card. If you are careful not to reveal the flap you can show the other two ordinary cards.

3

3 When the spectator turns over the card they believe to be the Queen, they will discover it has changed. They

TOP TIPS FOR TRICKSTERS

Have a look through the tricks in this book to see if you can put together your own act.

have been caught once again! If you wish, you can write a surprise personal message on the card. You could write, "You owe me £100" or "I hope that's taught you never to gamble with strangers!"

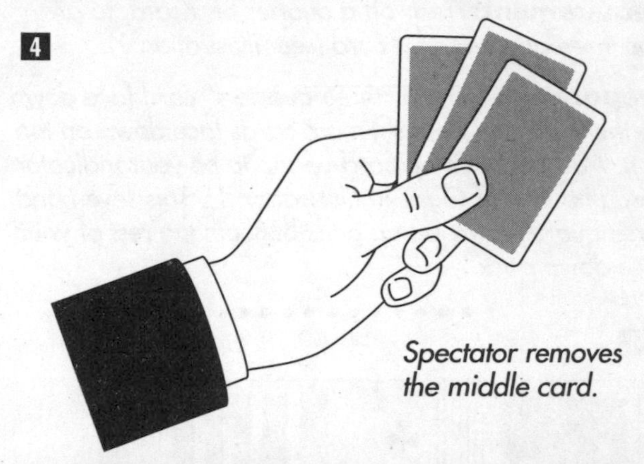

Spectator removes the middle card.

JOHANN N. HOFZINSER (1806-1875)

The Austrian Hofzinser was one of the first to transform card magic from the tricks of low conmen into sophisticated artistry. He frequently performed his sleight-of-hand magic for gentry and royalty. He created and developed many original effects, routines and plots which are still performed by close-up magicians around the world today. His book Hofzinser's Card Conjuring *is a classic among lovers of card magic.*

♠ CALCULATOR CARD ♣

Effect *The magician calculates that a freely chosen card is six and three-quarters from the top – and it is!*

Requirements *Tear off a quarter of a card, to give you three-quarters of a card (see illustration 1).*

Preparation *Set the "three-quarters" card face down on the table and deal six more cards face down on top of it. Add one face-up card on top to be your indicator card (the Two of Clubs in illustration 1). This seven and three-quarter card set-up goes beneath the rest of your face-down pack.*

1

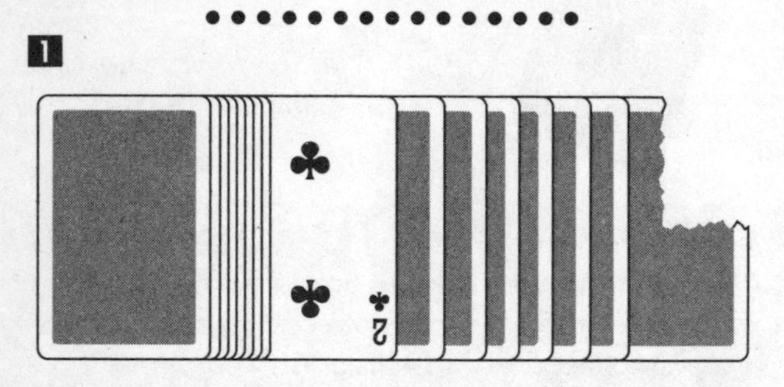

1 Fan the cards out face down for a spectator to select one. As you do this, be careful you do not fan too far and expose the face-up card.

2 Ask the spectator to remember the card and place it face down on top of the pack.

3 Ask the spectator to cut the pack wherever they like. Ask them to complete the cut (illustrations 2 and 3). Apparently the card is lost somewhere in the centre of the deck. In reality your prepared stack is on top of it.

Ask your audience if they think it would be a good trick if you went through the pack and found one card face up – and that was the freely selected card. They will probably agree that it would.

4 Say to them that you do not do good tricks – you only do miracles! Fan through the pack face down to reveal your face-up card. Cut it to the top. When the spectator says it is not their selection, explain that it is your calculator card that will calculate where their selection is. Pretend to listen to the face-up card and then announce the total is "six and three-quarters"! When you say "six and three-quarters" look slightly embarrassed, and look at your calculator card as though it really did talk to you. Apologise to your audience and say that the calculator card must be having an "off day". Once again you ask the calculator card the position of the chosen card. Again you pretend that it says "six and three-quarters". This a very funny situation with you talking and disagreeing with the calculator card.

5 Deal six cards off the top of the pack and then display the three-quarters card. The next card will be the chosen card. The calculator card is always correct!

♥ KINGS TO ACES ♦

Effect *A fan of four Kings changes into the four Aces!*

Requirements *For this effect you will need four Aces, four Kings, a Joker, some scissors and some glue. To make the special fake cards cut the four Kings diagonally in half from the bottom left to the top right corner (illustration 1). Glue half of each King into position on the corresponding Ace (illustration 2). Now the cards can be fanned to show either the four Kings or, when fanned the other way, the four Aces.*

Preparation *Set up the cards with all the Kings in the top left hand corner and the Joker on top (illustration 3).*

• • • • • • • • • • • • • • •

1

2

1 Display the Joker and explain that in many games the Joker is wild and can be used to represent any card. It is almost as if the Joker changes into any card. Explain that you can use your magical powers to do this to any card! Say that if you were playing a game of poker, a hand with four Kings and a wild Joker would be very good and you would probably bet a large amount of money on the outcome of the game.

TOP TIPS FOR TRICKSTERS

Never get talked into showing tricks that you haven't rehearsed fully.

2 Fan the cards to show the four Kings – as in illustration 3. The Joker covers the split on the face card.

3 Square the cards up and turn them around in your hand. Say your magical incantation and explain that

although you know the only hand that can beat your hand is the four Aces, you are going to use your magical powers to make sure you cannot be beaten. When you fan out the cards (illustration 4) they have changed into the four Aces. Wow!

You can use this same half card principle to apparently print blank cards (stick blank card on to the face of four cards as you did with the Kings). You can tell the tale of the Joker being a magical printer who changes

the four blank cards into regular cards. Or you could say how you made sure that you won a game of cards by making all the other player's cards vanish.

JEAN HUGARD (1872-1959)

Hugard was an Australian magician who performed all over the world, before finally making his home in America. In his stage show he featured the famous Bullet Catch effect. This is a highly dangerous and dramatic effect which has claimed the lives of 12 magicians. However, it is probably as an author that he is best remembered today, particularly for his highly recommended works with Fred Braue on card magic – The Royal Road to Card Magic *and* Expert Card Technique.

♥ SCARLET PIMPERNEL ♦

They seek him here, they seek him there,
those Frenchies seek him everywhere.
Is he in heaven? Or is he in hell?
That darned elusive Pimpernel.

Effect *The "scarlet" court card vanishes from a pile of three cards.*

Requirements *For this effect you will need three spot cards and one court card.*

Preparation *Cut the court card in half widthways and stick it on to the back of one of the spot cards (illustration 1). Discard the other half of the court card.*

• • • • • • • • • • • • • • •

1 Step the three cards in your left hand, as in illustration 2, so that the half court card is showing in the middle. Explain that the court card represents the famous Scarlet Pimpernel.

2 Pull out the card behind the court card (the Two of Diamonds in illustration 2). Turn it face down and slide it back behind the court card (illustration 3), but slide it square with the centre card. Now turn the pile over.

3 Pull out the face down card which is sticking out (illustration 4). In our effect this is the Two of Hearts. Turn it

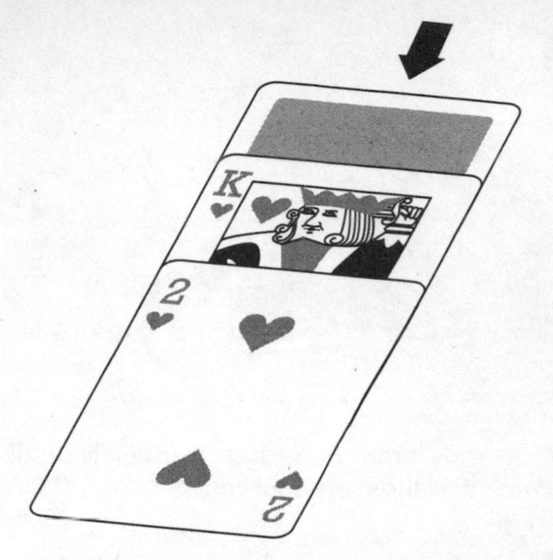

face up and replace it face up behind the other two cards (illustration 5). Turn the pile face down again.

4 Holding the cards in your left hand step the three cards away from you to show three backs as in illustration 6. Ask a spectator to guess which one of the cards is the court card. Most people will select the middle card but it doesn't matter if they don't.

TOP TIPS FOR TRICKSTERS

It is always good to finish with your best trick.

4

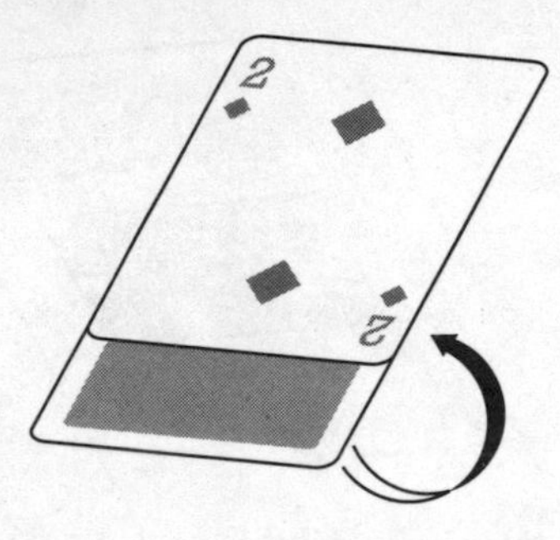

5 Turn over all three cards together (as in illustration 7) to show that all three are spot cards!

5

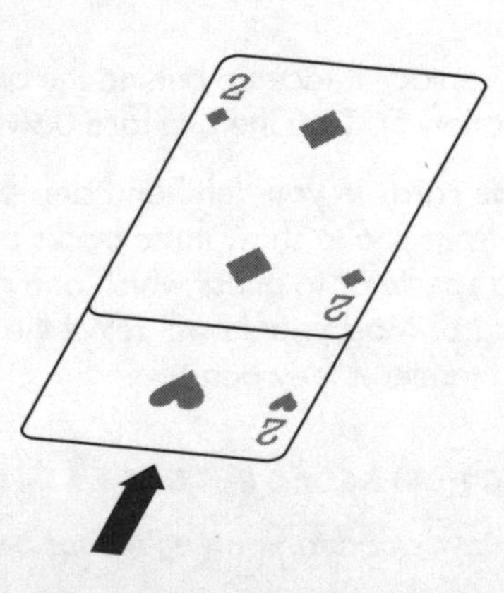

6

6 Deal the cards face up one at a time to show that the Scarlet Pimpernel has escaped once again!

7

THE GLIDE

♥ THE GLIDE MOVE ♦

The glide move enables you to secretly substitute one card for another. First we will teach you the move, and then some tricks which use it.

• • • • • • • • • • • • • • • • • • •

1 Hold a pile of cards in your left hand in the position shown in illustration 1. This displays the face card to the audience. Notice that your little finger of the left hand is curled around the edge almost touching the face card (the Two of Diamonds in the illustration).

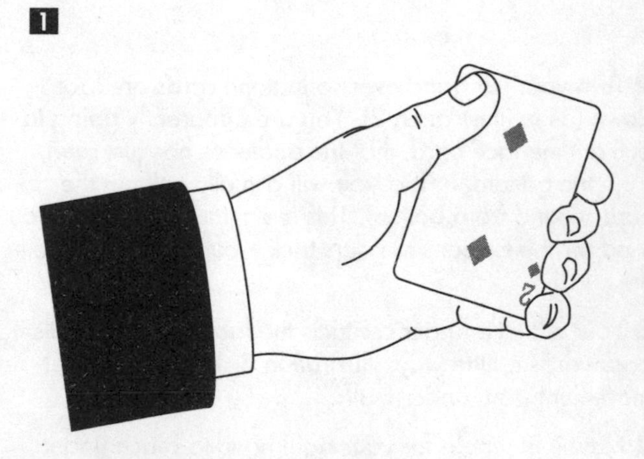

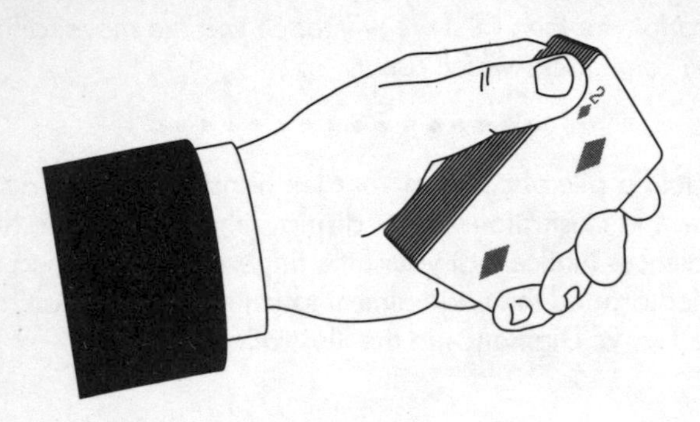

2 Turn your left hand over so that the cards are face down (as in illustration 2). You are apparently going to pull out the face card, that the audience has just seen, from the bottom. In fact you will actually pull out the card second from bottom. This is similar to the move you used for the Queens to Fours trick – but without a hole in the card!

3 Your left little finger contacts the face card and pulls it backwards a little way. Illustration 3 shows this secret movement from underneath.

4 Now it is simple for your right hand to reach under the pile and slide out the card which is one from the bottom (illustration 4). The audience believes this to be

3

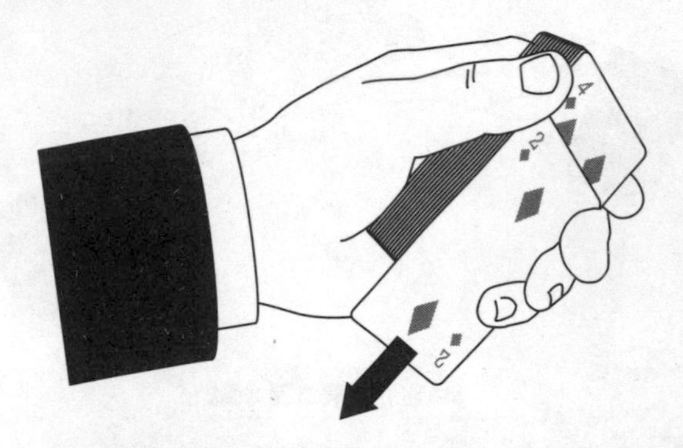

the card which they saw on the face a moment before. If you have difficulty pulling back the card with just the little finger you can use the right fingertips to push it back when they reach under to pull out the card.

As you will see in this section there are many great tricks you can do with this move, so it is worth learning and practising it until you can do it perfectly.

TOP TIPS FOR TRICKSTERS

Your audience will be more impressed if you do just one or two tricks really well, than several tricks poorly.

S.W. ERDNASE

The Expert at the Card Table *by S.W. Erdnase, first published in 1902, is generally considered to be the card magician's bible. It describes all the major card sleights necessary to cheat at gambling and to perform magic. Yet its author is shrouded in mystery. The book was written under the pseudonym of S.W. Erdnase as the author was a successful card cheat who was revealing the secrets of his dangerous livelihood. But many magicians believe the key to his true identity lies in his name – read backwards it hides Andrews. It is now generally thought that Erdnase was Milton Franklin Andrews, a professional gambler who became famous at the age of 33 – not as a magician, but for shooting three girlfriends and committing suicide. Not all magicians are nice people!*

Effect *This effect shows you how you can use the glide move to force a card.*

Requirements *You can use any pile of cards.*

Preparation *Set the cards so that you know the name of the bottom card.*

• • • • • • • • • • • • • • • •

1 Hold the cards face down in your left hand in position for the glide move. Do not let the audience see the card on the face.

1

2

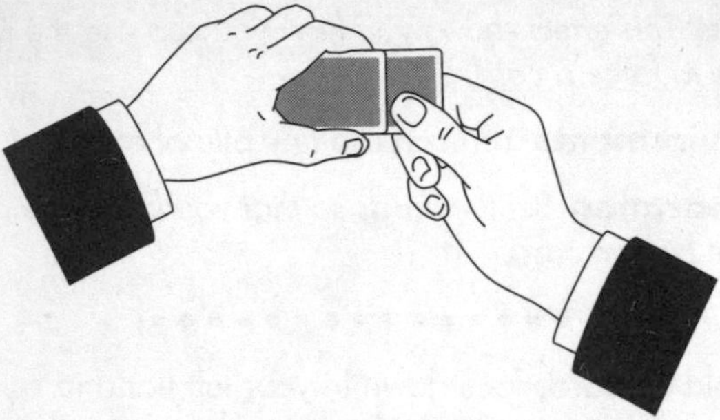

2 Ask a spectator to call "stop" at any time while you deal cards on to the table. Tell them that the card they call stop on is the one you will use.

3 Perform the glide move with your little finger (illustration 1). With your right hand pull the second card from bottom of the pack and deal it face down on to the table (illustration 2).

4 Reminding the spectator that they can call "stop" any time they wish, continue dealing keeping the known card – the force card – pulled back. Each time it is the card second from the bottom you deal on to the table.

TOP TIPS FOR TRICKSTERS

Use a new pack of cards for each performance. Grubby old cards look unprofessional.

5 When they say "stop", your right hand takes the real bottom card – your force card – and pulls that forward from the bottom of the pile (illustration 3). Hand this to the spectator. Even though they called stop whenever they wanted you can reveal the name of their card.

RICKY JAY

This outrageous Californian performer must be the only person to become the talk of New York and the theatre's "hot ticket" with a show consisting primarily of card tricks! His one-man show "Ricky Jay and his Fifty-Two Assistants" was an Off-Broadway hit in 1994. Jay also holds the World Record for throwing single playing cards the greatest distance.

♠ FAULTY FOLLOWER ♣

Effect *A spectator attempts – unsuccessfully – to follow the magician's simple instructions.*

Requirements *For this you require eight cards – four for you and four for your assistant.*

• • • • • • • • • • • • • • • •

1 Hold your cards in your lefthand face-down glide position. Get a friend to copy all your actions with their pile of cards. Ask them, "How good are you at following instructions? I have a simple test for you using just four cards. And if you do well you could win a prize!" At this point offer them a suitable outlandish prize like a new car or a round-the-world cruise.

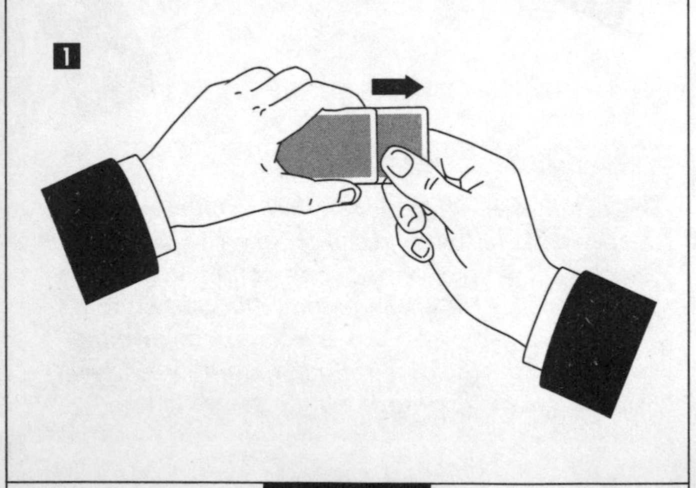

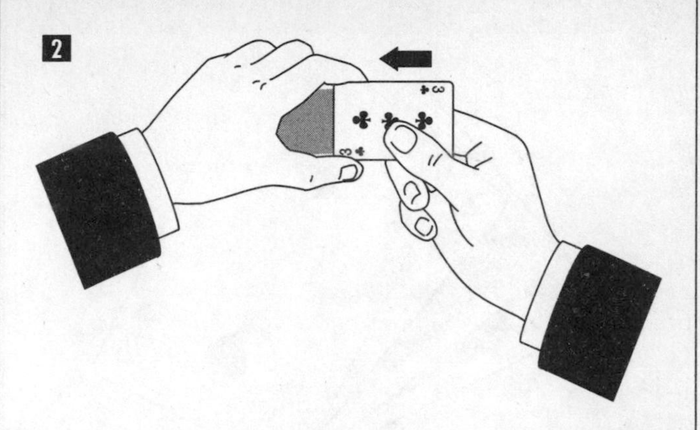

2 Say, "Now watch very carefully. All I do is . . . " Slide out the bottom card, turn it face up and place it on top of the pile (illustrations 1 and 2). Get your friend to do the same.

3 Slide out the new bottom card and place it on top without reversing it. Your friend does the same.

4 Slide out the new bottom card, turn it face up and place it on top of the pile. Your friend does the same. Turn both piles over.

TOP TIPS FOR TRICKSTERS

Remember that when you are performing card tricks your audience will be watching your hands closely. Make sure they are clean!

Performer's cards when dealt on the table.

5 Slide out the bottom card and deal it on to the table to show it is face down. Perform the glide move and show your next card is also face down. Fan the top two cards to show they are both face up. Because your friend does not know about the secret glide move their cards will be mixed up (illustration 4). Even though they followed you exactly they still got it wrong!

TOP TIPS FOR TRICKSTERS

Make sure you have a clean dry surface to work on. It might be worth buying a small piece of carpet to use as your "close-up mat".

TOP TIPS FOR TRICKSTERS

Never tell your audience what you are about to do. It spoils the surprise and they will know if things don't go according to plan!

Spectator's cards!

6 You can repeat this with someone else or do it with a group of people – each with four cards – all trying, unsuccessfully, to follow you. If you do repeat this over and over again it is a good idea to get progressively faster and faster. The more people that are involved, the better it will look. And as it gets faster it will seem more and more comical to the audience watching and those participating.

Effect *The spectator fails an observation test as a card magically changes.*

Requirements *For this you will require the four Kings and one odd card. We have chosen to use an Ace in the description. It is the Ace of Hearts in the illustration.*

Preparation *Set the pile face down with the Ace on top of the four Kings. The spectators must not know how many cards you have.*

● ● ● ● ● ● ● ● ● ● ● ● ● ● ● ●

1 Hold the pile in the left hand in the face-down glide position. Pull out the first King from the bottom of the pile and place it face up on the table. Pull out the second King and drop that face up on top of the first King.

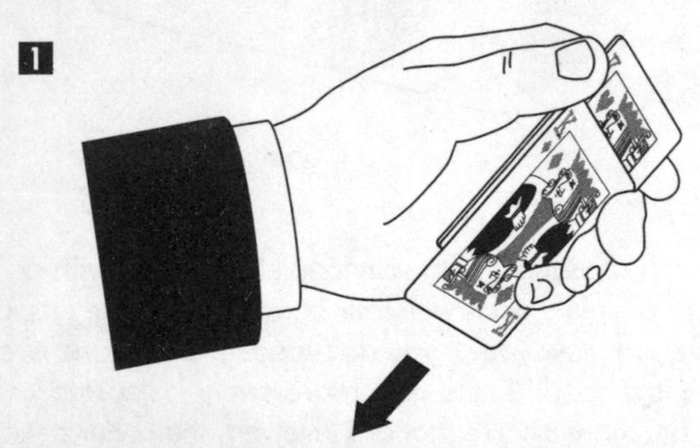

2 Perform the glide on the next card (illustration 1) and, with the right hand, pull out the top two cards squared

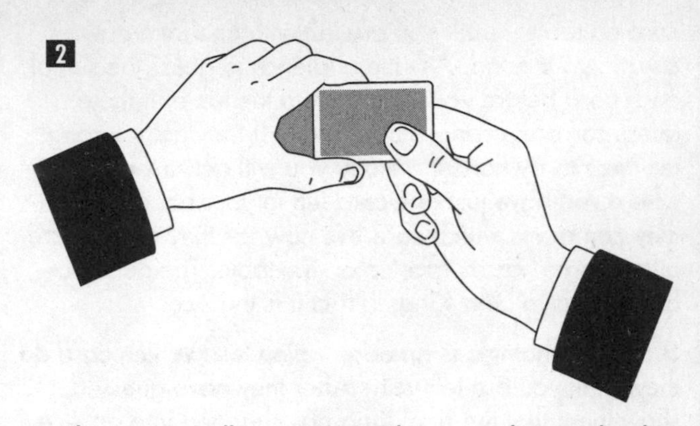

together as one (illustration 2). This is made easy by the glide. It appears you are just showing another King. Drop the two cards, as one, face up on to the pile on the table (illustration 3).

3 Finally display the last King and drop it face up on top of the pile. Pick up the pile apparently containing just the four Kings and mix the cards, keeping the faces towards you. You need to end up with the Ace in the third position and the King of the same suit on the top of the face-down pile. Challenge the audience to remember the order of the cards. Normally this would be quite simple – but when you shuffle them it becomes almost impossible to know the order.

4 Hold the pile, as you began, in the lefthand face-down glide position. Repeat the actions you did earlier – first card on table, second card on table, glide, double card on table – until you are left with one face-down card in your hand. Ask the audience to guess the suit of each card before you deal it on to the table. If they guess correctly, congratulate them. If they get it wrong, tell them to try harder. Finally you will get to the point where you have just one card left in your hand. Surely they can guess which card it is now, as they can see the other "three" cards face up on the table. The audience believe this to be a King. In fact it is the Ace.

5 Explain that this is an observation test. Which card do they think you are left with? After they have guessed show them that the final King has changed into an Ace. Let them examine the Ace while you scoop up the cards from the table.

3

♥ INSEPARABLE ACES ♦

Effect *The four Aces are inserted into different parts of the pack, but to prove the magician's claim that they are "inseparable Aces" they all move next to each other in the pack.*

Requirements *A normal pack of 52 cards.*

Preparation *None.*

● ● ● ● ● ● ● ● ● ● ● ● ● ● ●

This is another effect using a full pack which makes use of the glide move you have already learnt.

1

All the Aces are put behind cards of the same value.

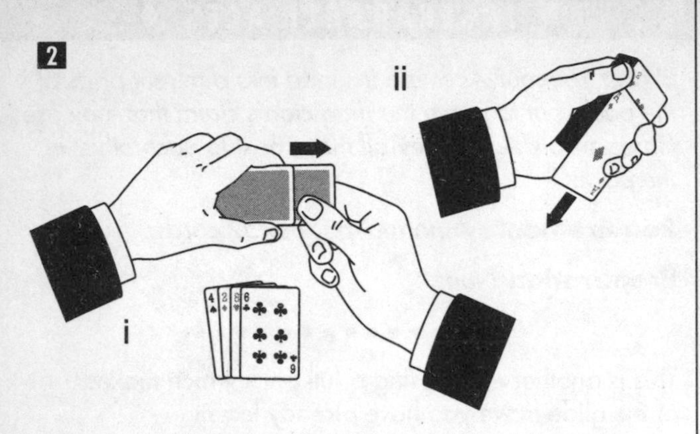

1 Remove the four Aces from the pack and place them face up on the table.

2 Evenly fan the pack in your left hand keeping the faces of the cards towards you.

3 Insert the four Aces into the pack. You apparently do this at random, but in reality all four Aces go to the left of cards of the same value. For example, all the Aces are inserted into the pack next to a Seven (as in illustration 1). These cards will be known as your indicator cards. The cards must be on the right of the Ace. Push the Aces square into the fan and square up the fan. The four Aces are apparently lost in the pack, but you know the cards which come before them.

4 Explain that the four Aces are inseparable and now you are going to prove it. Hold the pack face down in the left hand in glide position. Pull out the bottom card with the right hand and place it face up on the table. Do the same with the next card and continue through the pack (illustration 2 i) until you reach the first of your indicator cards that you know are next to the Aces. When you have dealt this card on to the table perform the glide move on the bottom card (illustration 2 ii). You know this bottom card will be one of the Aces because it was next to one of your indicator cards.

5 Keeping the first Ace pushed back, continue pulling out the cards above it one at a time and dealing them face up on to the table as you did before, until you reach the next of your indicator cards. When you have dealt the indicator card push the next card back with your right fingertips. This will put the first two Aces together. Then continue pulling out the cards above them. . .

6 Do the same thing after the third indicator card – pushing back the Ace with your right fingertips. When you pull out the final indicator card you know it is time to pull off all four Aces from the bottom of the pack – one at a time. All four Aces have moved together in the pack, proving they really are "inseparable Aces"!

BIG EFFECTS

These are card tricks which could be used on a platform or stage and still be effective.

Effect *The magician makes three cards fly invisibly from the pack to join ten cards inside a sealed envelope, which a spectator is sitting on!*

Requirements *For this you will need at least 20 cards and an envelope.*

Preparation *Secretly prepare for this effect by placing three cards inside the envelope (illustration 1).*

● ● ● ● ● ● ● ● ● ● ● ● ● ● ●

1 Ask someone to deal ten cards from the pack. Drop these cards into the envelope and ask someone to sit on them. Unknown to the audience there are now 13 cards in the envelope.

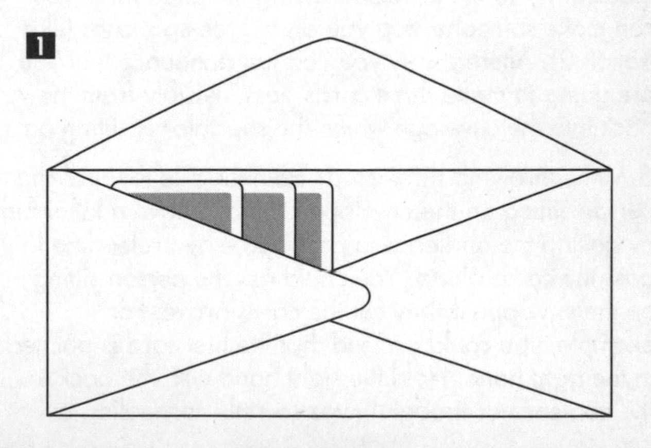

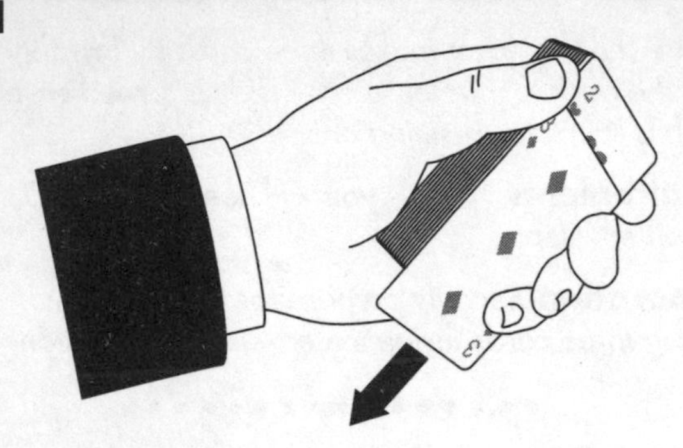

2 You announce that you need a number to be randomly selected by a member of the audience. The number chosen will indicate the number of cards to fly magically into the envelope. Using the glide force you can make someone stop you on a three-spot card (illustration 2). Alternatively you can just announce that you are going to make three cards pass invisibly from the pack into the envelope which the spectator is sitting on.

3 Mime throwing three cards from the pile towards the person sitting on the envelope. You can have a lot of fun by getting the audience to participate by pretending to pass the cards along. You could ask the person sitting on the envelope if they felt the cards arrive. For example, you could pretend that the first card is palmed in the right hand. Hold the right hand with the back to the audience as though it was secretly concealing a card. You say, "Of course if you do that you must not tell anyone or let them catch a glimpse of the card in your hand." As you say this you turn your right hand to show it really is empty. Explain the card is invisible and mime throwing it towards the envelope.

4 Apparently tie the second invisible card on to a length of invisible string, and ask your assistant sitting on the envelope to reel in the string and place the card in the envelope. Daft as it may seem, they usually enjoy doing this and hamming it up to earn you a few more laughs from the audience.

5 Explain that the third card is the toughest of them all. Take another invisible card from the pack and throw it into the air. Pretend to follow its invisible flight around the room – "and it lands in that gentleman's pocket!" Indicate a man in the audience, but as he reaches into his pocket continue quickly, "but it doesn't stop there!" The card crawls down his leg, along the floor and up into the envelope.

6 Ask your assistant to open the envelope and count aloud the number of cards now inside the envelope. Amazingly there are now 13. Do not ignore this trick because of its simplicity – it will have people talking for a long time after your performance.

TOP TIPS FOR TRICKSTERS

Always make sure that your flies are done up!

♠ COMICAL CARD TRICK ♣

Effect *A spectator manages to select the only card from a contrasting suit. It looks as if the magician has goofed – but it all ends up okay.*

Requirements *For this you need 26 cards – two complete colour contrasting suits. In the description we use Hearts and Clubs. You will also need a prediction (illustration 3) and some Copydex glue.*

Preparation *To prepare for this you will need to lightly glue a red card on to the back of each black card so that you have 13 double cards. You only need a couple of dabs of Copydex on the back of each black card to do this (illustration 1). You also need a written prediction saying "YOU WILL CHOOSE A HEART".*

●●●●●●●●●●●●●●●

1

1 Hand the sealed prediction to someone to guard it for you. Tell them that no-one is to go near the prediction. If you are doing this trick on a stage it is better to invite the volunteer on to the stage to look after the envelope so that everyone can see all is fair and above board. They are to read it out when you ask them.

2 Ask someone on stage to assist you. Explain that you have predicted which suit they will choose. As you say this fan the cards to the audience. They will only see clubs in the fan (illustration 2). This will get a laugh when they realise how you are going to trick your assistant!

3 Do not show the faces of the cards to your assistant on stage, but ask them to touch the back of any card. Make sure they keep their finger on it as you cut it to the top of the pile.

4 Peel the top card off of the back of the Club. Because you have only used a couple of spots of glue it should separate quite easily. Hand them this card, but don't let anyone see the face of it.

5 Ask your prediction keeper to read out what it says. When they do you should get another big laugh from the audience, who only saw Clubs. Pretend that the trick has gone wrong. Ask the spectator who was looking after the envelope if anyone has changed the envelope for another one. Ask them if they are trying to ruin your trick? The prediction should say that they would choose a black card, a Club.

6 Everything ends with a big laugh when your assistant on stage turns the card around to reveal they chose the only Heart (apparently!) from all those Clubs. This will get another big laugh and hopefully a well deserved round of applause. All's well that ends well!

3

Rope & Ring Tricks

GLOSSARY OF TERMS

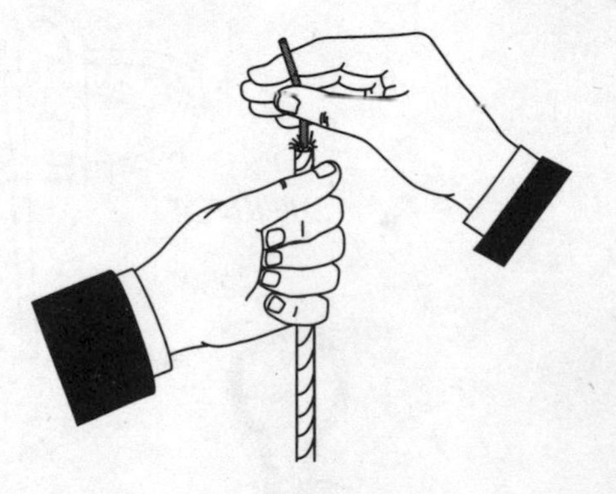

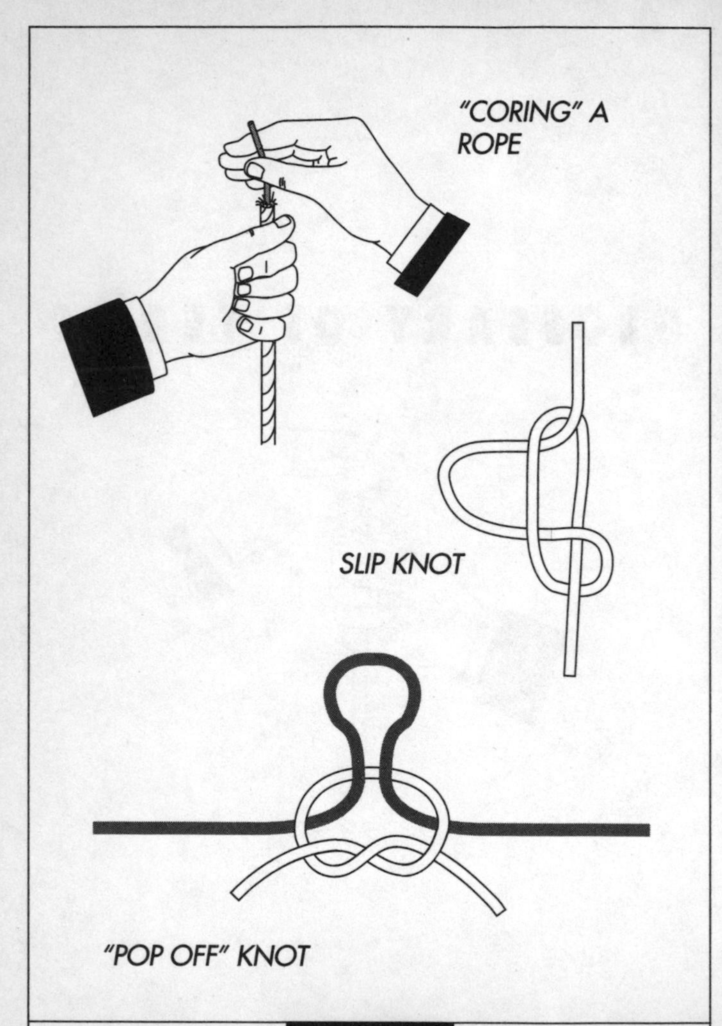
"CORING" A ROPE
SLIP KNOT
"POP OFF" KNOT

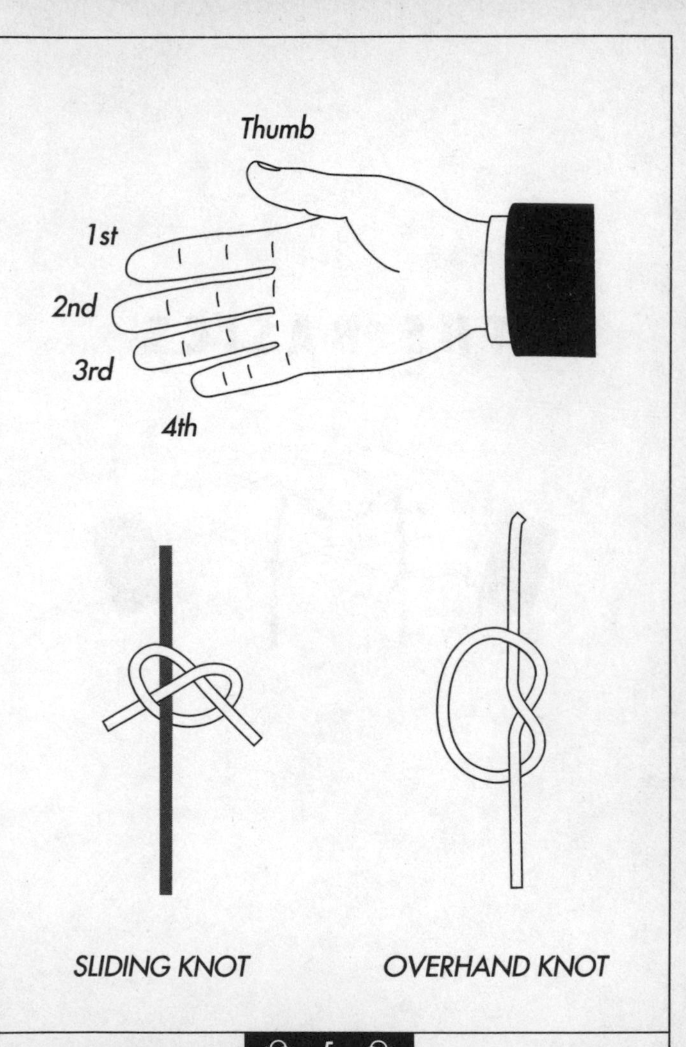
Thumb
1st
2nd
3rd
4th
SLIDING KNOT
OVERHAND KNOT

THE BASICS

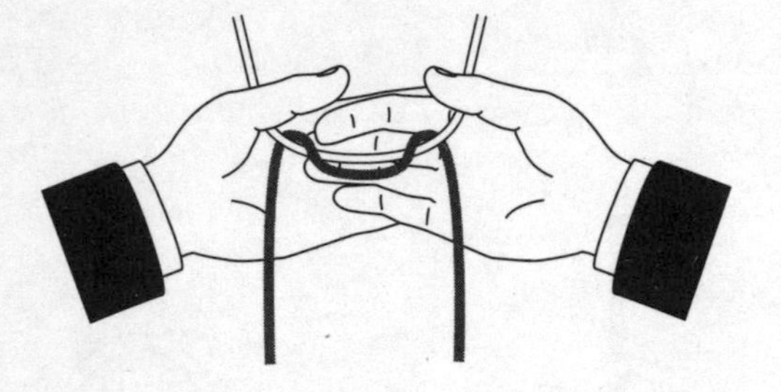

ONE-HANDED KNOT

Effect *The magician ties a knot in the end of a length of rope using only one hand.*

Requirements *A length of rope about 75cm/30in long.*

Preparation *At one end of the rope tie an overhand knot (see Glossary) and conceal it in your right hand.*

• • • • • • • • • • • • • • • •

1 Dangle the rope from your right hand, keeping the knot concealed inside your hand. We will refer to the knotted end of the rope as end A and the unknotted end as end B (see illustration 1).

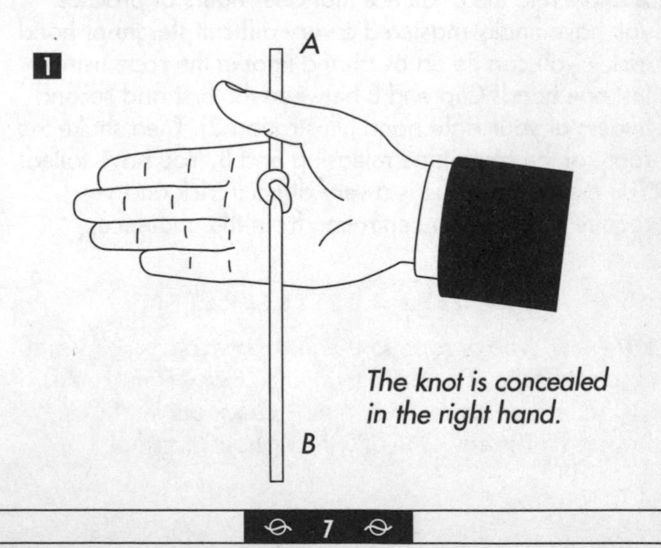

The knot is concealed in the right hand.

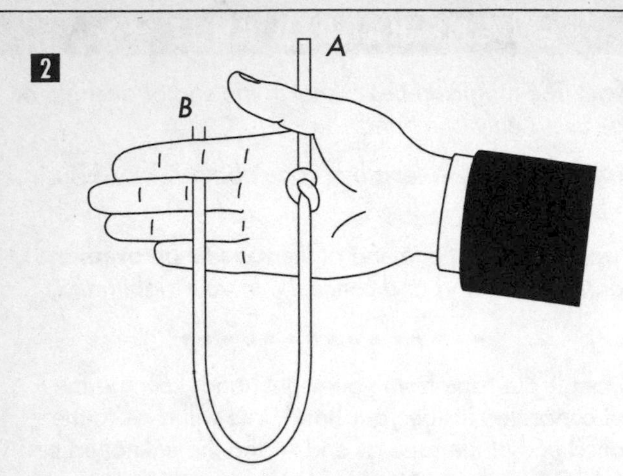

2 Explain to the audience that after hours of practice you have finally mastered a very difficult sleight-of-hand trick – you can tie an overhand knot in the rope using just one hand! Clip end B between the first and second fingers of your right hand (illustration 2). Then shake the rope, at the same time releasing end B. You have failed! You explain that this is a very difficult trick and you require absolute concentration from the audience.

TOP TIPS FOR TRICKSTERS

The best type of rope to use in these tricks is soft white cotton rope. There are many tips that will make this rope even easier to handle – check out the ROPE PREPARATION TIPS throughout this book.

3 Offer to attempt to do it again. Once again, bring end B up to your right hand and clip it between your fingers. Shake the rope, but this time hold on to end B and release end A (illustration 3). It seems you have magically tied an overhand knot in the end of the rope with just one hand. All those hours of practice paid off!

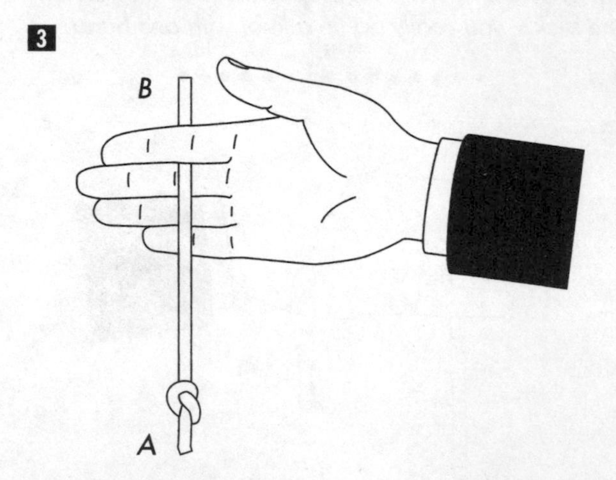

TOP TIPS FOR TRICKSTERS

Soft cotton rope consists of a woven outer shell that contains an inner core. It is available from magic shops and suppliers or from the haberdashery section of department stores.

ANOTHER ONE-HANDED KNOT

Effect *The magician ties a knot in a rope using only one hand.*

Requirements *A piece of rope about 65cm/25in long.*

Preparation *There is no preparation for this version of the trick – you really do tie a knot with one hand.*

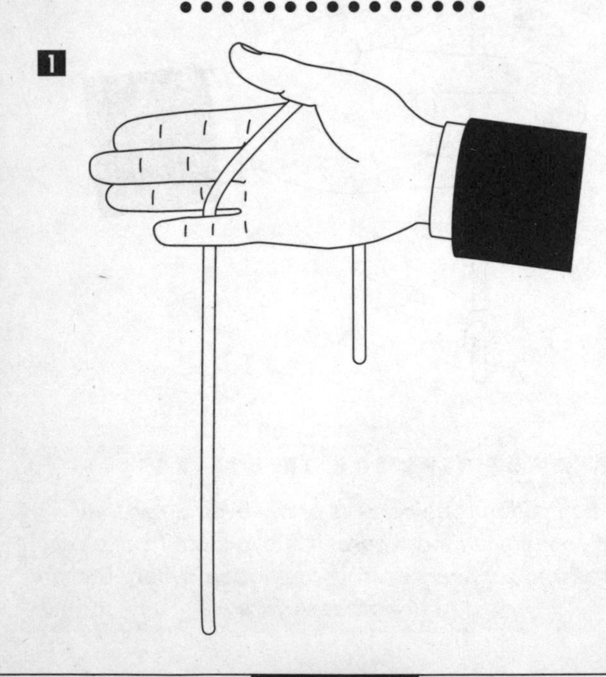

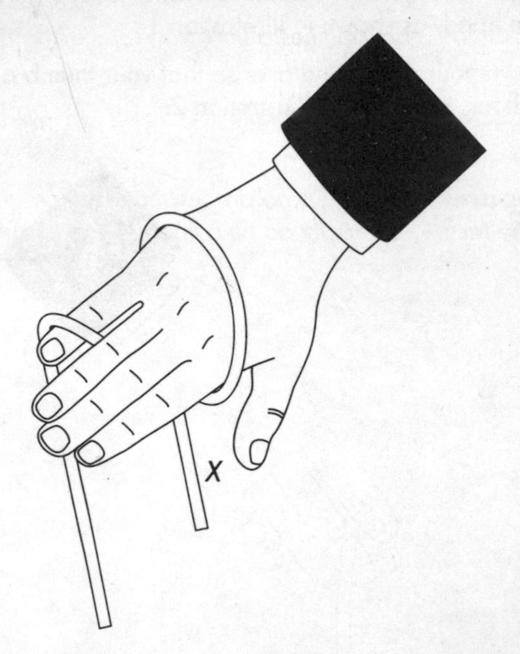

1 Drape the rope over your right hand as shown in illustration 1. The end hanging at the back should be slightly shorter than the end hanging at the front.

ROPE PREPARATION TIP

To make your rope even more flexible you can remove the inner core. This is known as "coring" a rope.

2 Clip the rope between the little and third fingers of the right hand, as shown in illustration 1.

3 Turn your right hand over so that your thumb points to the floor, as shown in illustration 2.

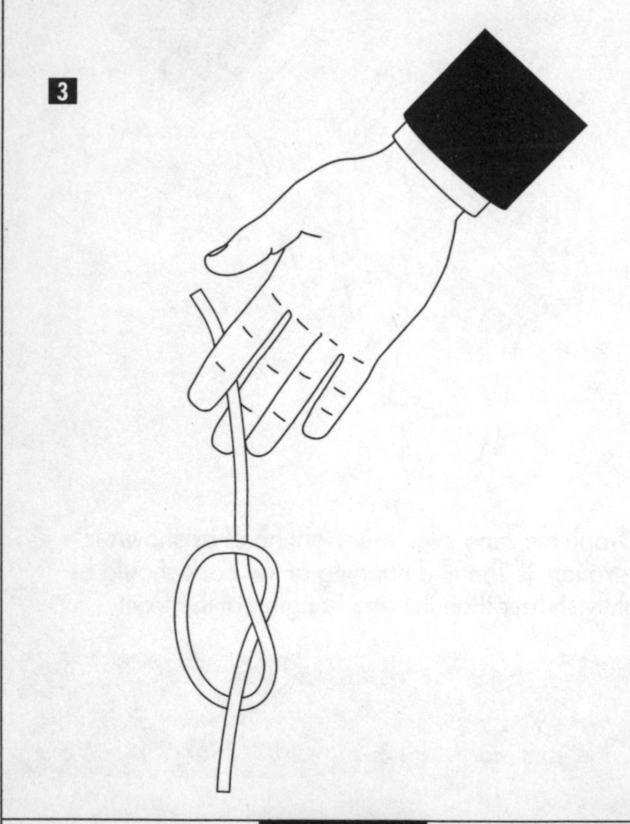

4 As your hand twists, your first and second fingers bend inwards and catch hold of the rope at the back just below the hand (at X on illustration 2). Give the rope a shake so that it falls off your hand. The piece of rope held by the first and second fingers will be pulled through the loop to form a knot (illustration 3).

5 As the rope falls, grab the other end with your left hand and pull it tight.

6 A knot will appear in the middle of the rope – as if by magic (illustration 4).

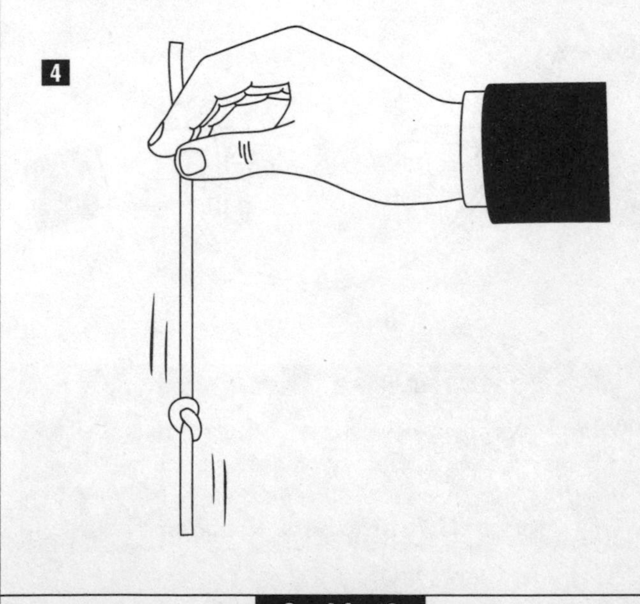

QUICK KNOT

Effect *A knot mysteriously appears in the centre of a length of rope.*

Requirements *A rope about 75cm/30in long.*

Preparation *No preparation is required.*

• • • • • • • • • • • • • • • •

1 Hold end A of the rope in the left hand with the end pointing up. Drape end B over the back of the right hand so that end B rests in the right palm (illustration 1).

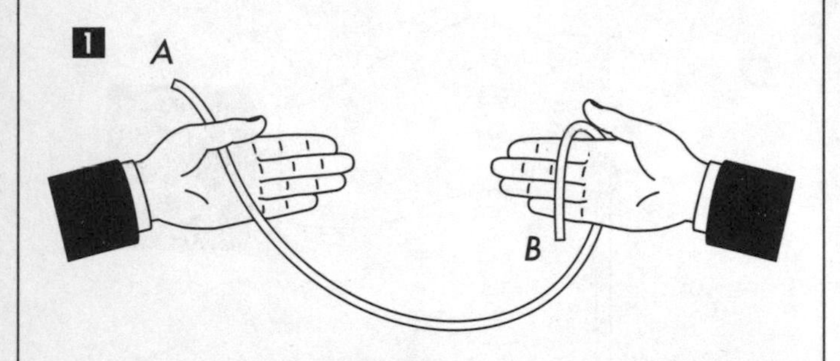

TOP TIPS FOR TRICKSTERS

When using newspaper for your tricks, remember to rub over the newsprint with a tissue to remove any excess ink. This will ensure that you finish your performance as clean as you started!

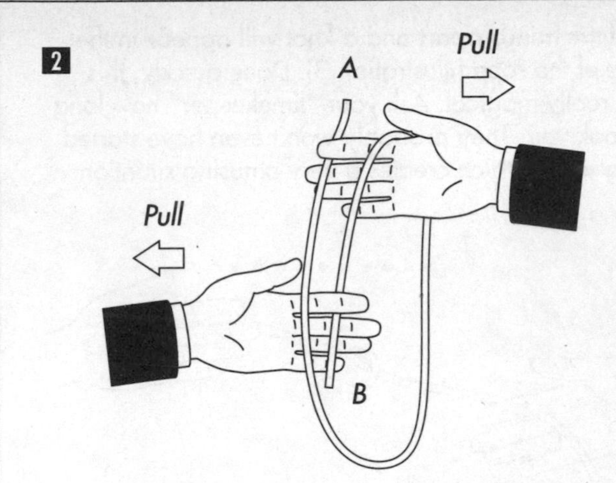

2 Move your hands towards each other. The righthand first and second fingers clip end A above the left hand. At the same time the lefthand first and second fingers clip end B (illustration 2). As your hands move together ask a spectator to time you with their watch to see how long it takes you to tie a knot in the centre of the rope. You can explain that it takes most people about ten seconds.

ROPE PREPARATION TIP

To "core" a length of rope, open the threads at one end, grasp the inner core and slide off the outer shell by pulling on the core and bunching up the shell.

3 Pull the hands apart and a knot will appear in the centre of the rope (illustration 3). Done quickly, this looks really magical. Ask your "timekeeper" how long that took you. They probably won't even have started timing you – which creates a very amusing situation.

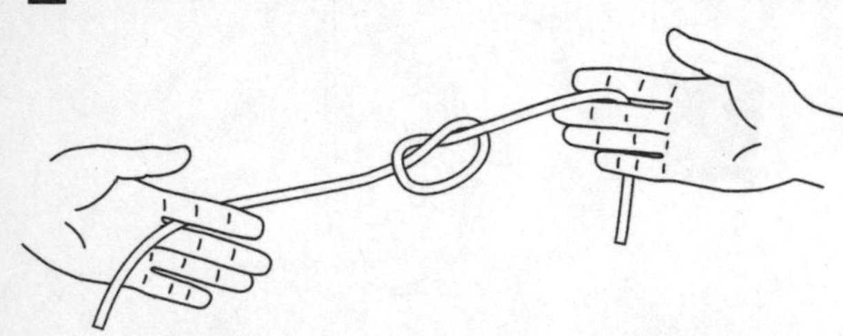

HARRY HOUDINI (1874-1926)

Houdini was famed all over the world for his daring and dangerous escapes from packing cases, handcuffs, straitjackets – and rope. Although some of the escapes described in this book may seem simple, a number of the methods were used by Houdini to help make him into the legend he is today. He died after a student punched him in the stomach to see if he was as powerful as he claimed. His death, on 31 October (Halloween) 1926, was ironic, as he had spent the years since the death of his beloved mother investigating and debunking spirit mediums.

QUICK SLIP KNOT

Effect *A knot dissolves when it is pulled.*

Requirements *A length of rope at least 60cm/2ft.*

•••••••••••••••

1

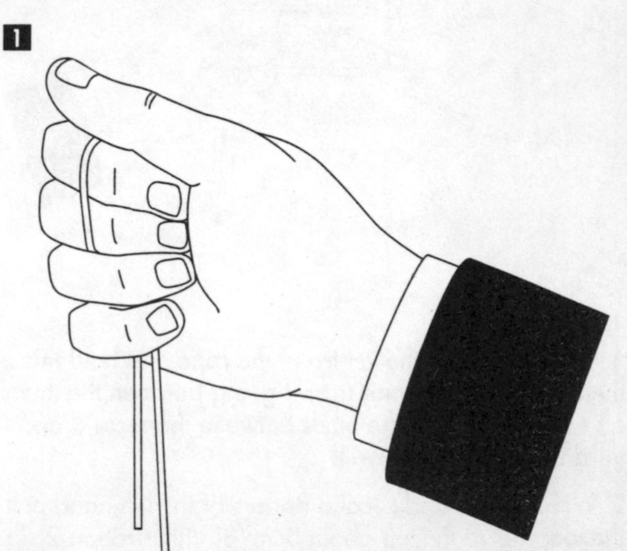

ROPE PREPARATION TIP

It is a good idea to "fix" the ends of any pieces of rope you may be using in your performance as this will prevent them from fraying.

2

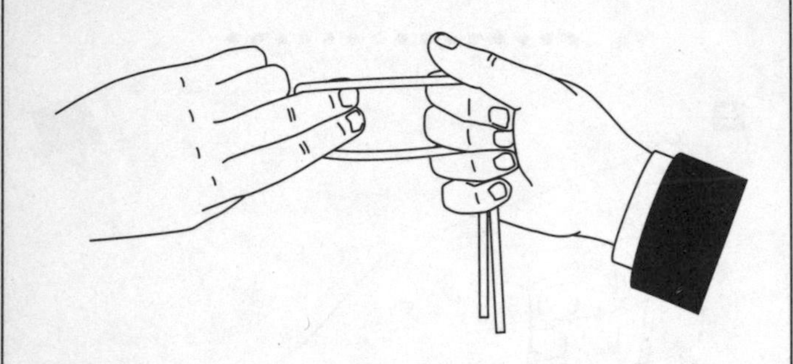

1 Make a loop at the centre of the rope and hold this in the right hand with one strand going between the thumb and first finger and the other between the second and third finger (illustration 1).

2 With the first and second fingers of the left hand pull the loop out to the left about 8cm/3in (illustration 2).

ROPE PREPARATION TIP

One way to "fix" the ends of a length of rope to stop them fraying is to dip them in white glue (for example, Copydex) and allow them to dry overnight.

3

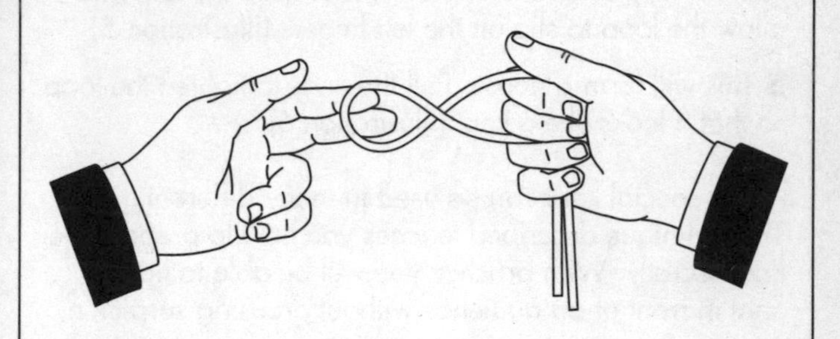

3 Twist the left hand to put a single twist in the loop (illustration 3).

4

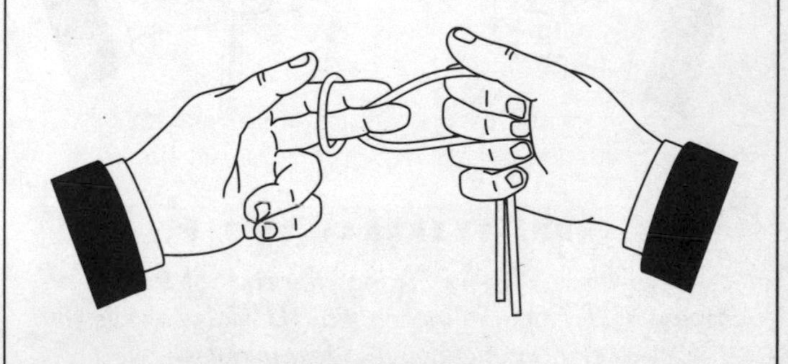

4 Slide the left first and second fingers through the loop and clip hold of the upper strand of rope (illustration 4). Pull the clipped strand through the loop to the left, and allow the loop to slip off the left fingers (illustration 5).

5 This will form a noose. Pull the ends to tighten the loop so that it looks like a knot (illustration 6).

This special knot can be used in many different tricks. The technique described teaches you how to prepare the knot secretly. With practice you will be able to tie this knot in front of an audience without arousing suspicion.

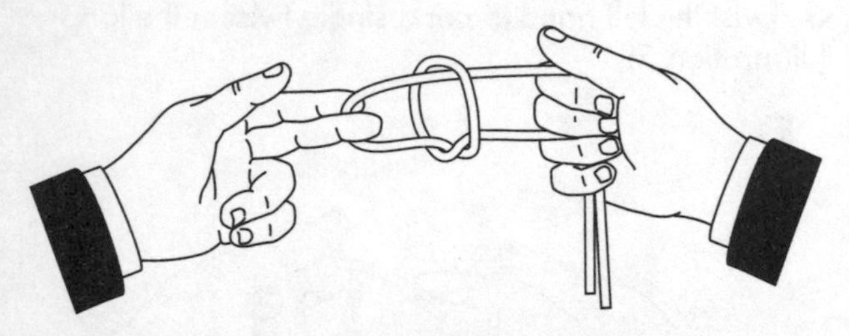

ROPE PREPARATION TIP

Another alternative for "fixing" the ends of a piece of rope is to dip them in molten wax. Unlike glue this will dry and harden in a few minutes.

6

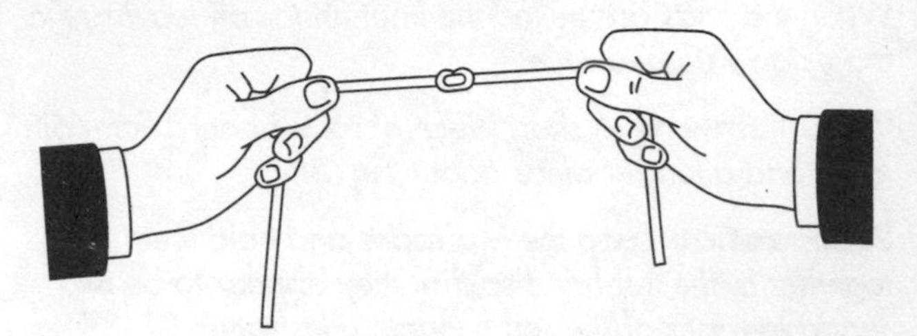

When the ends are pulled hard, the knot will disappear.

THE INDIAN ROPE TRICK

In reports of this effect an Indian street magician (fakir) throws a long coil of rope into the air where it remains vertically rigid. A boy climbs to the top and promptly vanishes. The magician follows the boy to the top of the rope carrying a large knife and vanishes as well. The boy's severed limbs fall from the sky and are collected in a basket by the magician upon his return. Finally, the boy emerges unharmed from the basket. So few people can lay claim to having seen this trick performed that it is generally considered to be a myth. Various magicians have managed to replicate the effect on stage, but as yet no one has performed the trick successfully in the open air.

THE POP-OFF KNOT

Effect *The magician ties two ropes together with a knot. When the ends are pulled the knot jumps off leaving the magician with one rope.*

Requirements *A short piece of rope about 15cm/6in long, and a longer piece about 1m/3ft.*

Preparation *Loop the two ropes and hold them together in the left hand so that they appear to be two separate ropes of the same length (illustration 1).*

• • • • • • • • • • • • • • •

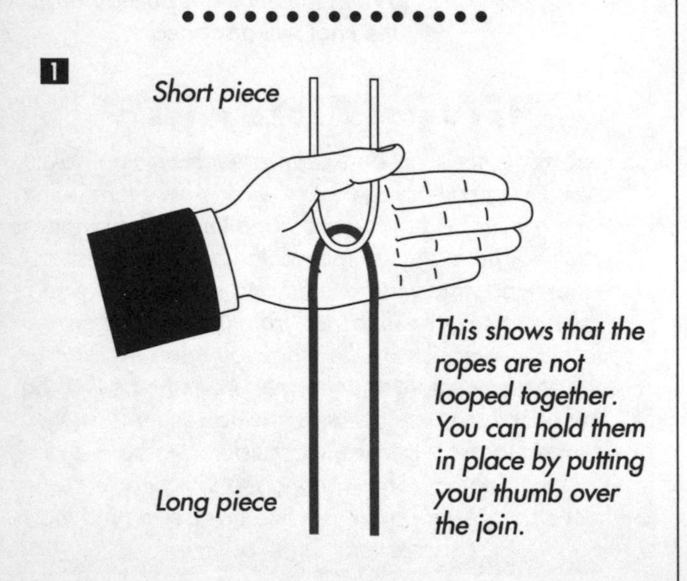

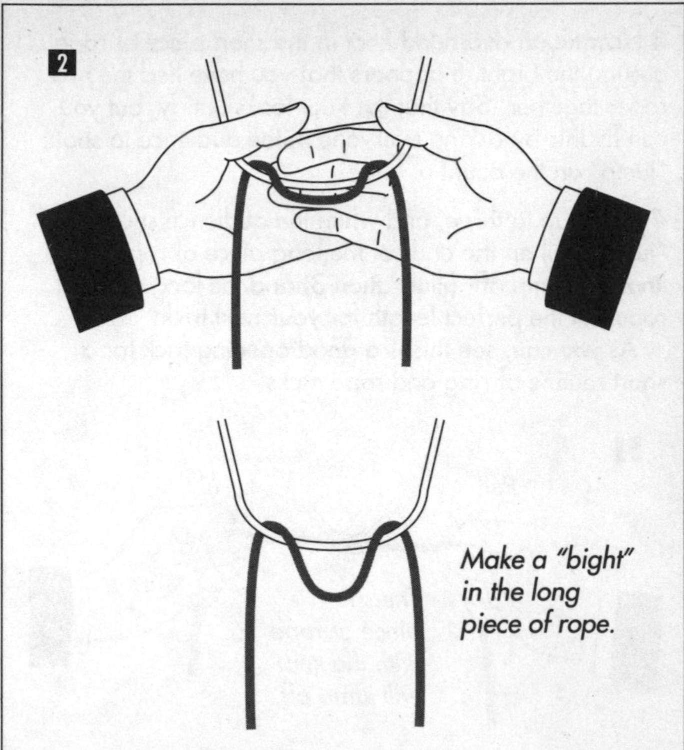

Make a "bight" in the long piece of rope.

1 Display the rope as two pieces of rope of equal length (illustration 1). Explain that neither rope is long enough so you are going to tie them together.

2 The right first finger pushes the centre of the long piece through the loop of the short piece (illustration 2). This forms a loop or "bight" in the long rope.

3 Now tie an overhand knot in the short piece of rope around the bight. It appears that you have tied the two ropes together. Say that the knot looks untidy, but you can fix this by asking everyone in the audience to shout "jump" on the count of three.

4 Count up to three, and when the audience shouts "jump" pull on the ends of the long piece of rope. The knot will jump off (illustration 3) and the long piece of rope will the perfect length for your next trick!

As you can, see this is a good opening trick for a short routine of ring and rope tricks.

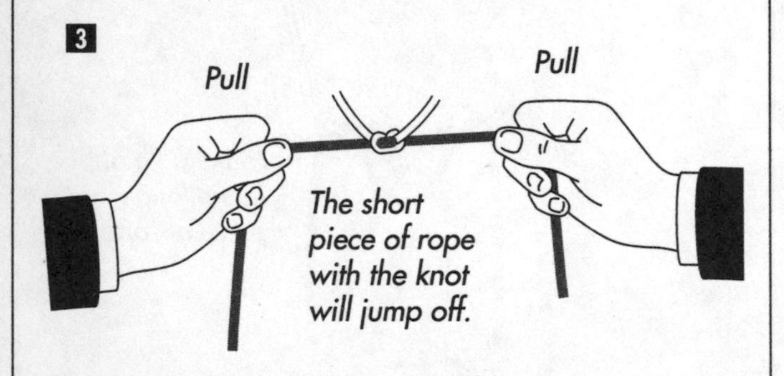

ROPE PREPARATION TIP

You can sew the ends of the rope to "fix" them and prevent them fraying, or simply wrap the ends in white cotton to stop them unravelling.

THE SIMPLE SLIDING KNOT

Effect The magician knots together two ropes of equal length. The magician then slides the knot down to the bottom of one piece of the rope and unties it – to show one short rope and one long rope.

Requirements A short piece of rope (20cm/8in long) and a long rope (about 1m/3ft).

Preparation Loop the short piece of rope around the centre of the long piece (illustration 1).

• • • • • • • • • • • • • • •

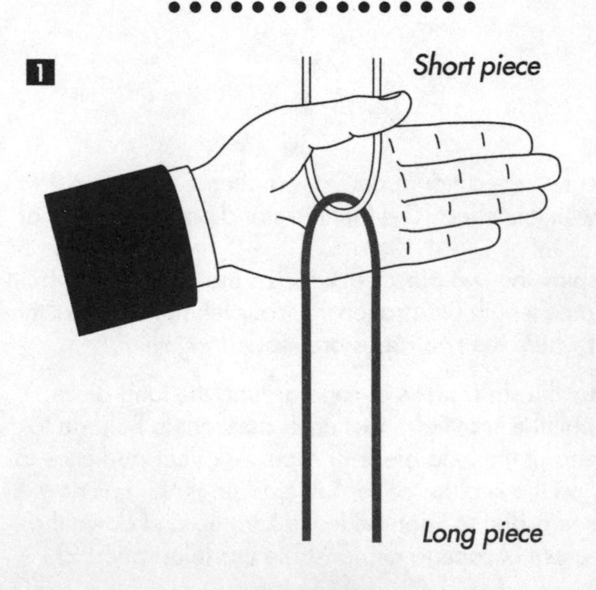

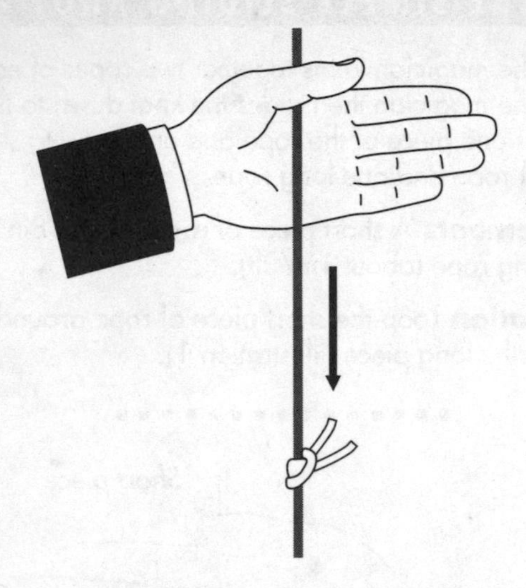

1 Get two spectators from your audience up to assist you with this effect. Get them to stand one either side of you.

Display the two pieces of rope as though they are both the same length (illustration 1). Your left hand covers the point where the two ropes are looped together.

2 Knot the short piece of rope around the long piece, and pull the knot tight. Get each assistant to hold on to one end of the long piece of rope. Ask your audience to blow on the knot to "soften" it. Explain that it has now become a sliding knot. Slide the knot up and down the long piece of rope to demonstrate this (illustration 2).

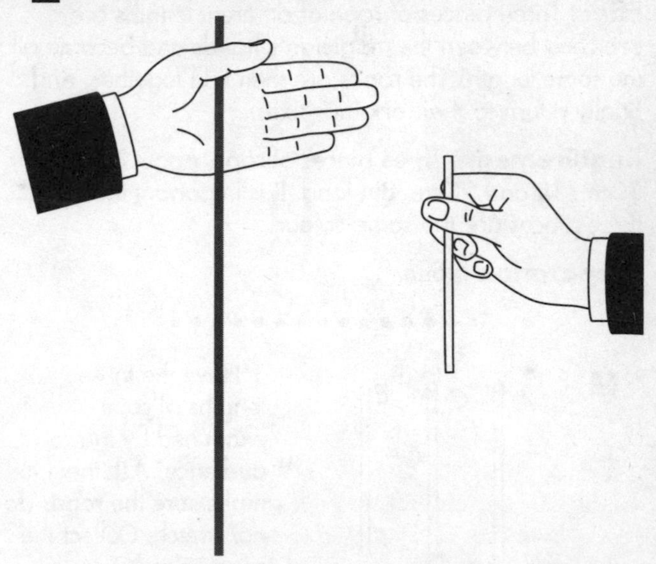

3 Slide the knot down the rope to about 10cm/4in from the end (illustration 2). Ask the person holding that end of the rope to let go, so that you can untie the knot.

4 Hold the knotted portion in your left hand and untie the knot with your right.

5 Separate the ropes to show one is now four times longer than the other (illustration 3). The ropes can be examined and kept by your two volunteers as souvenirs.

THE EQUAL UNEQUAL ROPES

Effect Three pieces of rope of different lengths are stretched between the magician's hands and become all the same length! The ropes are then tied together, and finally return to their original sizes.

Requirements Three pieces of rope, about 60cm/2ft, 30cm/1ft and 20cm/8in long. It is important that all three pieces are the same colour.

Preparation None.

• • • • • • • • • • • • • • • •

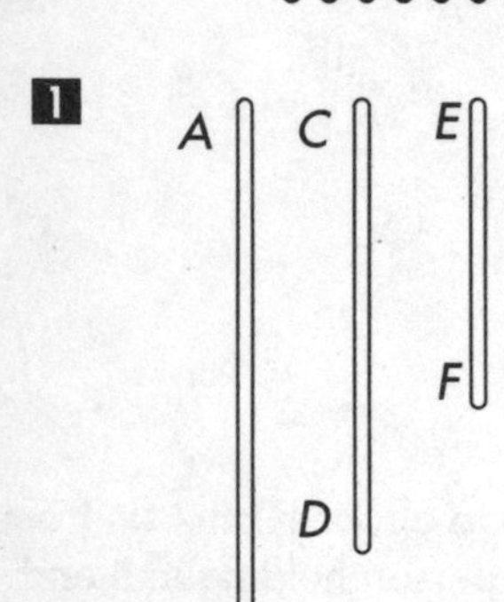

1 Have the three lengths of rope examined by the audience. Ask them to make sure the ropes do not stretch. Collect the ropes together.

2 You must clip one end of each rope between the left thumb and first finger. The order of the ropes must be as in illustration 1, so that the longest rope (AB) is nearest the thumb crotch.

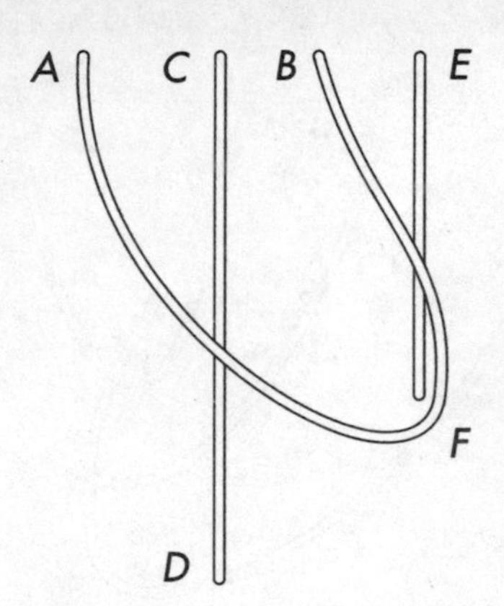

3 With your right hand bring end B up to the left first finger and thumb, so that it it clipped between ends C and E. Make sure that the rope passes over the top of rope EF as in illustration 2.

4 Now with your right hand bring up ends F and D into the left hand, placing them to the right of the other ends being clipped (illustration 3). You will see from the illustration that this procedure loops ropes AB and EF together. This prepares you for the "big stretch"!

5 Take ends A, C and B in your left hand and E, F and D in your right hand and slowly pull your hands apart. Amazingly it will appear that all three ropes stretch between your hands to become the same length (illustration 4). Keep your right hand closed around the point where the short and long ropes are linked.

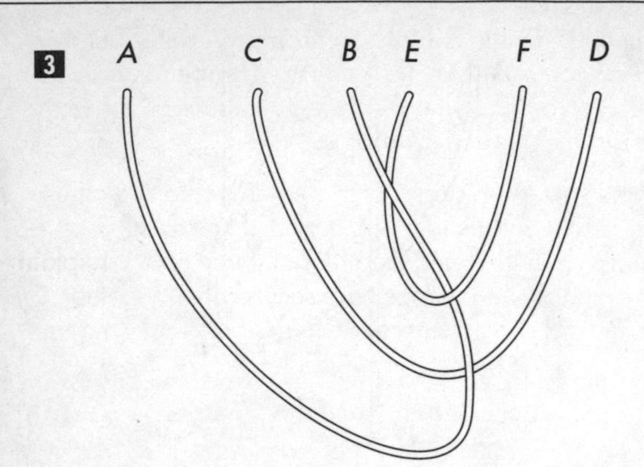

6 To convince the audience that the three ropes really are of the same length you now perform a special false count. You appear to count the ropes singly from hand to hand – concealing the fact that two of them are looped together. Here's what really happens . . .
The right hand takes rope CD from the left hand as you say "one". The right hand then appears to take one of the two ropes in the left hand. It cannot do this as they are connected! So it swaps the single rope for the looped ropes. It does this by putting rope CD back into the left hand (clipped in the thumb crotch), and grasps the looped ropes with the right second and third fingers. Your right hand moves to the right as you say "two". The left hand then passes rope CD to the right hand again as you say "three".

7 Tie ends EF into a knot around rope AB. It should appear you are just tying two ends of rope together, but in reality you are tying the short piece around the long piece to make a sliding knot.

8 When the knot is tight and is not going to slip off the rope, let go and tie end B to end C. It should appear you are making a long length of all three ropes. Explain that even though the ropes are securely tied together you can still make them return to their original lengths.

9 Wrap the ropes around your left hand, but as you do so, slide the knot at the same time. Secretly move the knot until it is about 15cm/6in from one end of the long rope it is tied around.

10 Show the ropes coiled around your hand. Then snap your fingers – and uncoil the ropes to show they have now returned to their original length. It appears that you now have a short piece, tied to a long piece, tied to a medium-length piece of rope. All three ropes can be untied and examined by the audience.

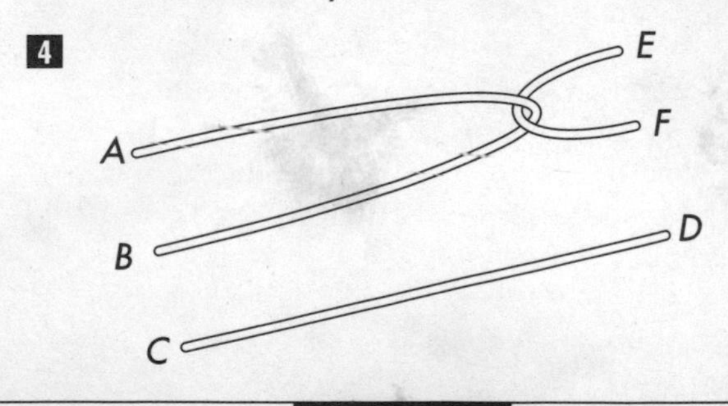

RINGS AND ROPE

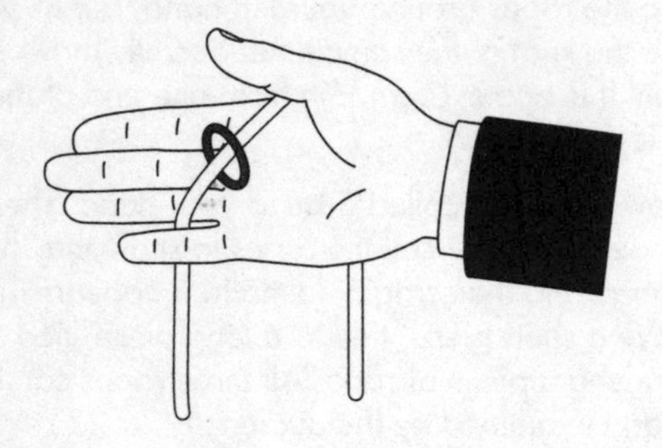

THE MAGIC BANGLE

Effect *A bangle mysteriously penetrates on to a rope tied around both the magician's wrists.*

Requirements *A piece of rope about 120cm/4ft long and two identical bangles.*

Preparation *Slide one of the bangles on to your arm and up your sleeve so that it is hidden (illustration 2).*

• • • • • • • • • • • • • • •

2

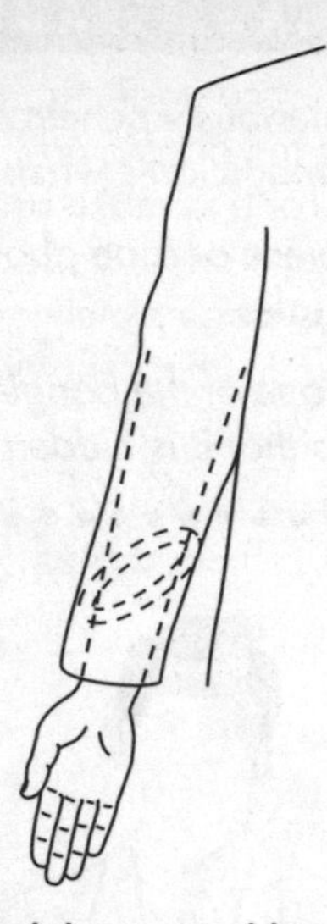

1 Give the rope and the second bangle to the audience so that they can be examined. Ask them to check that there are no slits, cracks or holes in the bangle – except for the hole in the middle!

Then ask someone to tie the rope around your wrists. It is important that it is tied tightly so that the audience do not think you can slip the rope over your wrists. Take the examined bangle and turn around (illustration 1).

2 With your back to the audience place the examined bangle in your breast pocket and slide the duplicate bangle down your sleeve, over your wrist and on to the rope.

3 Turn around to show that the bangle is now on the rope (illustration 3)! Once again, you can get the audience to examine the bangle now that it is dangling on the middle of the rope to make sure you have not tampered with it to get it on to the rope. Of course, unknown to them, it is a completely different bangle! You can also get them to check that the rope is still securely tied around your wrists.

4 You can have them untie the rope to release the bangle or reverse the actions to make it "escape".

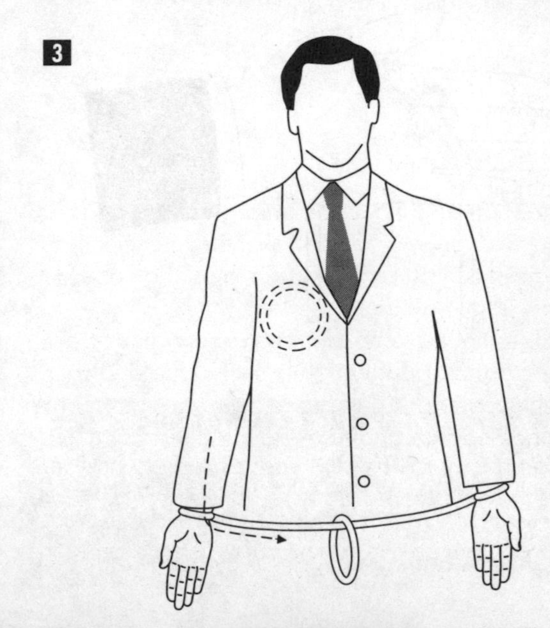

APPEAR-RING

Effect *A knot appears in the centre of a length of rope with a finger ring tied in it!*

Requirements *A piece of rope and a finger ring.*

Preparation *Thread the ring on to the rope. Hold the rope in your right hand with the ring concealed in your fist (illustration 1).*

1

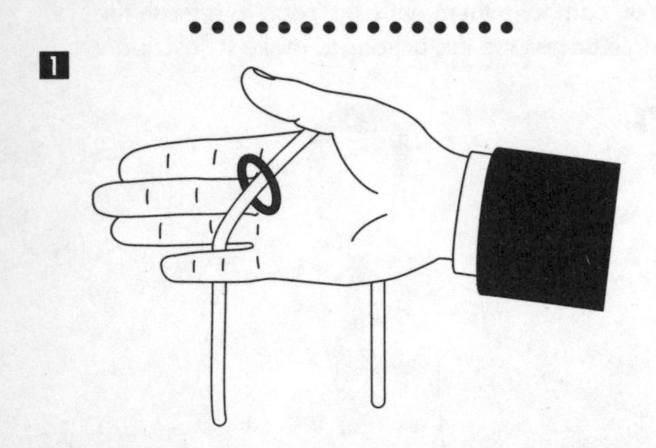

TOP TIPS FOR TRICKSTERS

The quickest way to "fix" the ends of rope to prevent fraying is to wrap them with white or clear sticky tape. However, this is not suitable for some tricks in this book where the ends are switched for a cut piece of rope.

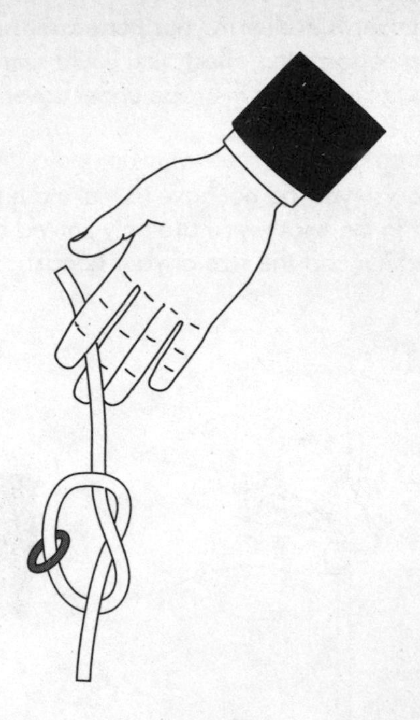

1 Perform "Another One-handed Knot" with the ring in position (illustration 2).

2 Keep the ring concealed with the back of your hand as you make the knot. It will appear tied on the centre of the rope when the knot appears (illustration 3).

To make this an even more impressive effect you could borrow a ring from a member of the audience and make it vanish earlier in your performance. When you come to perform this effect, you could secretly slide the ring on to the end of the rope under cover of your other "props" on the table.

Of course you do not have to make a finger ring appear in the knot – you are only limited by your imagination and the size of your hands!

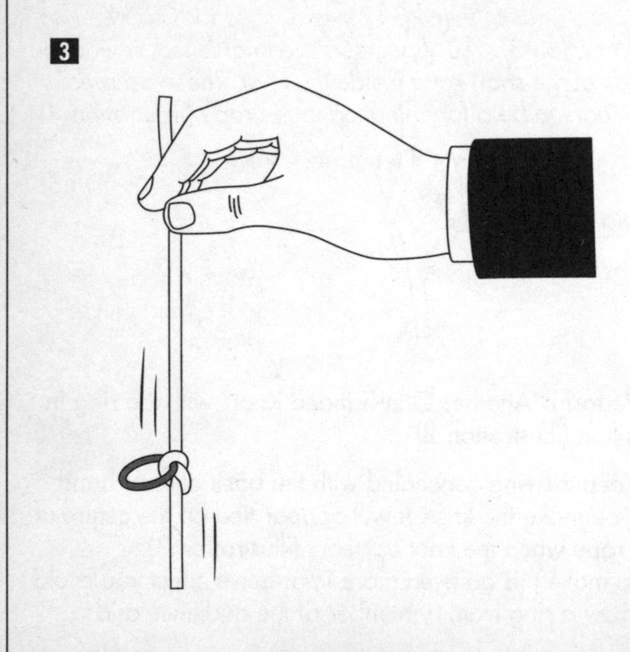

RING OFF ROPE

Effect *A ring, securely knotted on the centre of a rope, is magically released.*

Requirements *A ring, a long piece of rope (about 1m/3ft) and a short piece (about 25cm/10in).*

Preparation *Tie a slip knot in the centre of the long rope, but do not pull the loop tight (illustration 1). Pass the short piece of rope through the ring (illustration 2). Slip the ends of the short piece of rope into the slip knot (illustration 3). The slip knot is then tightened to hide the ends of the short rope inside the knot. The extra piece appears to be a loop knotted in the rope (illustration 4).*

• • • • • • • • • • • • • • •

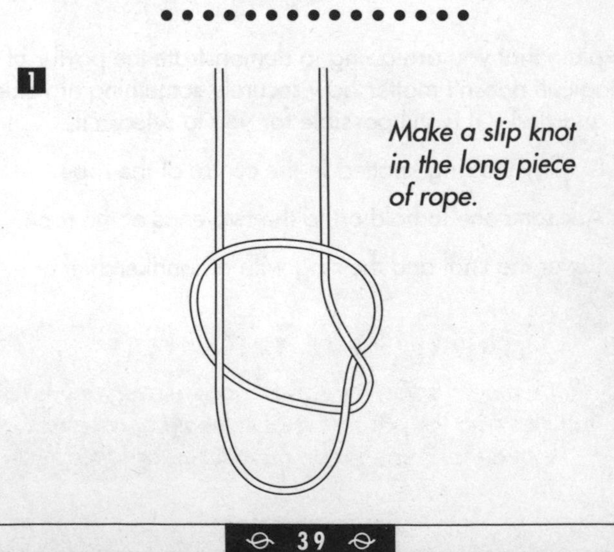

Make a slip knot in the long piece of rope.

2

Thread the short piece of rope through the ring.

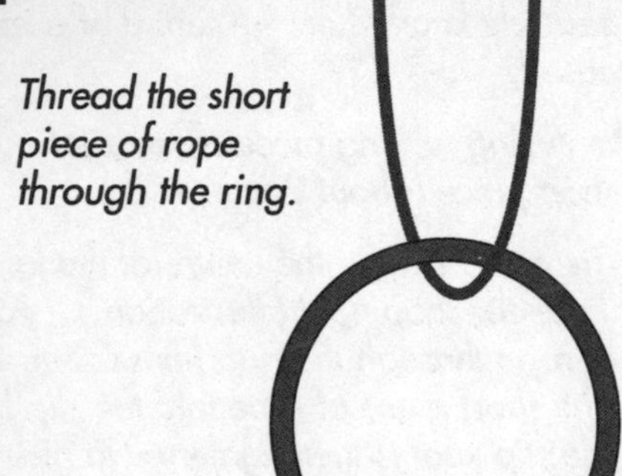

Explain that you are going to demonstrate the power of magic. It doesn't matter how securely something of value is guarded – it is still possible for you to release it.

1 Display the ring knotted in the centre of the rope.

2 Ask someone to hold on to the two ends of the rope.

3 Cover the knot and the ring with a handkerchief or

TOP TIPS FOR TRICKSTERS

Rope magic is very effective because everyone is familiar with the properties of a length of rope and knows that it cannot be gimmicked or faked.

3

Then thread the ends of the short piece of rope through the slip knot.

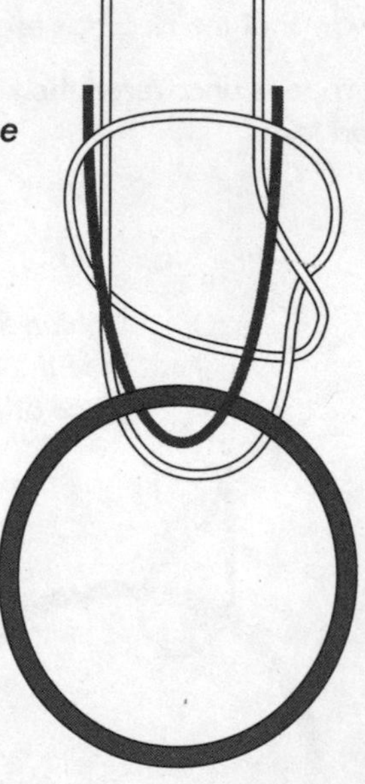

TOP TIPS FOR TRICKSTERS

In all the tricks using rings or bangles it is far more effective if you are able to borrow these objects from members of the audience.

jacket. Dissolve the slip knot, releasing the short piece of rope.

4 Slip the ring off the short piece of rope and, keeping the short piece of rope hidden (under the handkerchief or jacket), show that the ring has escaped.

5 When the rope is uncovered the knot in the centre will have vanished too!

4

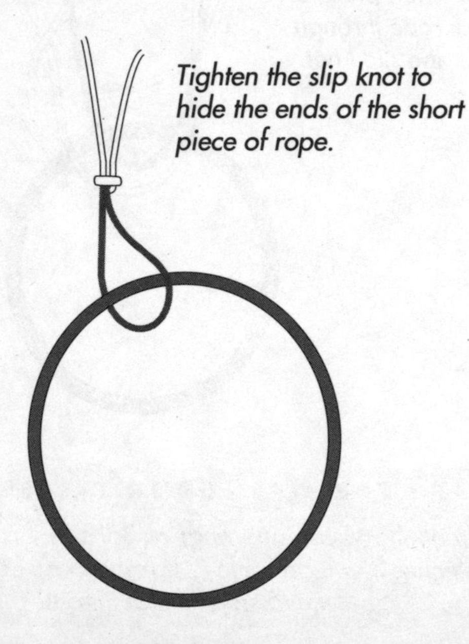

Tighten the slip knot to hide the ends of the short piece of rope.

KNOTTY BRACELET

Effect *The magician throws a borrowed bangle into a knot.*

Requirements *A length of rope and a bangle borrowed from a member of the audience.*

Preparation *None.*

• • • • • • • • • • • • • • •

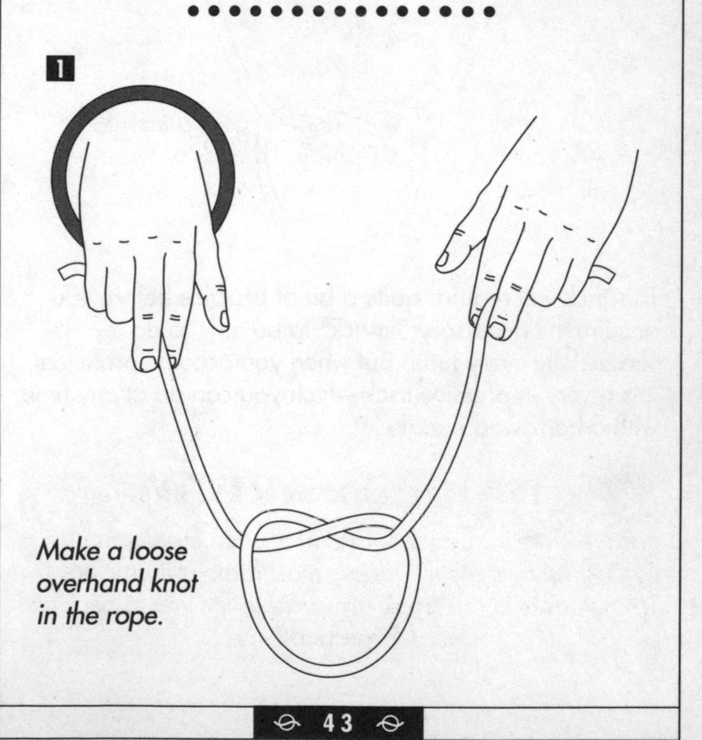

1 *Make a loose overhand knot in the rope.*

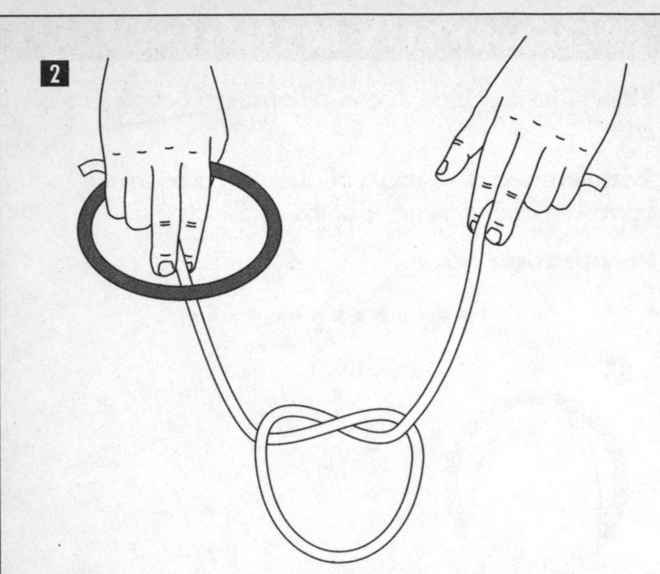

This trick will require quite a bit of practice before you acquire the necessary "knack" to be able to do it successfully every time. But when you become proficient, it is a very impressive trick which you can do at any time with a borrowed bangle.

TOP TIPS FOR TRICKSTERS

Rope magic is very visual and is often featured in the stage shows of the world's most famous magicians. Many tricks in this book are suitable for you to perform to a large audience.

1 Tie a loose overhand knot in the centre of the rope. Put the bangle on your right wrist. Hold the ends of the rope between the first and second fingers of each hand (illustration 1).

2 Slip the bangle over the hand on to the rope. At the same time the right thumb clips the rope to prevent the bangle from sliding down (illustration 2).

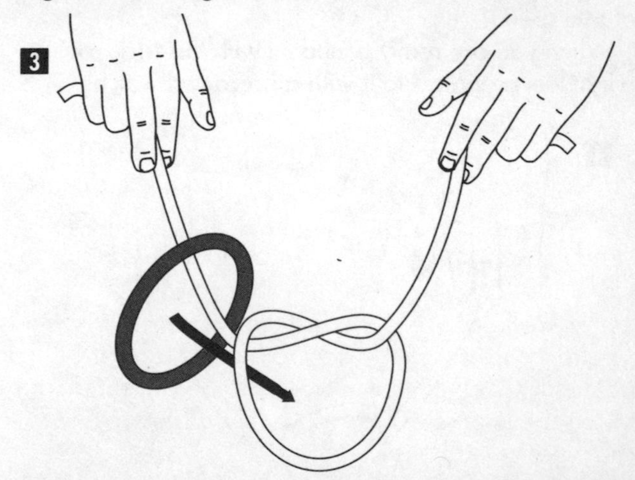

TOP TIPS FOR TRICKSTERS

To make your rope magic more visible to the audience try to hold the props at your chest level. This also encourages you to keep your head up and make eye contact with the audience.

3 The right hand throws the bangle through the loop of the knot (illustrations 3 and 4).

4 When the bangle is through, pull the knot tight. The bangle appears tied in the knot at the centre of the rope.

What actually happens is that the original overhand knot melts away and a new knot forms itself around the bangle. It is even more amazing in slow motion than it is at true speed!

When you are really confident with this trick you might feel prepared to it with a borrowed watch!

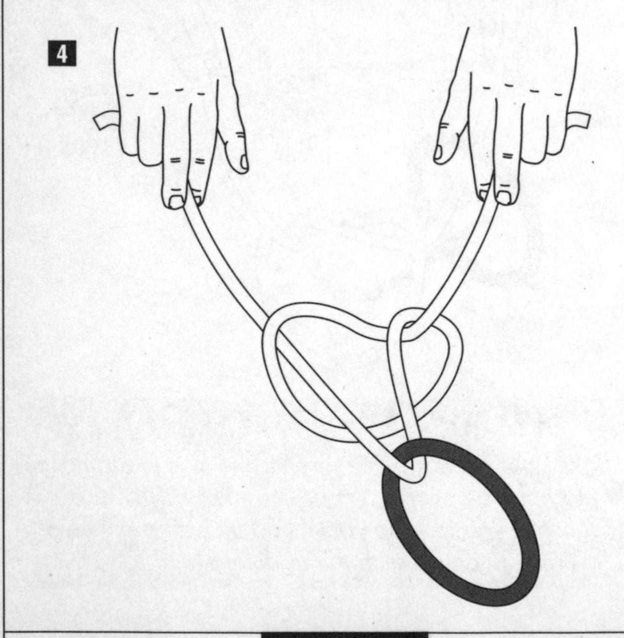

KNOTTY TRICKS

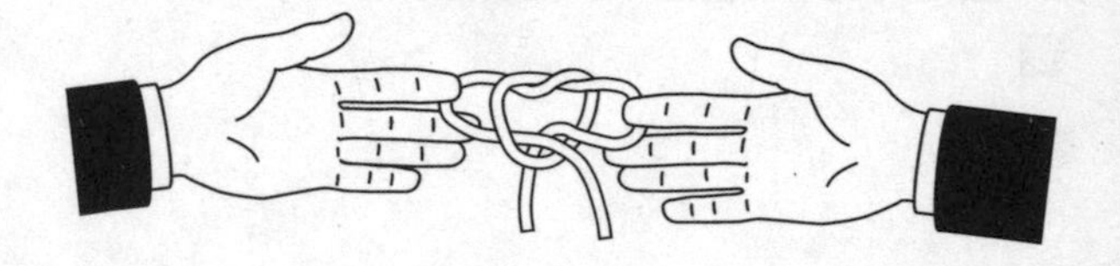

Effect *Three knots magically appear on a rope.*

Requirements *A rope about 65cm/25in long.*

Preparation *Tie a knot about 8cm/3in from each end (illustration 1).*

• • • • • • • • • • • • • • •

1 Hold the rope as in the Quick Knot with the knots concealed in your hands (illustration 1). The backs of your hands are towards the audience.

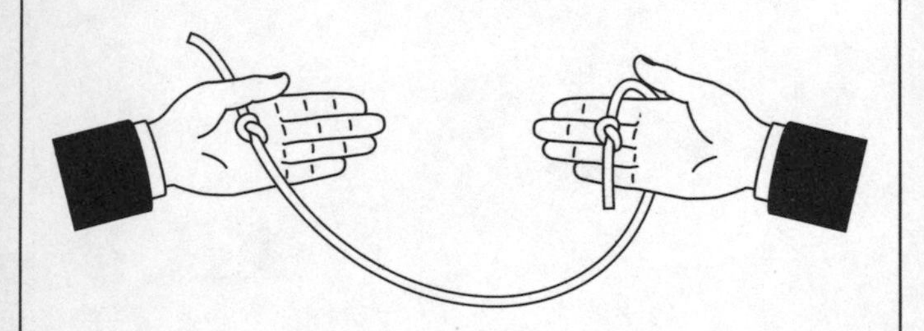

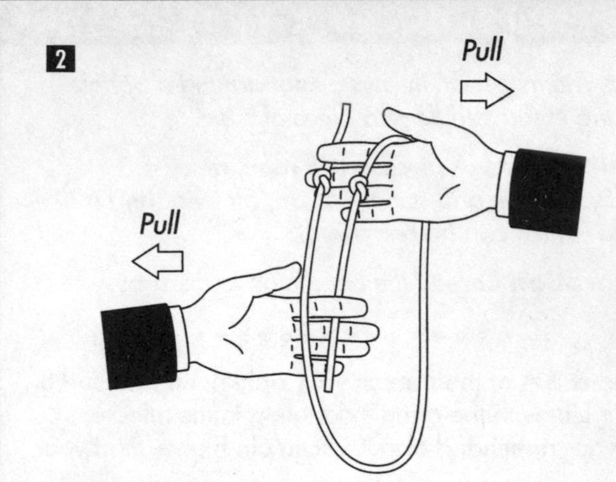

2 Perform the Quick Knot as described (illustration 2).

3 The Quick Knot will appear in the centre and the two end knots will now be seen (illustration 3).

4 All the knots seem to have appeared at the same time!

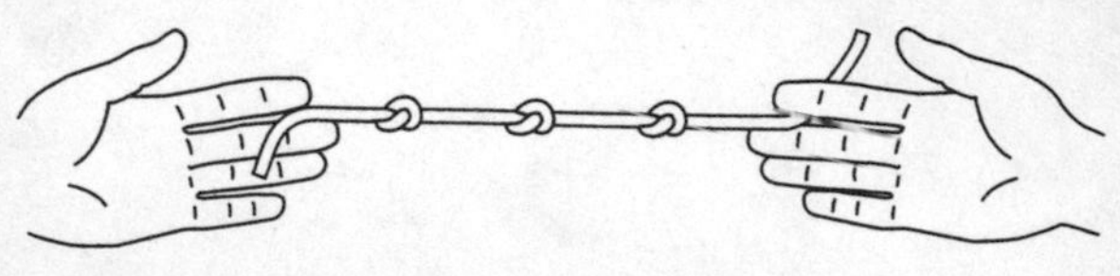

THROWING A KNOT

Effect *The magician throws a knot around a bangle dangling in the middle of a piece of rope.*

Requirements *A piece of stiff rope, at least 1cm/0.5in thick and about 150cm/5ft long, and a bangle (which can be borrowed).*

Preparation *Thread the bangle on to the rope.*

••••••••••••••••

1 Hold end A of the rope in your right hand and end B in your left, with the bangle dangling in the middle. Hold your right hand about 15cm/6in higher than your left.

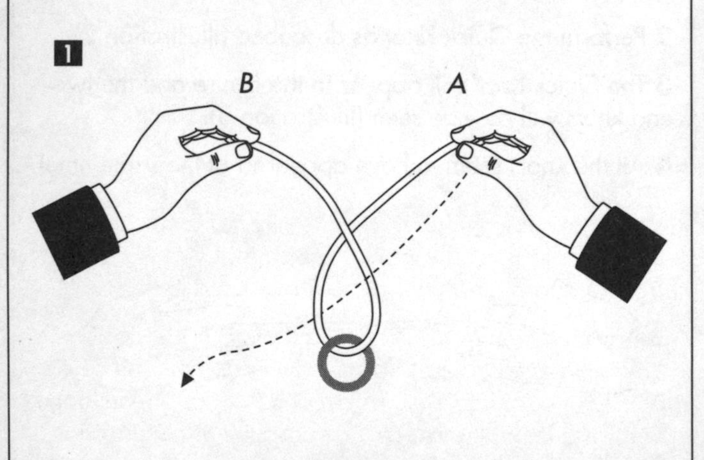

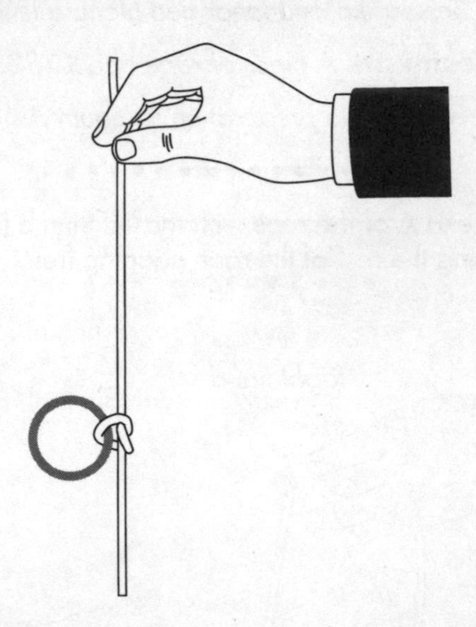

2 Move your right hand horizontally to the left and the left hand horizontally to the right so that end A passes in front of end B, and your arms are crossed over.

3 Now move your arms back to their original position. You will see that a loop forms momentarily in the centre of the rope. Act quickly. Throw end A through the loop to form a knot (illustration 1), and pull tight (illustration 2). This is a very impressive effect.

Effect *Several knots appear tied along a length of rope.*

Requirements *A piece of rope about 180cm/6ft.*

Preparation *No preparation is required.*

• • • • • • • • • • • • • • •

1 Clip end A of the rope with the left thumb (illustration 1) leaving the rest of the rope hanging free.

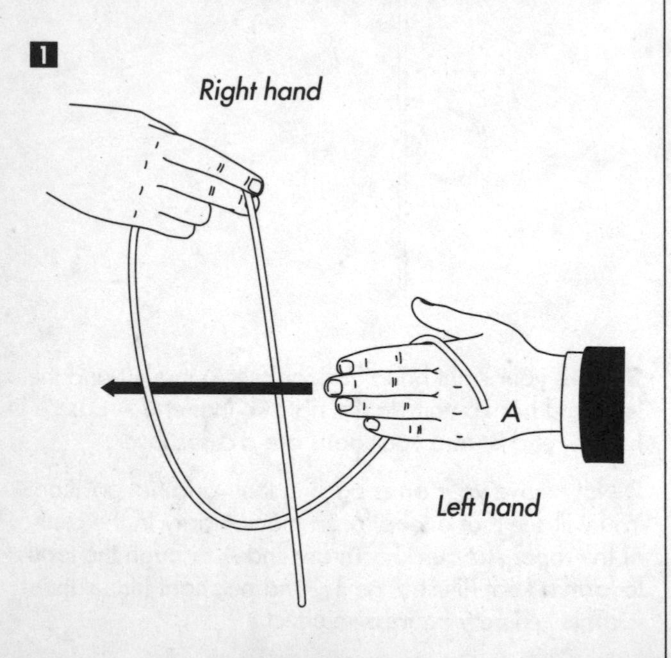

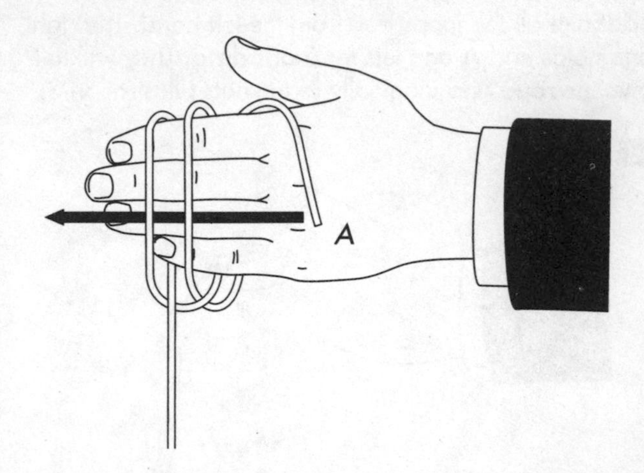

2 Take hold of the free rope at the centre with the right hand and lift it up with the first and second fingers (illustration 1). Twist the fingers away from you and hang the resulting loop on the left hand (illustrations 1 and 2).

3 Repeat step 2 to form another loop and drape this over the left fingers.

4 The number of loops you can make will depend on the length of the rope. The number of loops will equal the number of knots that appear.

5 Slip the first and second fingers of your right hand through the loops on your left hand (illustration 2) and grip end A of the rope. Pull end A through the loops and shake all the loops free from the left hand. The right hand holds end A and lets the loops drop. They will fall down the rope and magically form knots (illustration 3).

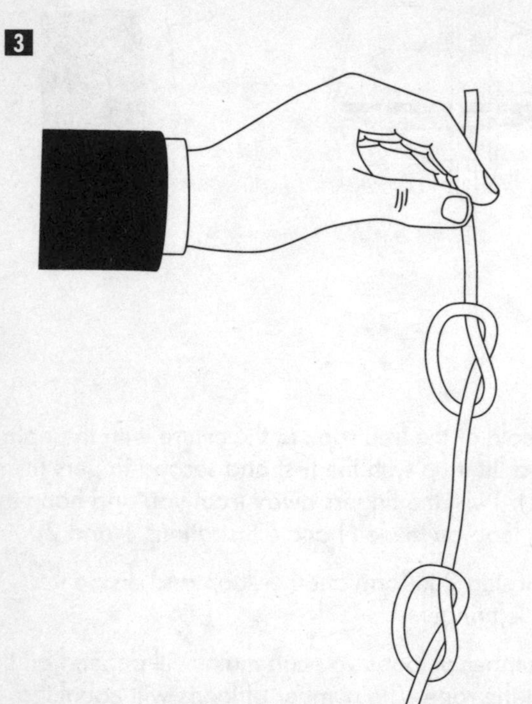

THE SLIDING KNOT

Effect *The audience watch the magician tie a genuine knot in a piece of rope. The magician then slides the knot along the rope and it comes off the end! The audience can keep the knot as a souvenir!*

Requirements *A long length of rope and a short piece of rope tied into a knot.*

Preparation *Place the knot in a pocket on your right side. Tie a slip knot (see page 17) in one end of the rope (we will call this end A). Hold end A in your left hand keeping the knot concealed (illustrations 1 and 2).*

• • • • • • • • • • • • • • •

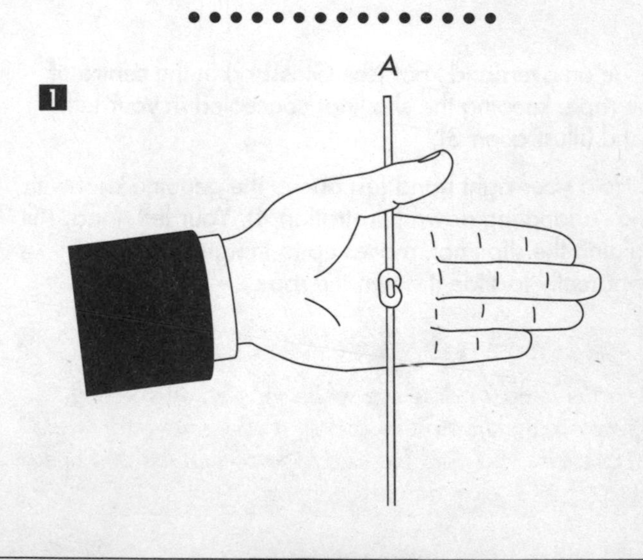

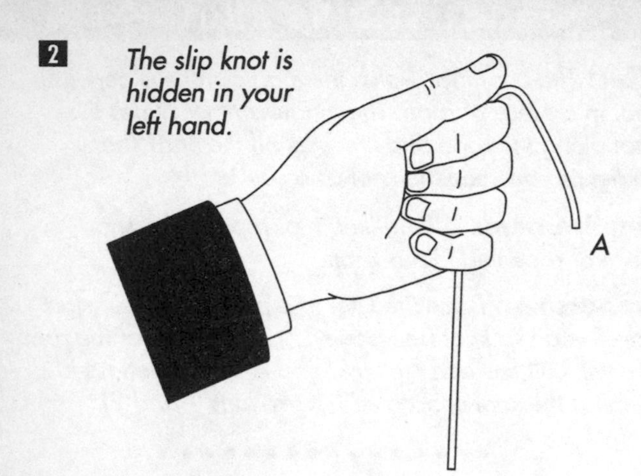

1 Tie an overhand knot (see Glossary) in the centre of the rope, keeping the slip knot concealed in your left hand (illustration 3).

2 Hold your right hand just above the genuine knot with end A dangling down (illustration 4). Your left hand, still holding the slip knot, moves up to the genuine knot, apparently to slide it down the rope.

TOP TIPS FOR TRICKSTERS

Remember not to use white rope when you are wearing a white shirt or jacket. If you must wear white, make sure you use coloured rope so that the audience can see the props!

3 But in fact your right hand covers the genuine knot as your left hand slides down the rope towards end A (illustration 5). Open the left hand to show the slip knot. The audience will believe this to be the genuine knot.

4 Now move the left hand and end A to the top, keeping the right hand over the genuine knot. Reverse the action in stage 3, moving the right hand up to the slip knot (taking the genuine knot with it) and apparently sliding the knot back to the centre.

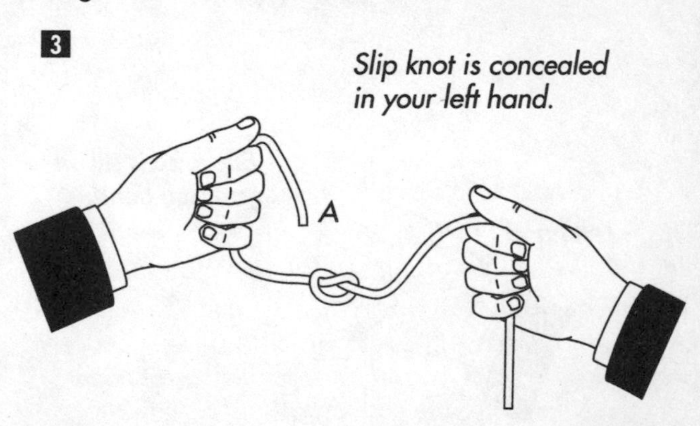

TOP TIPS FOR TRICKSTERS

As rope is very inexpensive it is always a good idea to finish your routine by passing your piece of rope out to the audience to keep as a souvenir.

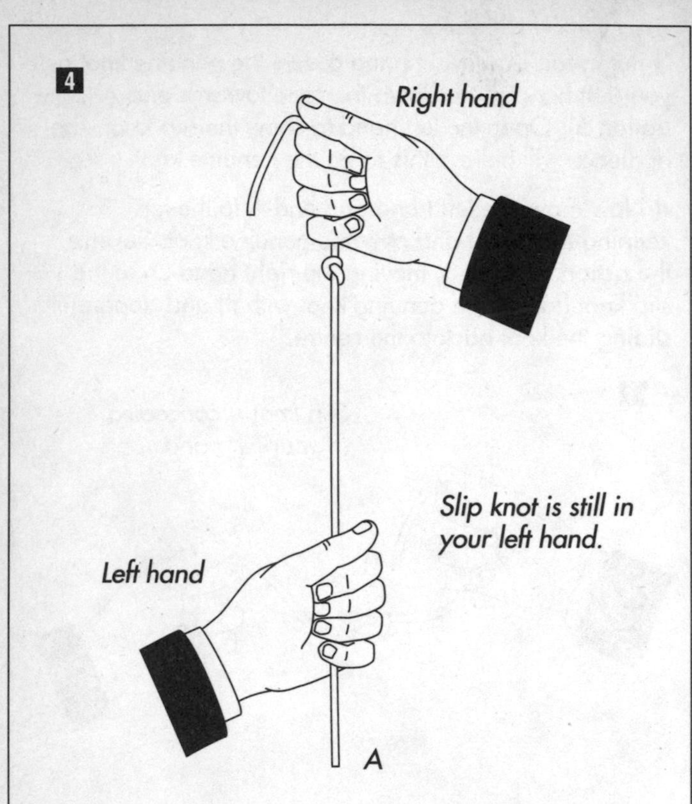

5 While the right hand covers the slip knot, tug on the rope with the left hand to "vanish" the slip knot. At the same time slide the right hand to the centre. Remove the right hand to show the knot is back where it began – in the centre.

6 You can have the rope and knot examined at this stage. While the audience are doing this, slip your right hand into your pocket and secretly take hold of the loose knot.

7 As you take back the rope, secretly slip the second and third fingers of your left hand into the loop of the genuine knot. Show the audience the knot in your hand.

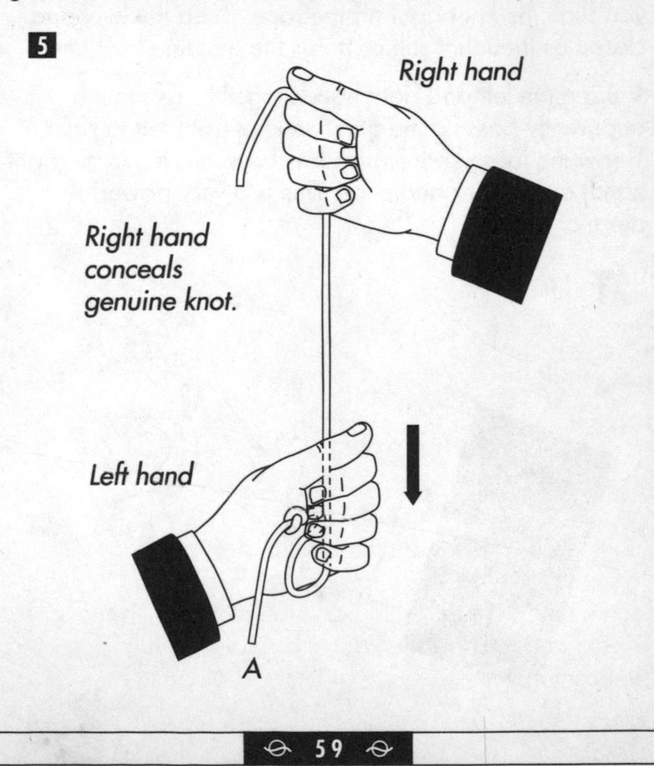

Close your left hand into a fist, keeping the fingers towards you to conceal the loop of rope running over them (illustration 6).

8 With the right hand hold tightly to the rope coming out of the top of the fist and slide your left hand down. The knot will slide down the rope. Continue to the end of the rope, where the knot will untie. It looks as though you slide the knot right off the rope. Keep the left hand closed as though it still contains the genuine knot.

9 Bring the left and right hands together as though apparently passing the genuine knot from left to right. Throw the loose knot (which has been hidden in the right hand) out to your audience. This is a very powerful piece of magic!

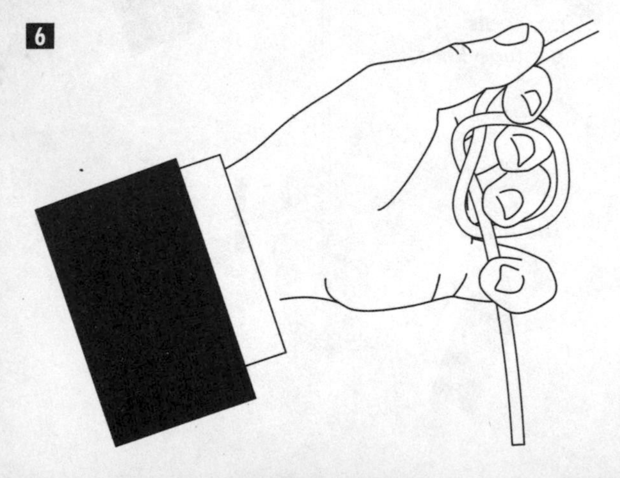

THE SHOELACE ROPE TIE

Effect *The magician ties a bow in a rope and pulls the ends through the bow to make a giant knot. When the audience blows on it the knot melts away.*

Requirements *A piece of soft white rope about 1m/3ft long.*

Preparation *None.*

• • • • • • • • • • • • • • •

1 Drape the rope over your hands as shown in illustration 1. Your right hand should be behind your left and slightly higher. The palms of your hands are facing you and the backs are towards your audience.

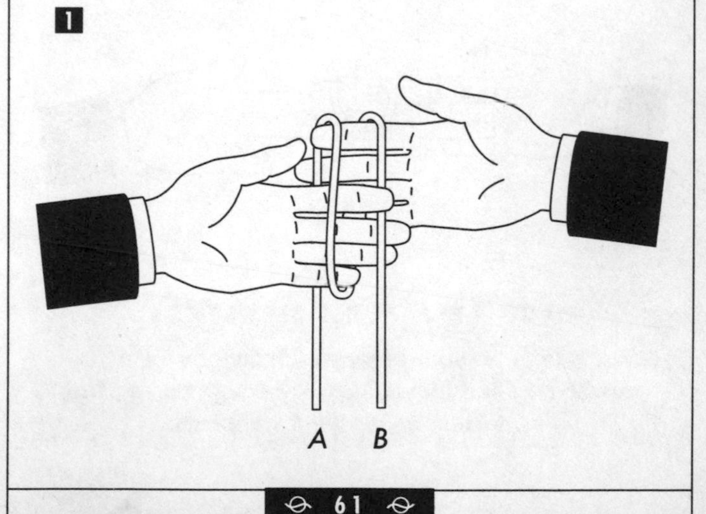

2 Clip the rope between the first and second fingers of each hand as shown in illustration 1.

3 Holding tightly to the bits of rope clipped between your fingers, move your hands slowly apart. As your hands move apart the clipped portions will form two loops of a bow (illustration 2). Continue pulling until the bow is pulled tight. You can then ask your audience if they ever get knots in their shoelaces – and explain that this is what you do if you are a magician!

4 Transfer the loops to the third finger of each hand. With the left thumb and first finger reach through the left loop and pull end A through (illustration 3).

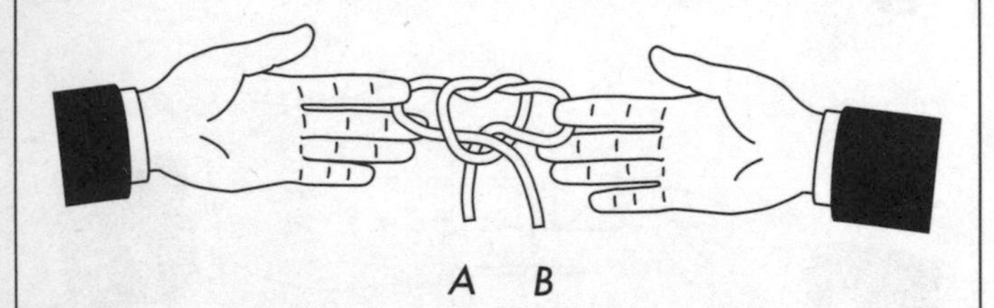

TOP TIPS FOR TRICKSTERS

You can make your escape tricks more exciting by pretending that something has gone wrong or that something unusual has happened.

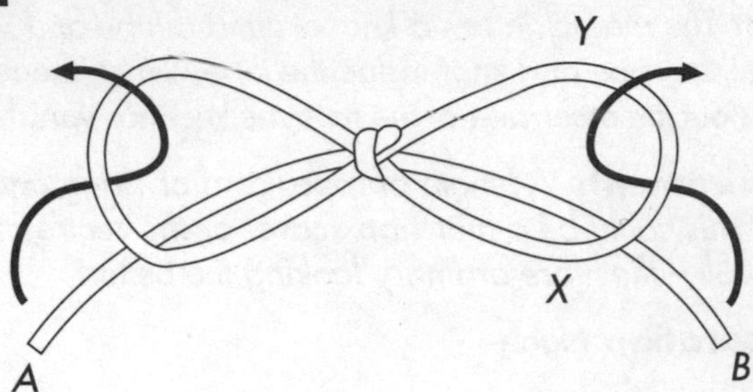

5 Give the right hand loop a half twist, bringing Y forward towards you. Then with your right thumb and first finger reach through the right hand loop and pull end B through (illustration 3).

6 Pull on the two ends of the rope and the bow will get smaller, becoming what appears to be a tangled knot. In fact this is a dissolving knot all set to vanish!

7 Ask your audience to blow on the knot. As they do so, pull hard on the ends and the knot will vanish!

TOP TIPS FOR TRICKSTERS

You may think that some of the methods in this book are too simple too fool anybody. Don't worry! All the best tricks are based on simple principles.

THROUGH THE TUNNEL

Effect *The magician ties a knot around a tube and pushes the rope and knot inside the tube. When the rope comes out the other side of the tube the knot has vanished!*

Requirements *A length of rope, cord or string and a tube. This could be a matchbox cover or the centre of a toilet roll – the more ordinary looking the better!*

Preparation *None.*

• • • • • • • • • • • • • • •

1 Ask the audience if they have ever heard of black holes. Explain that you have one with you, and bring out your tube! You can say, "Don't laugh, this is a

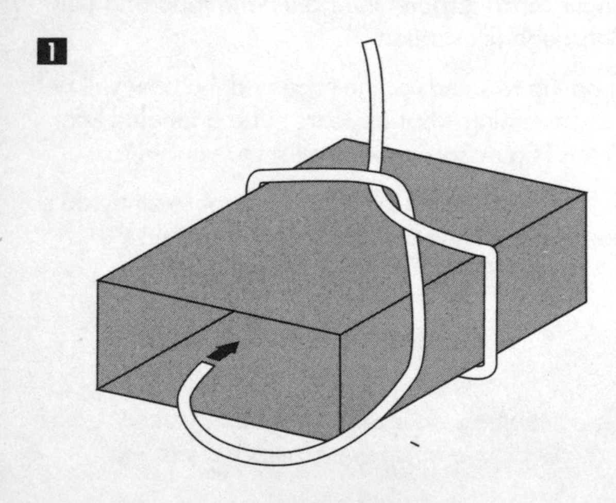

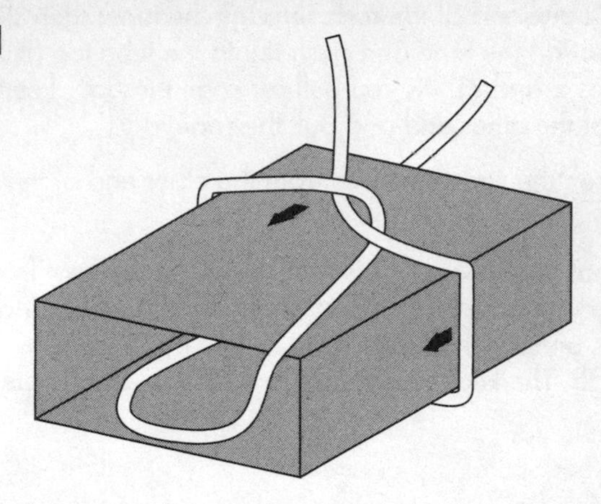

serious scientific experiment to discover what happens in black holes."

2 Drape the rope over the tube and tie a regular overhand knot around the tube (illustration 1).

3 Explain that anything can exist outside a black hole – like the knot, for example – but when things go through a black hole, anything can happen!

TOP TIPS FOR TRICKSTERS

Coloured rope is available from the haberdashery section of most department stores.

4 Push one end of the rope through the tube, then slide the knot off the tube and push it into the tube too (illustrations 2 and 3). As you pull the rope through, keep hold of the other end and pull the rope taut.

5 When the rope emerges from the other end of the tube the knot has completely vanished!

6 What really happens is this: removing the knot from around the tube forms a slip knot (illustration 3), and this comes undone inside the tube as you pull the rope through. The knot has disappeared into a black hole!

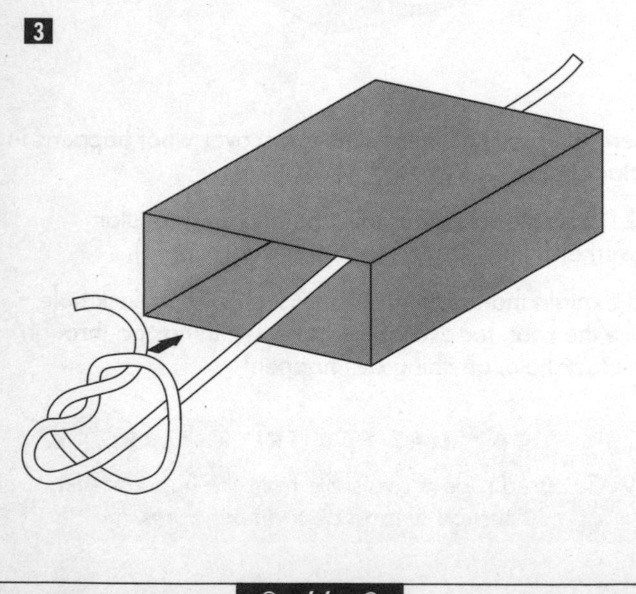

SIMPLE ESCAPES

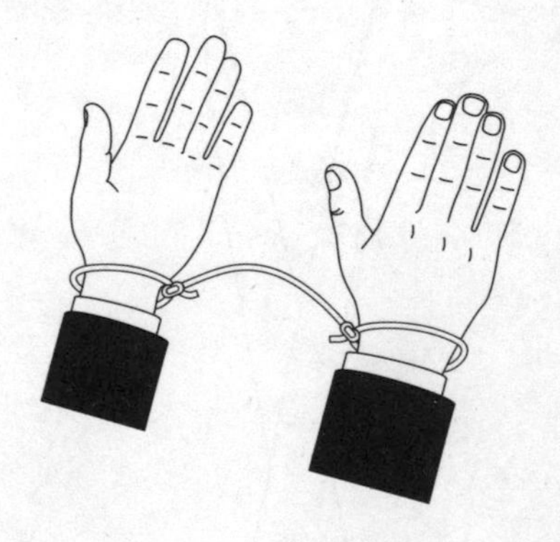

SCISSOR ESCAPE

Effect *A piece of string is tied securely around the handle of a pair of scissors – yet the scissors magically escape!*

Requirements *A pair of scissors and a piece of string.*

Preparation *No preparation is needed.*

●●●●●●●●●●●●●●●

1

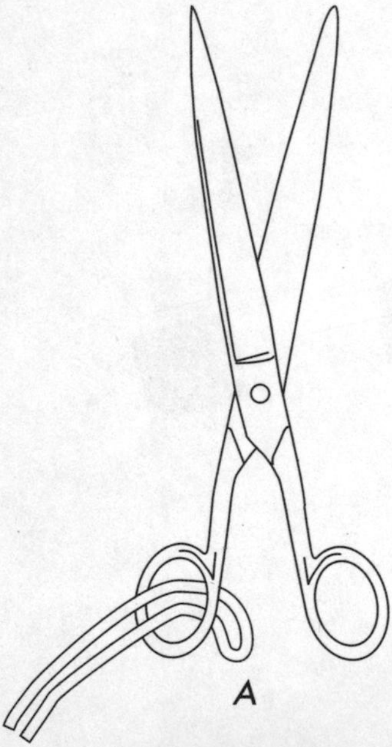

A

2

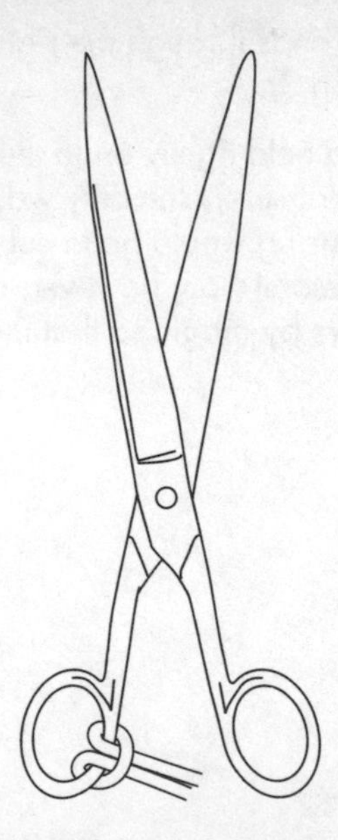

1 Double the string and thread the centre loop A through the left handle of the scissors.

2 Thread the loop A over the two ends of the string and pull tight (illustration 2).

TOP TIPS FOR TRICKSTERS

It is worth remembering that rope tricks are very versatile and can be performed for children, a group of friends or before a large audience.

3 Thread the two ends through the right handle of the scissors (illustration 3).

4 Ask someone to hold tightly on to the two ends of the string. Point out that surely the only way to release the scissors from the string would be to cut through the string with the scissors! You, however, are going to remove the scissors by magic so that the string remains undamaged.

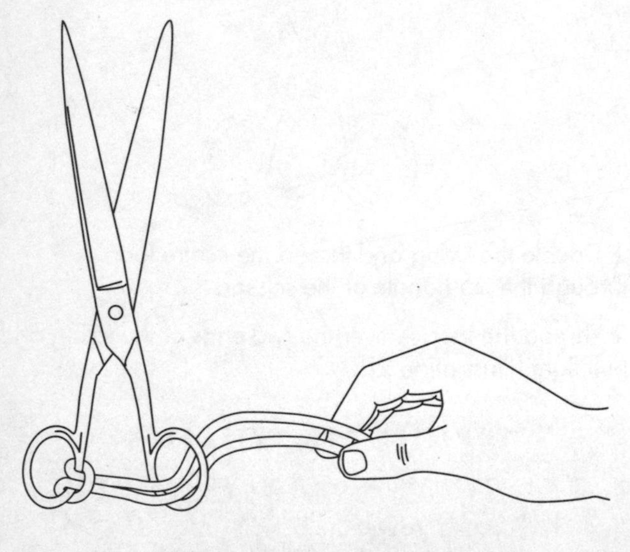

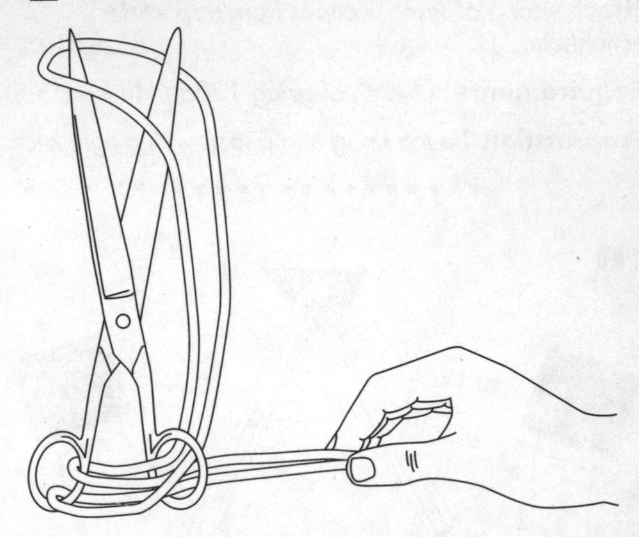

5 Pull the loop A through the right handle and up over the point of the scissors (illustration 4). Then bring the loop right down over the scissors.

6 Ask whoever is holding the two ends to pull hard and the scissors will come free!

You could use yourself in place of the scissors! Tie a large bangle to each of your ankles using cord. Then thread the rope through the bangles as you would through the handles of the scissors.

BUTTONHOLE RELEASE

Effect *A loop of string escapes from a spectator's buttonhole.*

Requirements *A length of string 120cm/4ft long.*

Preparation *Tie the string into a loop with a tight knot.*

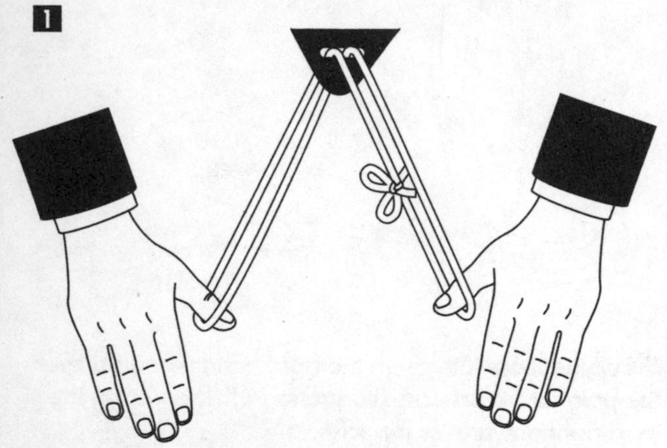

TOP TIPS FOR TRICKSTERS

Remember that white rope can get dirty very quickly when you rehearse with it. Always try to use a fresh piece of rope for each performance.

2

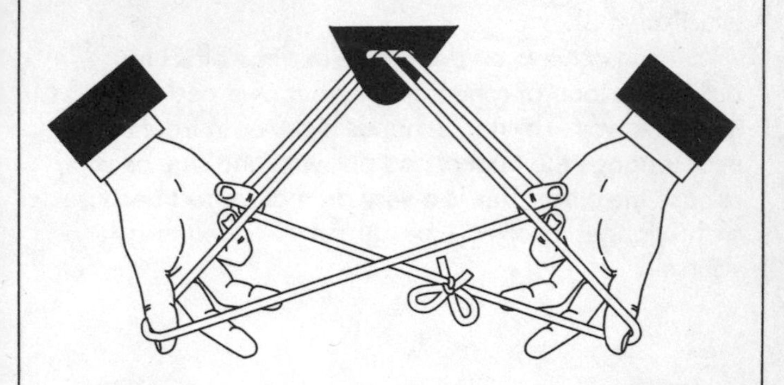

1 Thread the loop through the buttonhole of a spectator, and hook your thumbs through each end of the loop (illustration 1).

2 Bring your hands together. Insert the little fingers as shown in illustration 2 – each picks up the lower strand from the opposite side.

TOP TIPS FOR TRICKSTERS

When using silk handkerchiefs in your rope magic always ensure that they are ironed and pressed before each performance. Audiences DO notice.

3 Release the left little finger and the right thumb, at the same time pulling the loop tight. The loop will appear to pass through the buttonhole without damaging it (illustration 3).

You can achieve an even more exciting effect by pulling the loop of rope through your own neck! It works the same way – bring the hands together in front of the neck, engage the fingers and pull with one side as you release the other. This is a very dramatic effect because of the danger involved – be careful you don't throttle yourself!

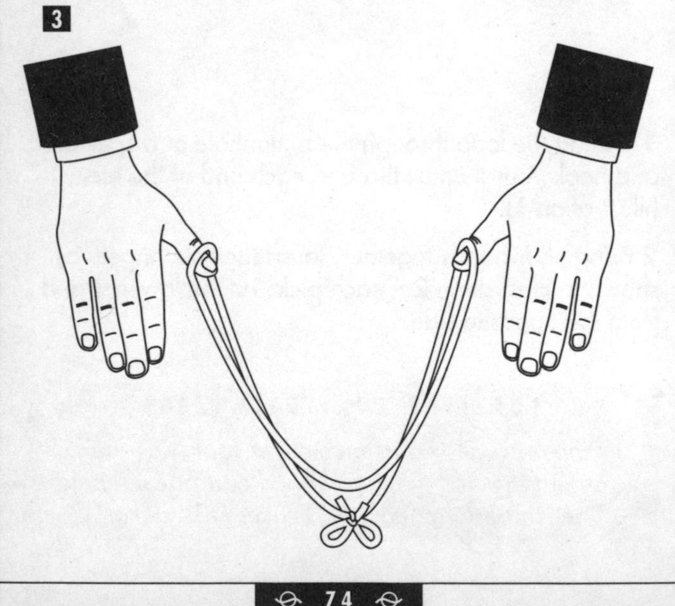

DOUBLE ESCAPE

Effect *The magician and a spectator are tied securely together, but they manage to escape by magic.*

Requirements *Two ropes, each 120cm/4ft long.*

Preparation *No preparation is required.*

• • • • • • • • • • • • • • •

1 Tie one of the ropes around the wrists of the spectator (illustration 1).

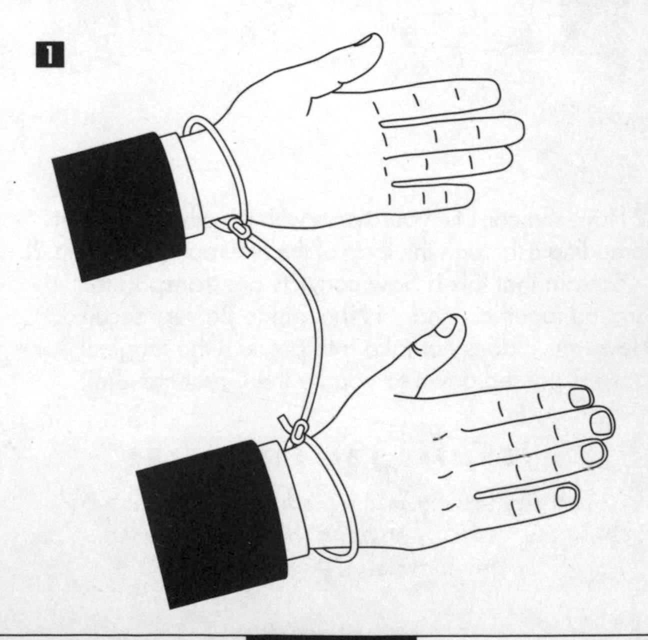

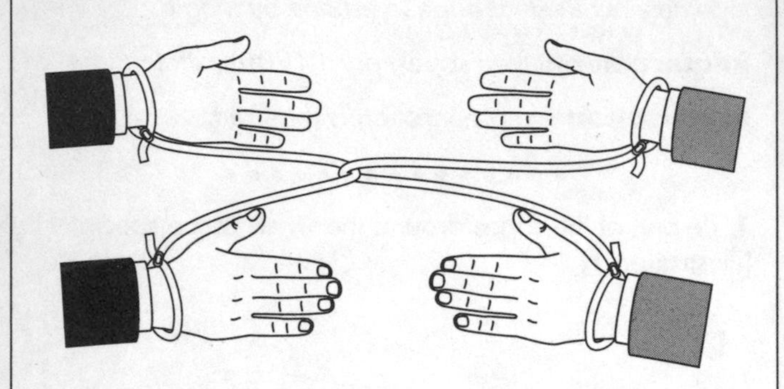

2 Have someone tie your wrists with the other rope, first threading it through the loop of the first rope (illustration 2).

Explain that this is how convicts are transported around together, and it is thought to be very secure. However, it does not take into account the magical powers passed down to you by the Great Houdini!

TOP TIPS FOR TRICKSTERS

Escapes are much more effective if you use the strongest looking person in the room to tie the knots and make sure you are secure.

3 It seems impossible for you to escape, but it can be done. Pull the centre loop A of the spectator's rope and thread it under the loop tied around your left wrist. When you have enough rope pulled through pull it over your left hand (illustration 3).

4 If the spectator now steps back you will both be free! With practice you can learn to do step 3 in just a few seconds.

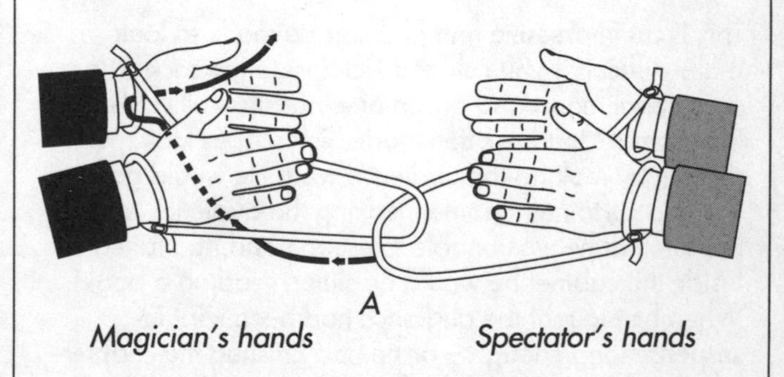

TOP TIPS FOR TRICKSTERS

Your rope will stay cleaner and whiter longer if you ensure your hands and nails are kept clean before practice sessions, rehearsals and performances.

SACK ESCAPE

Effect *The magician escapes, like the Great Houdini, from a big canvas sack.*

Requirements *A canvas sack, big enough for you to sit in comfortably, which has eyelets around the top with a long piece of rope threaded through them. You also need a screen or cover.*

Preparation *There is no preparation.*

• • • • • • • • • • • • • • • •

This is an impressive feat and can be made to look really difficult if you roll and kick inside the sack. The occasional moan and groan of exhaustion all adds to the drama! Houdini often made his escapes look more difficult by making the audience wait. He would go inside a curtained cabinet, leaving the audience to believe that he was unable to escape and had failed. Inside the cabinet he would be sitting reading a book! When he thought the audience had been kept in suspense long enough – or he had finished the chapter! – he would stumble out of the cabinet, as though he was exhausted, free once again!

TOP TIPS FOR TRICKSTERS

If you are performing for children it is always a good idea to use coloured rope to add visual appeal.

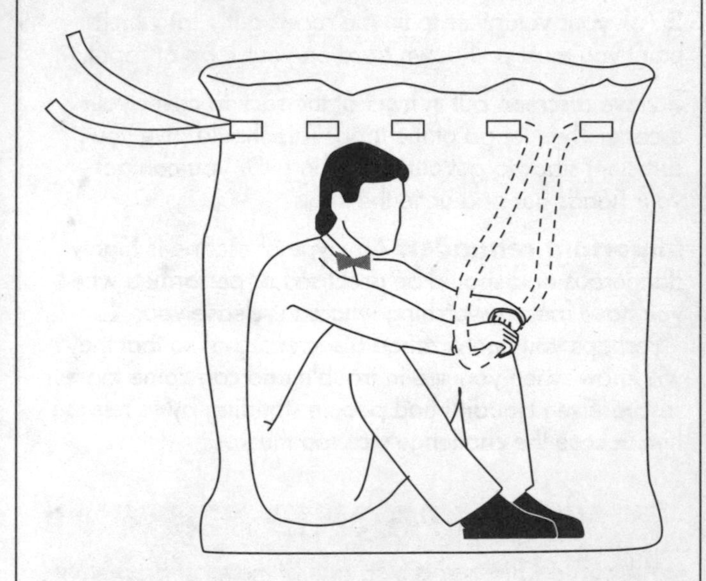

TOP TIPS FOR TRICKSTERS

One of the main reasons for Houdini's fame was the challenge aspect that his escapes offered. People enjoy the tension of a challenge – remember this when performing your escapes.

1 Climb into the sack and ask someone to tie you into it. As you climb inside pull a loop of the rope inside with you (at least 60cm/2ft).

2 Ask your volunteer to tie the rope tightly (at which point you must pull down hard on your loop of rope).

3 Have a screen put in front of the sack to cover your escape. Then let go of the loop. This should give you sufficient slack to get out of the bag. Or you can get your hands out and untie the knots.

Important reminder: Any type of escape is highly dangerous and should be practised or performed when you have friends watching who can release you.

Perhaps you can arrange a secret signal so that they will know when you are in trouble and can come to your rescue. Even Houdini had people standing by to release him in case the challenge was too much.

MILBOURNE CHRISTOPHER

Milbourne Christopher was one of the most prominent American magicians in the second part of the twentieth century. He toured the world with his own big illusion show, appeared on Broadway and starred in some of America's first televised magic "specials", paving the way for the likes of Doug Henning and David Copperfield. But the show's highlight was a rope routine, admired by magicians the world over.

HANDKERCHIEF TRICKS

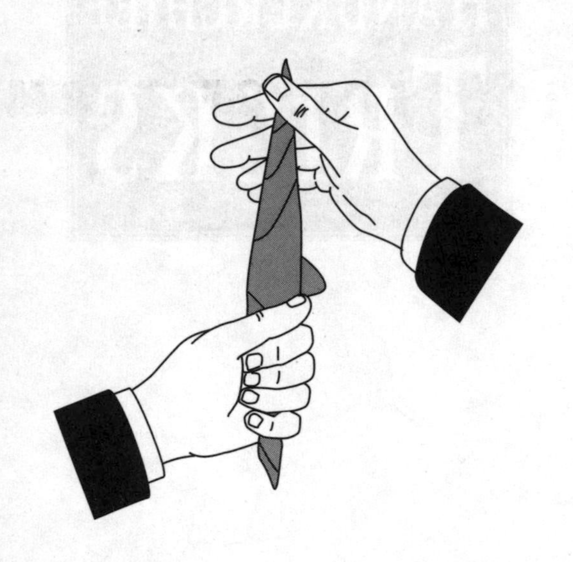

GLOSSARY OF TERMS

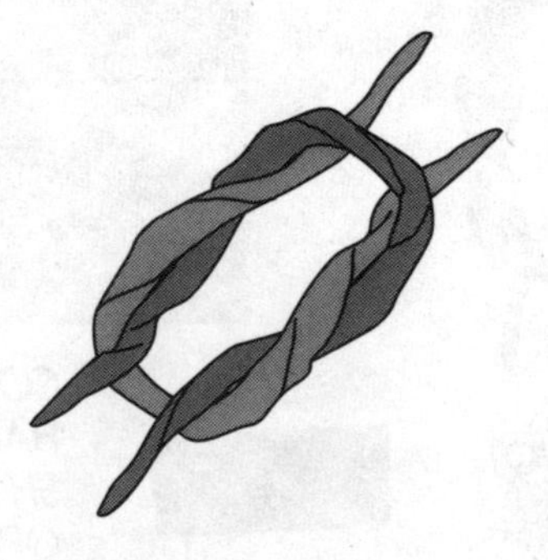

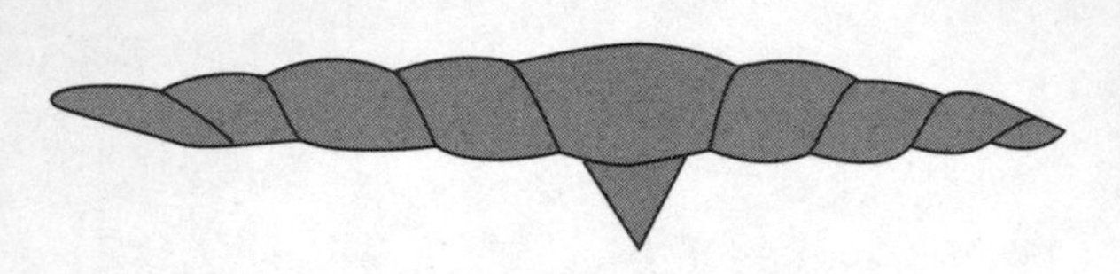

TWISTING A HANDKERCHIEF INTO A "ROPE"

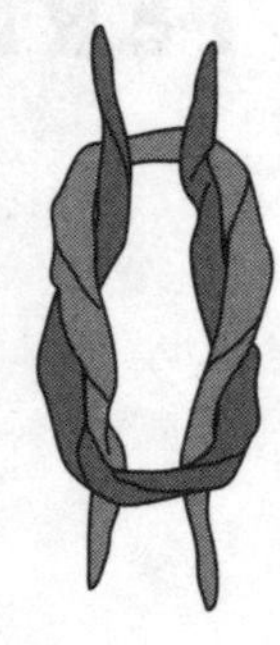

REEF KNOT

CORNER OF A HANDKERCHIEF SHOWING THE OPENING IN THE HEM

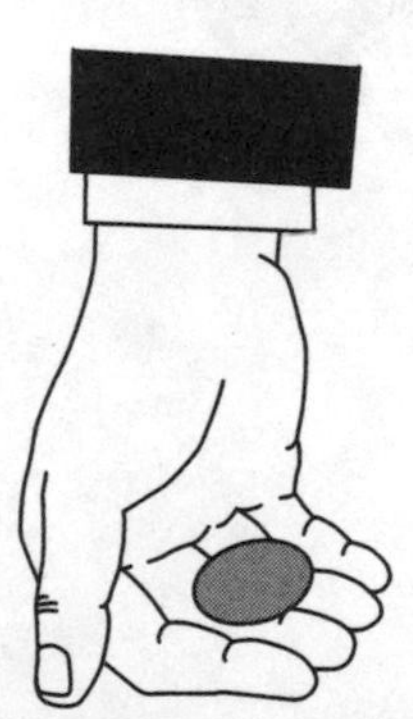

FINGER PALM OF A COIN

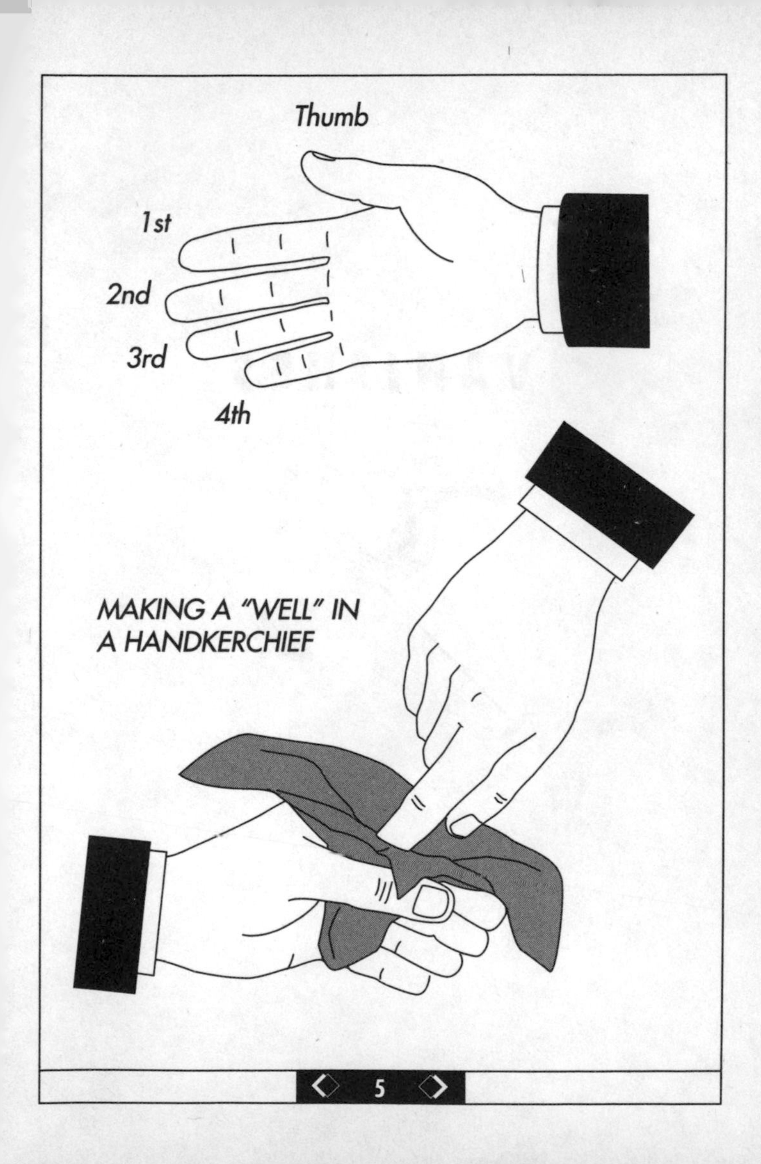
Thumb
1st
2nd
3rd
4th
MAKING A "WELL" IN
A HANDKERCHIEF

VANISHES

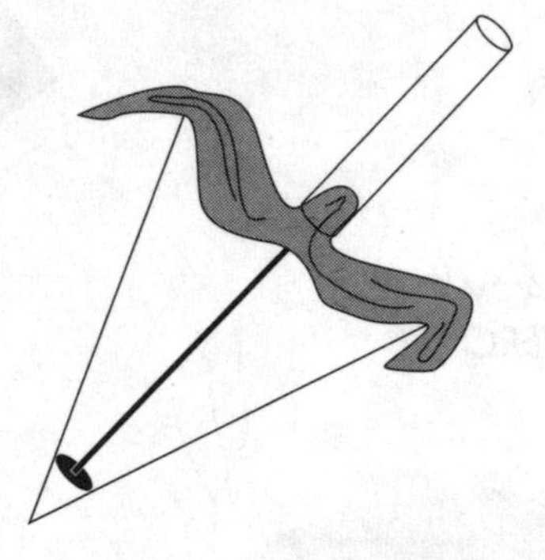

◇ DISSOLVING KNOT ◇

Effect *The magician ties a knot in the centre of a silk handkerchief. When the spectators blow on the knot it simply melts away.*

Requirements *A silk handkerchief or scarf 45 x 45cm/18 x 18in.*

Preparation *None.*

• • • • • • • • • • • • • • •

1 Hold the handkerchief by diagonally opposite corners between the first and second fingers of the left hand (end A) and the right hand (end B). Twist the handkerchief into a "rope" as shown in illustration 1.

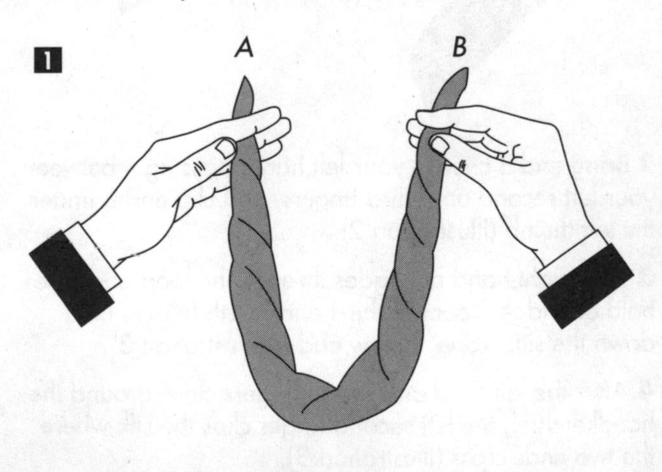

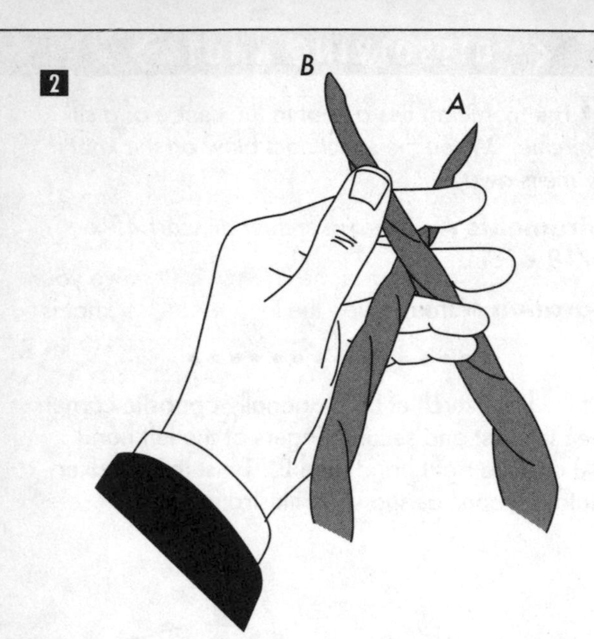

2 Bring end B over to your left hand, passing it between your left second and third fingers, and clip end B under the left thumb (illustration 2).

3 Your right hand now goes through the loop and takes hold of end A. Your left third and fourth fingers hold down the silk "rope" below end A (illustration 3).

4 After the left third and fourth fingers close around the handkerchief, the left second finger clips the silk where the two ends cross (illustration 3).

5 Pull end A through the loop with your right hand. End B is held tightly between the left thumb and first finger. The left third and fourth fingers release their grip around the silk as your left second finger hooks and pulls the lower portion of end B through the loop (illustration 4).

6 As you pull on end A a knot will form around the loop held by the second finger of the left hand. Remove your left second finger from inside the loop when the knot is tight enough to hold its own shape. This appears to be a genuine knot, but it is actually a slip knot.

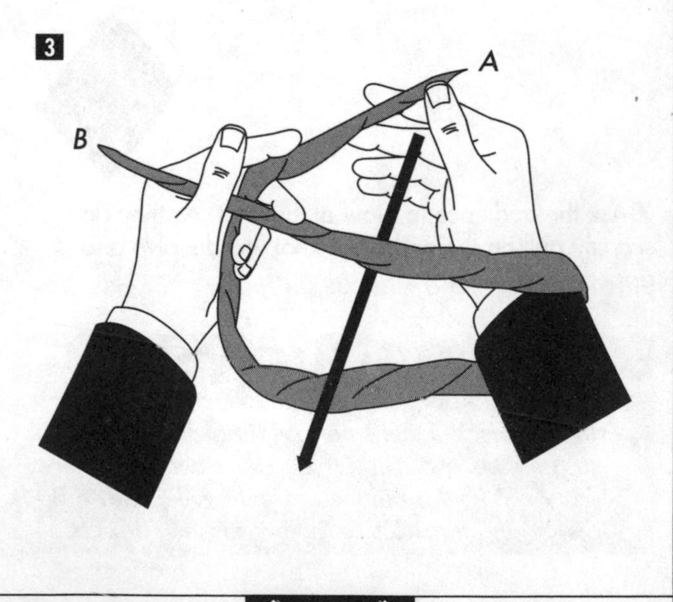

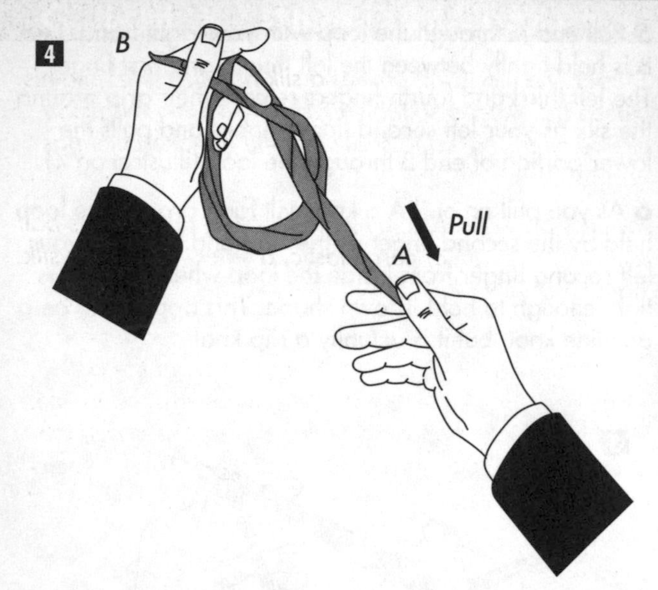

7 Ask the audience to blow at the knot. As they do, secretly pull on the ends. The knot will dissolve and appear to melt away.

ADE DUVAL (1898-1965)

Many magicians use silk handkerchief in their performances, but the American magician Ade Duval was one the few to create an entire act of "Silken Sorcery". With this unique act he travelled the world performing in exclusive glamourous night spots.

◇ THE HANDKERCHIEF VANISH ◇

Effect *The magician pushes a silk handkerchief into his closed fist. After a suitable mystical pass the magician slowly opens his fist to show that the handkerchief has vanished!*

Requirements *A small hollow ball (a table tennis ball is ideal), a length of cord elastic, a safety pin and a silk handkerchief.*

Preparation *You will need to make a special prop known as a "pull". Cut a hole in one side of the ball large enough for the handkerchief to be pushed inside. Attach the ball to one end of the elastic and attach the safety pin to the other end (illustration 1). Pin the safety pin on the inside left of your jacket (illustration 2).*

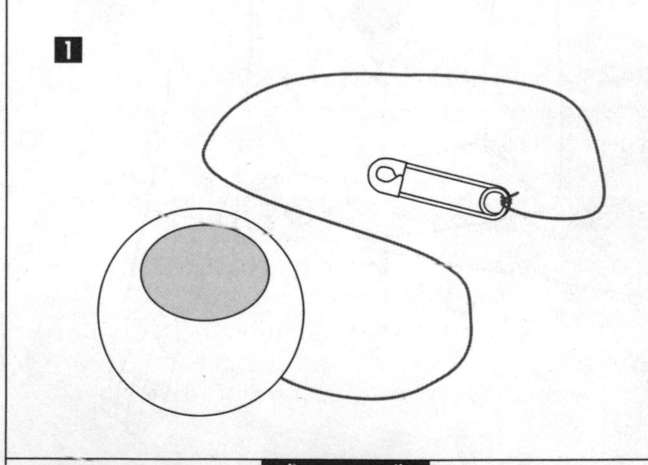

You will have to adjust the length of the cord elastic so that when it is stretched, the ball can be held comfortably in your right hand. When you release the ball the elastic should pull it up into your jacket. You need to experiment to get the right length of elastic for you.

Prepare by pinning the elastic inside your jacket as already described, and stretching the elastic so that you can hold the ball concealed in your closed right hand with the opening at the top (illustration 2) .

●●●●●●●●●●●●●●●

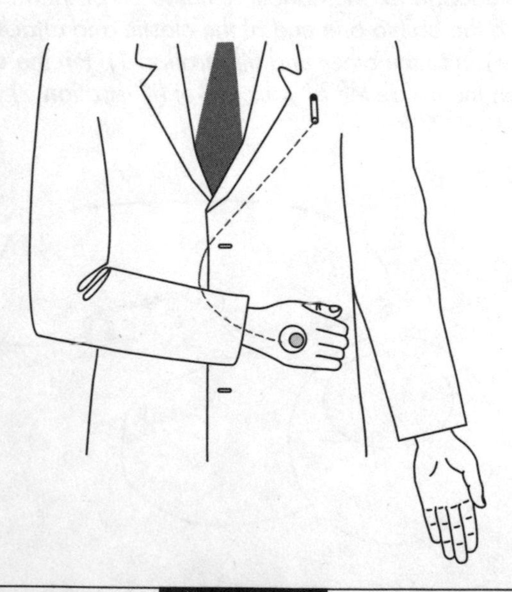

1 Display the handkerchief and push it inside your closed fist, ensuring it goes inside the ball (illustration 3).

2 Wave your empty hand over your closed fist, at the same time releasing the ball, allowing it to shoot quickly inside your jacket, taking the handkerchief with it.

3 After a sufficient build-up you can slowly open your hand to show that it is completely empty.

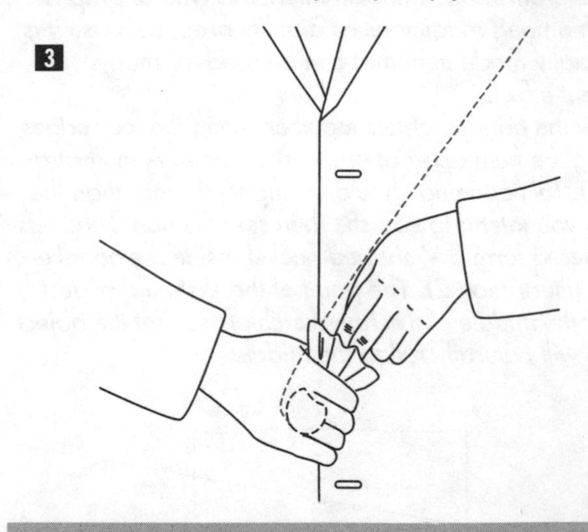

TOP TIPS FOR TRICKSTERS

Magic with coloured silk handkerchiefs is ideal for entertaining young children because it is bright, bold and uses a prop which they can all relate to.

◇ THE HANDKERCHIEF VANISHER ◇

Effect *A coin, ring or card is wrapped in a handkerchief and then vanishes!*

Requirements *Two identical pocket handkerchiefs, preferably with a colourful pattern or design.*

Preparation *The two handkerchiefs are made into a special "vanishing" handkerchief. This type of prop is known among magicians as a utility prop, because it is a specially made item that can be used for many different effects.*

Sew the handkerchiefs together along the four edges, leaving the hem open at one corner (point A in illustration 1). This opening should be slightly bigger than the object you intend to vanish. Then sew the handkerchiefs together to form a V-shaped pocket inside the handkerchiefs (illustration 2). The point of the V should be just below the middle of the handkerchiefs so that the object inside will naturally fall to the middle.

1

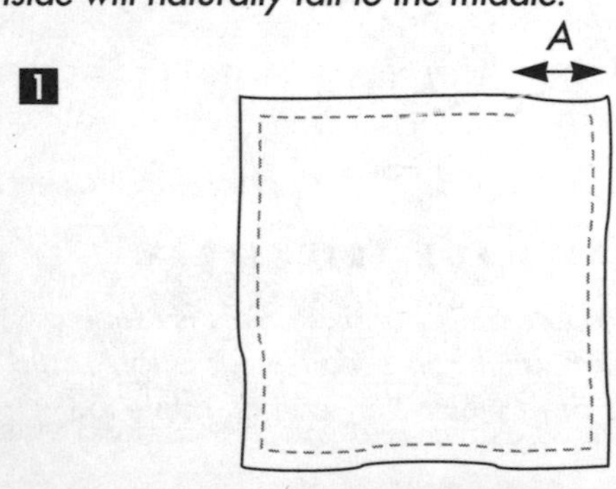

2

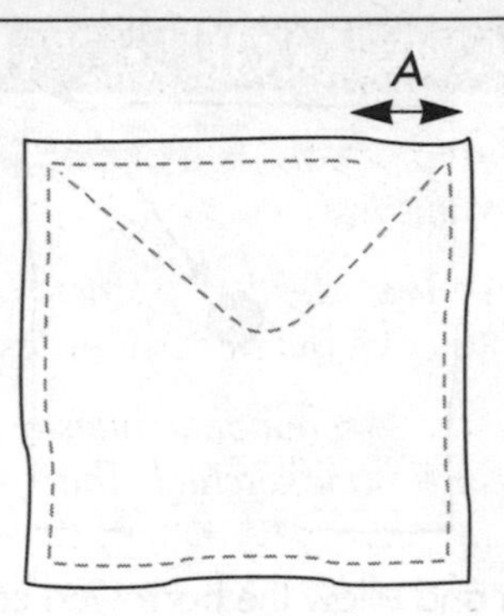

To give you an example of how to use the vanisher we will assume you want vanish a borrowed coin. Prepare by inserting a duplicate of the coin you intend to use inside the secret pocket (illustration 3).

• • • • • • • • • • • • • • •

1 Hold the handkerchief by the corners at the top of the sewn V (due to the nature of the material the audience will be unable to see where it has been sewn). Drape the handkerchief over your open empty left palm so that the hidden coin rests on your hand.

2 Borrow a coin and place it directly on top of the secret hidden coin.

3 With your right hand pick up both coins together – the borrowed one and, through the layer of material, the hidden coin. Turn everything upside down so that the handkerchief covers the coins and your hand. Hang on to

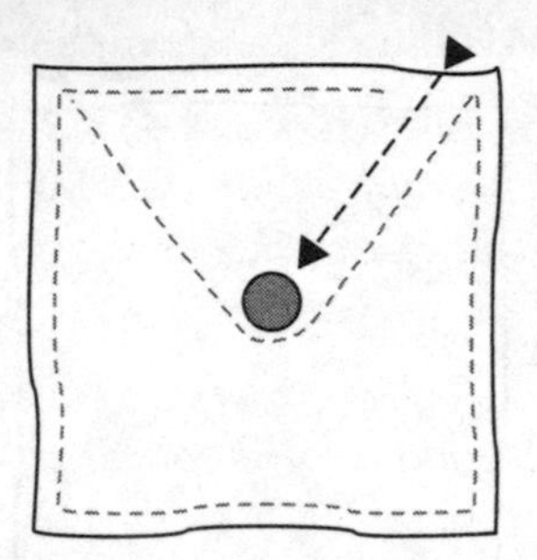

the hidden coin and allow the borrowed coin to slip into the palm of your hand where you can keep it concealed.

4 Ask a member of the audience to hold the coin through the handkerchief. They will feel the coin inside the handkerchief and hold it believing it to be the borrowed coin. When they have taken hold of the handkerchief and coin, allow your right hand to drop naturally to your side with the borrowed coin concealed in your curled fingers. You can secretly dispose of it in your pocket or load it somewhere to be reproduced later.

5 To vanish the coin hold one corner of the handkerchief and pull it from the spectator's grasp. They will feel the coin being pulled from their fingers, but fail to see it fall. It looks as though the coin has magically vanished in mid-air!

This is a very effective vanish and can be used in many other effects.

◇ VANISHING WAND ◇

Effect *The magician makes a cone out of newspaper and pushes a silk handkerchief inside with a magic wand. The magician tears the newspaper into pieces to show that the silk handkerchief has completely vanished!*

Requirements *A newspaper, a silk handkerchief and a special magic wand (see "Preparation").*

Preparation *As the title of the effect suggests, it is the magic wand which makes the handkerchief disappear. To make this you will need a long thin hollow tube, plus a length of thin dowelling. Glue a circle of black card slightly larger than the diameter of the tube to the end of the dowelling (see illustration 1). Paint the tube black and white so that it looks like a magic wand.*

•••••••••••••••

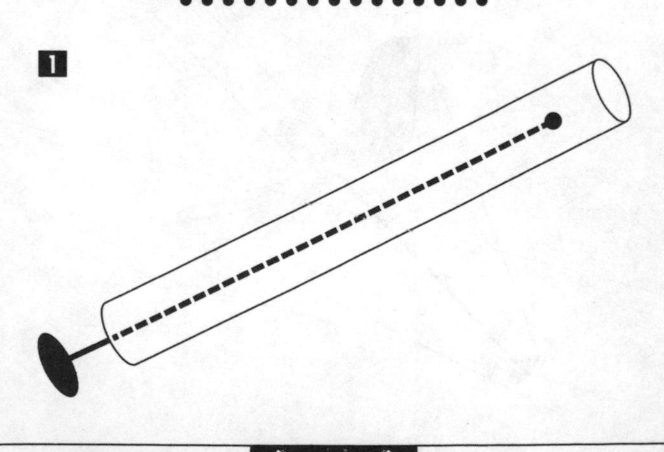

1 Form the newspaper into a cone. Rattle the magic wand inside the cone to prove it is empty. Secretly allow the rod to slide out and remain inside the cone. Drape the handkerchief over the mouth of the cone.

2 Using the magic wand you appear to push the silk down into the cone. In reality the wand slides over the rod and the rod and handkerchief are pushed up inside the hollow wand.

3 Remove the wand from the cone (with the rod and handkerchief tucked inside it) and set the wand down to one side.

5 Say the magic words and tear open the newspaper cone to show that it is completely empty!

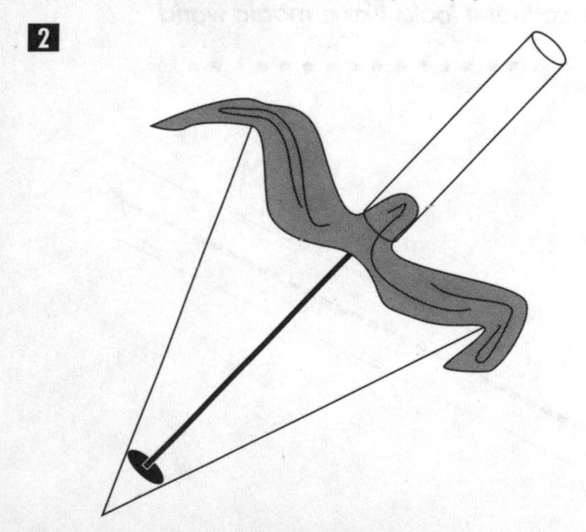

ANIMATION

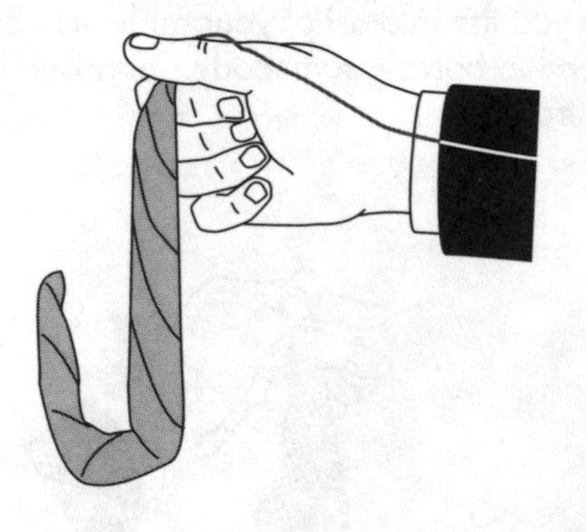

Effect *The magician hypnotises a handkerchief and it moves mysteriously as though obeying commands.*

Requirements *A pocket handkerchief.*

Preparation *None.*

• • • • • • • • • • • • • • • •

1 Claim to be able to hypnotise any pocket handkerchief. This is an impressive and unusual claim and will surely gain you the interest of your audience. Explain that you need to borrow somebody's handkerchief to be "put into a trance".

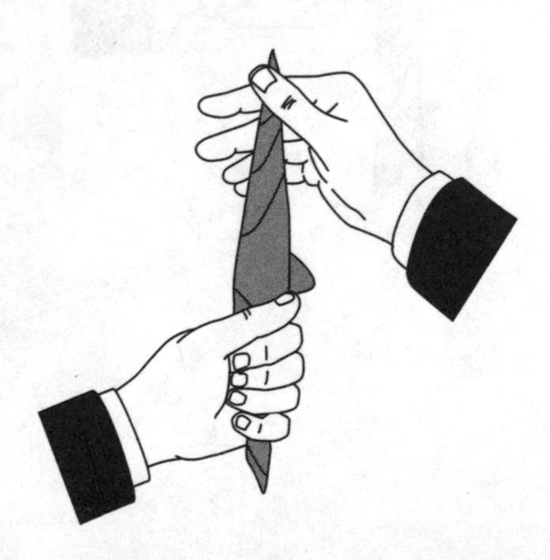

2 When you have borrowed a handkerchief spread it out flat on the table (it always worth having a handkerchief of your own in your pocket in case nobody in your audience has one in a suitable state!).

3 Grab the top lefthand corner of the handkerchief with your left fingers and thumb, and with your right fingers and thumb hold the left edge about halfway down. Lift up the handkerchief and twist it between your hands to form a tightly twisted "rope".

4 Hold the handkerchief up vertically with your right hand at the top and the left hand below (illustration 1).

5 Keep hold with the right hand and move your left hand to a position about halfway up. As you do this make sure the handkerchief remains tightly twisted.

6 Pull the handkerchief tight between your hands and slowly let go with your right hand. The handkerchief will remain rigid as though hypnotised. "There you are," you say, "completely under my control!"

7 Gaze at the handkerchief and say in your most commanding tones, "Forward, forward, forward!" At the same time gently move your left thumb down the handkerchief and it will lean towards you.

8 Continue, "Back, back, back!" and move your left thumb back up the handkerchief. It will gradually slowly move away from you.

9 Repeat this a number of times, then move your left hand to hold the handkerchief horizontal to show it is rigid and completely in a trance. Say, "But it can be woken. On the count of three, when I snap my fingers it will wake up and will be unable to remember any of the things that have happened in the last few minutes!"

10 Return the handkerchief to its vertical position, click your fingers and flick open the handkerchief. Return it to its owner with a warning that it may never be the same again!

TOP TIPS FOR TRICKSTERS

Magic with silk handkerchiefs is often best when performed "silently" to a musical background, without the usual magician's patter.

◇ FATIMA THE DANCING HANKY ◇

This is not a baffling trick, but an amusing "bit of business" to perform either between tricks or to entertain a group of children at a social event. It would be a nice follow up to the "Hypnotised Hanky".

Effect *The magician transforms a pocket handkerchief into a doll-like replica of a ballet dancer. At the magician's command the figure seems to come alive with a high kicking spinning flourish!*

Requirements *A pocket handkerchief.*

Preparation *None.*

• • • • • • • • • • • • • • •

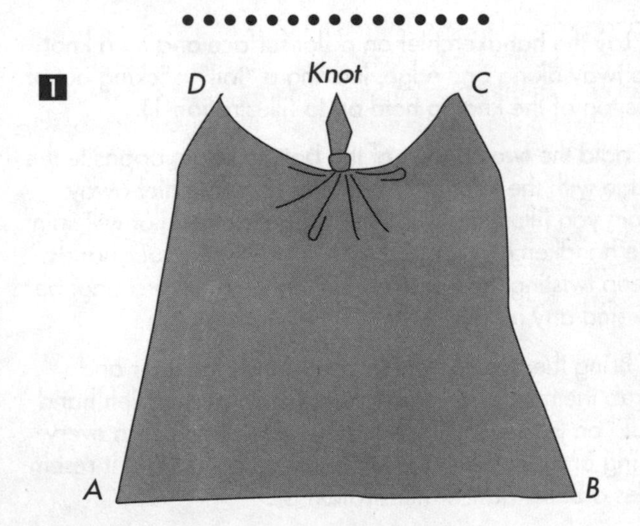

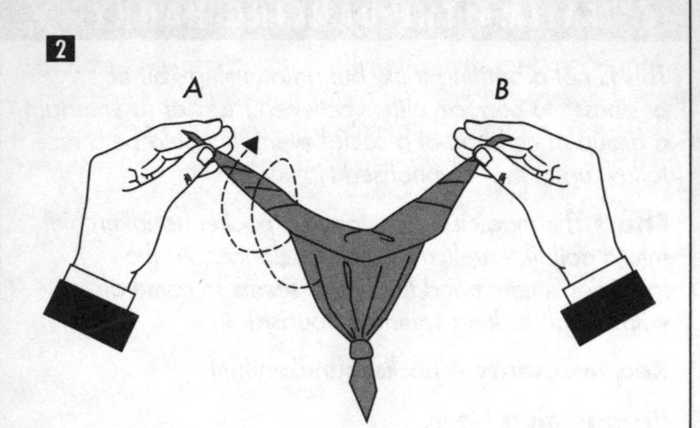

1 Lay the handkerchief on a flat surface and tie a knot halfway along one edge, leaving a "tail"' sticking out of the top of the knot to hold on to (illustration 1).

2 Hold the two corners of the bottom edge, opposite the edge with the knot in it. Twirl the handkerchief away from you (illustration 2). The weight of the knot will spin the handkerchief around the hem between your hands. Keep twisting the handkerchief tightly, until it cannot be twisted any further.

3 Bring the two corners in your hands together and grab them both in your right hand. With your left hand hold on to the "tail" sticking out of the knot. Turn everything around – with the knot at the top – so that it resembles a ballet dancer (illustration 3).

4 By moving your hands you can animate the "ballet dancer" so that she swings her hips or bows. If you let go of one corner with the right hand you can make her perform a high kick (illustration 4), and then go into a dramatic spin, until you are just left with a hanky with a knot in it! A ballet dancer's career is always short!

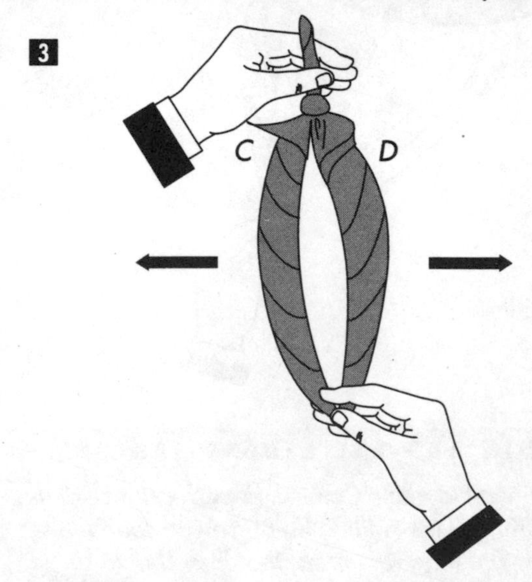

TOP TIPS FOR TRICKSTERS

Silk handkerchief magic tends to appeal to female audiences in particular. They seem to prefer this kind of magic to card tricks!

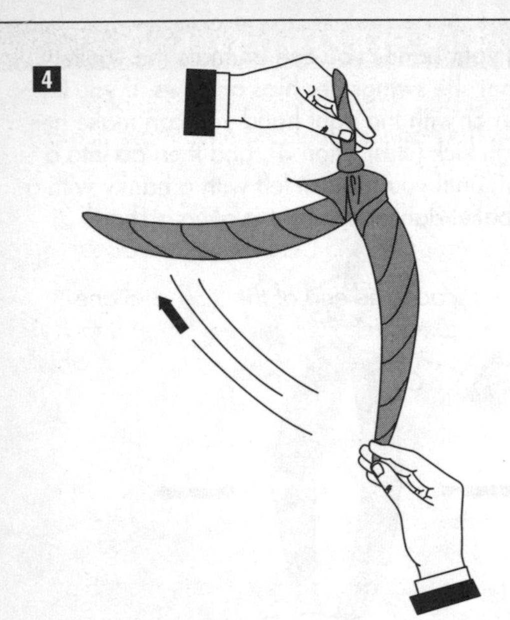

HOUDIN AND THE KING'S HANKIES

During Robert Houdin's Command performance at the palace of King Louis Phillipe he borrowed six handkerchiefs. The King requested that they should be magically sent under the last orange tree outside the palace. A guard was sent to the tree while Houdin vanished the bundle of hankies. An iron box was found buried under the selected tree and locked inside were the six borrowed handkerchiefs!

◇ THE SERPENT SILK ◇

Effect *The magician ties a knot in the middle of a handkerchief. The handkerchief begins to move like a snake and unties the knot!*

Requirements *A silk handkerchief 45 x 45cm/18 x18in and 180cm/6ft of fine black nylon thread .*

Preparation *Attach one end of the thread to one corner of the handkerchief. Attach the other end to your table. Fold the handkerchief and place it on your table alongside the length of thread.*

• • • • • • • • • • • • • • • •

1 Pick up the handkerchief and stand about 1m/3ft to the side of the table. Hold the handkerchief by the corner knotted to the thread. We will call this end A. The thread should pass under your right arm to the table

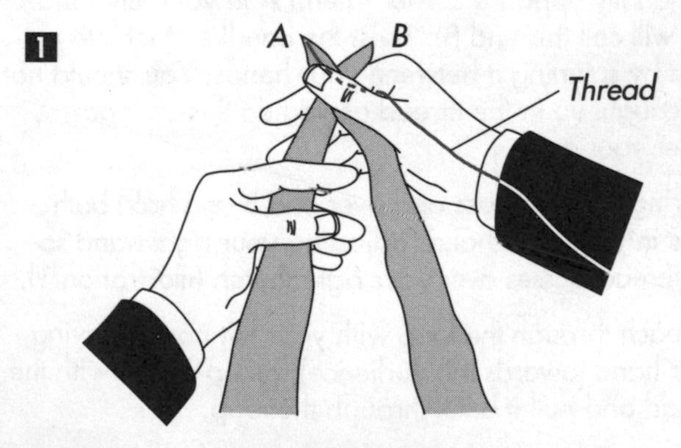

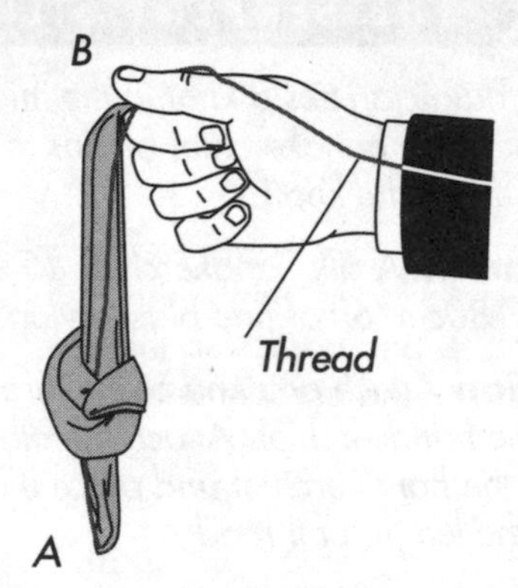

top. Do not worry about anybody seeing the thread. The attention of the audience is on you and what you do with the handkerchief.

2 What you do with the handkerchief is to take the diagonally opposite corner to end A in your left hand (we will call this end B). Twist the handkerchief into a rope by spinning it between your hands. You should not get caught up in the thread as you do this as it passes under your arm.

3 Bring end A across and over end B and hold both ends in your right hand, adjusting your right hand so the thread passes over your right thumb (illustration 1).

4 Reach through the loop with your left hand (moving your hand towards the audience), grasp end A with the thread and pull it back through the loop.

5 Pull your hands apart slowly so that a knot forms in the centre (illustration 2). Unknown to the audience the thread passes through the loop in the knot. It is important the thread runs over your right thumb.

6 Release end A, so the handkerchief is held in the right hand. The thread is attached to the bottom corner A of the handkerchief and passes up through the knot, over your right thumb and across the table.

7 So if you move your right arm forward, the thread will pull end A up and through the knot (illustration 3). Gently move forward to pull end A up to your right hand. The knot will appear to melt away. When end A reaches your hand, release your hold of end B and grasp end A (illustration 4). Drop the handkerchief back on to your table, concluding your performance of the world's first untying knot!

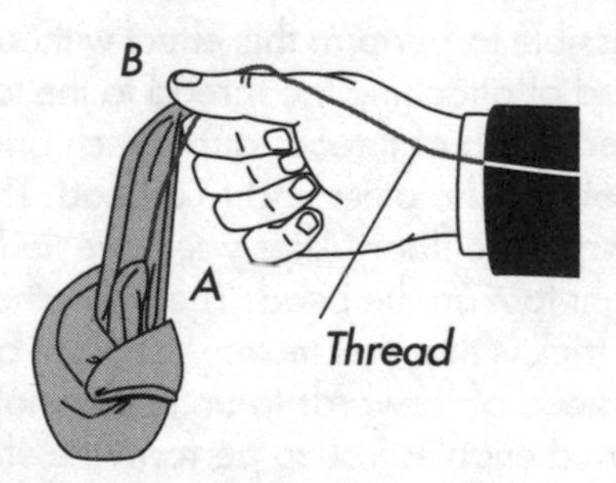

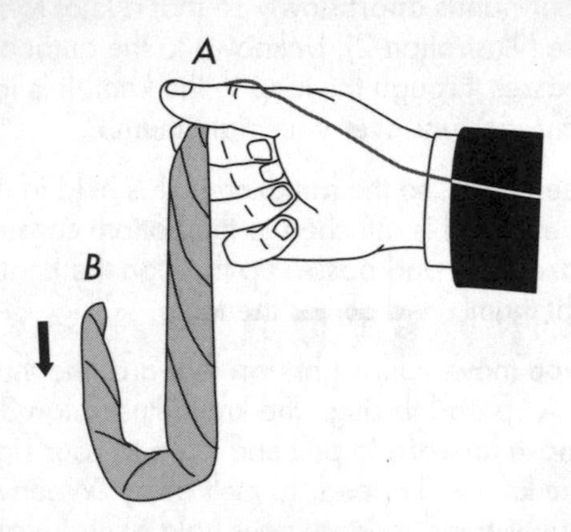

This is a stunning visual effect that is in the repertoire of many of the world's best professional magicians. It is important that you spend plenty of time practising, rehearsing and mastering this effect before you attempt to show it to anyone.

It is also possible to perform this effect without using a table. Instead of attaching the thread to the table you use a shorter length of thread, and attach one end to the handkerchief and the other end to a bead. The bead will dangle down to the floor. After you have tied the knot, put your right foot on the bead. The only other difference in the trick is that you move your right arm upwards instead of forwards to untie the knot.

This method enables you to perform the effect almost impromptu.

PENETRATIONS

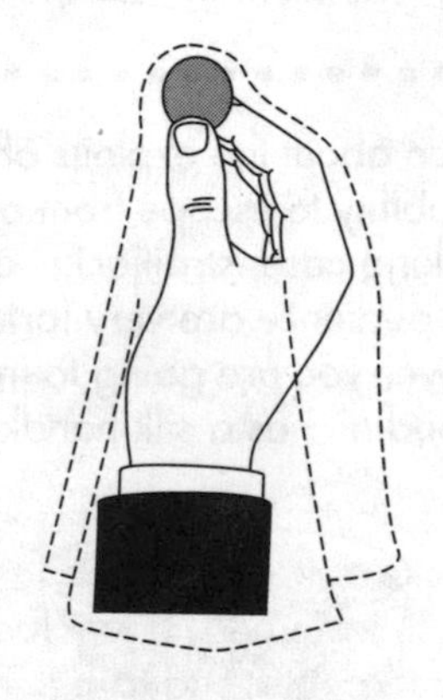

Effect *A silk handkerchief – representing the world famous escape artiste Harry Houdini – escapes from a sealed glass tumbler.*

Requirements *Two different coloured silk handkerchiefs, a large silk scarf, 25cm/10in of cotton thread, a glass tumbler and an elastic band.*

Preparation *Tie the cotton thread to one corner of the handkerchief that you want to "escape".*

•••••••••••••••••

1 Tell the audience about the exploits of the Great Houdini and his ability to escape from any confinement – prison cell, packing case, straitjacket or handcuffs. Explain that your audience are very fortunate because for the first time ever you are going to introduce the reincarnation of Houdini – as a silk handkerchief!

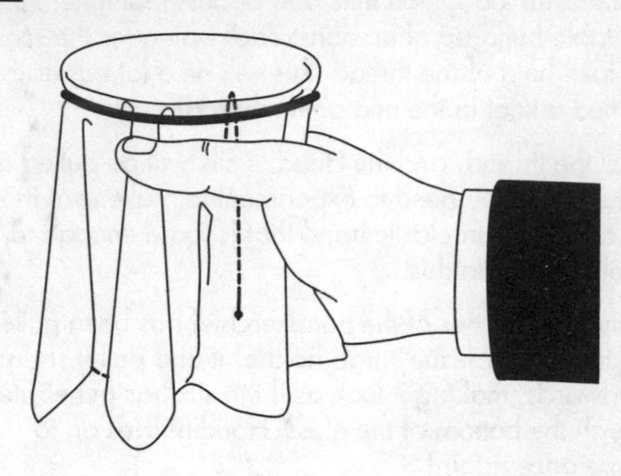

2 Display the "Houdini silk" to the audience and push it down into the bottom of the empty tumbler. As you do this make sure that you leave the thread hanging outside the glass.

3 Introduce the second handkerchief as a prison guard and stuff it into the tumbler on top of the first handkerchief (illustration 1).

4 To make extra sure that the handkerchief is unable to escape, throw the scarf over the mouth of the tumbler and hold it in place with the elastic band (illustration 2). You could call this the padded cell – or perhaps this is taking the analogy a bit too far!

5 Now tell the audience that this escape used to take 30 minutes! But today you intend to double that time! After a suitable build-up of tension, reach up under the scarf and take hold of the thread (this will be a lot easier if you tied a knot in the end of the thread).

6 Pull the thread, and the Houdini silk will be pulled out of the glass. You need to experiment to make sure that you are using an elastic band that is loose enough to enable you to do this.

7 Once the corner of the handkerchief has been pulled past the rubber band, grab hold of it and pull it sharply downwards, making it look as if the silk has penetrated through the bottom of the glass. Houdini lives on to escape once again!

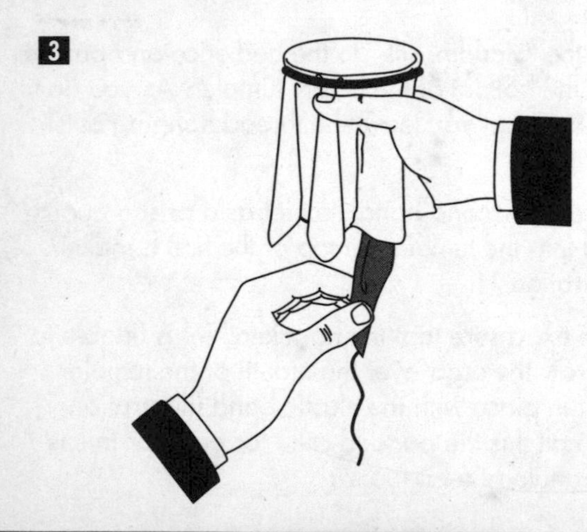

HANKY THROUGH HANKY

This is based on the "Dissolving Knot" and it is highly recommended that you learn and perfect that effect before attempting this one.

Effect *The magician displays two silk handkerchiefs, which are then twisted into ropes. A spectator holds one outstretched between his hands. The handkerchiefs are securely knotted around each other, creating two knotted linked loops of silk. Like the classic "Chinese Linking Rings" the handkerchiefs seem to melt apart with their knots still intact.*

1

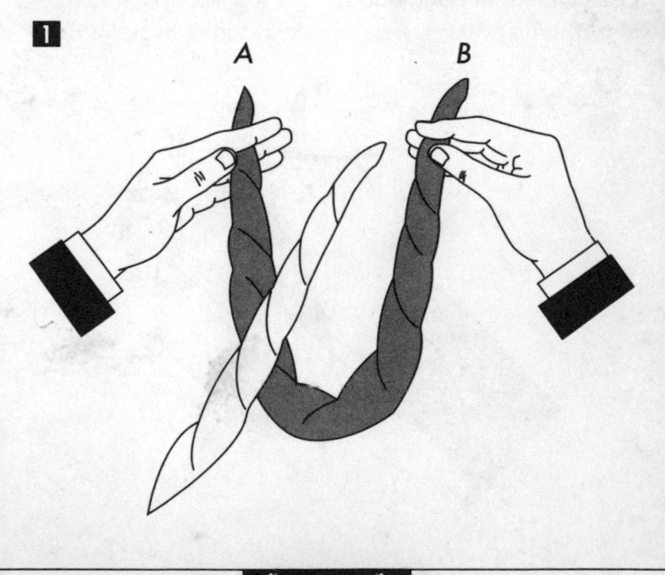

Requirements *Two silk handkerchiefs 45 x 45cm/18 x 18in, preferably of contrasting colours.*

Preparation *None.*

••••••••••••••••

1 Hold the first handkerchief by its diagonally opposite corners and twist it into a rope. Hand it to a member of the audience, requesting them to hold on tightly to the two ends.

2 Twist the second handkerchief and thread it underneath the first (illustration 1). Hold an end of your handkerchief in each hand.

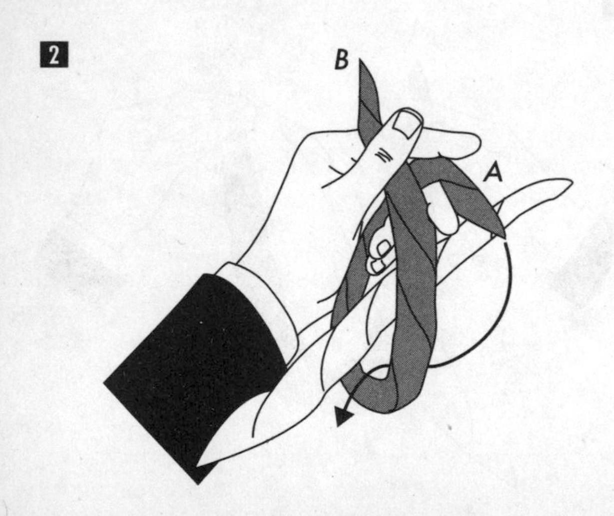

3

3 Move the righthand end (end B) over to the left hand and clip the two ends exactly as in the "Dissolving Knot" (illustration 2). Insert your right hand through the loop and grab end A. Pull this end back through the loop to form the "Dissolving Knot".

4 Pull the two ends of your rope in opposite directions to tighten to the knot. As you do this, keep your left second finger in the small loop. When the knot becomes tight you can slide out your left finger and the knot will hold itself together.

5 Loop your handkerchief underneath the spectator's handkerchief again and tie a regular secure reef knot (see Glossary) above the slip knot to make "an unbreakable circle of silk" (illustration 3).

6 Ask the spectator to tie the two ends of his handkerchief together in a secure knot. As they do this, hold on to the slip knot to ensure it is not accidentally pulled apart. It seems that the two handkerchiefs are now securely linked together.

7 Ask the spectator to hold on to the two ends of their handkerchief. You do the same with yours. Get the audience to blow on the handkerchiefs as you gently pull. The slip knot will dissolve and the two handkerchiefs will melt apart in a very magical fashion.

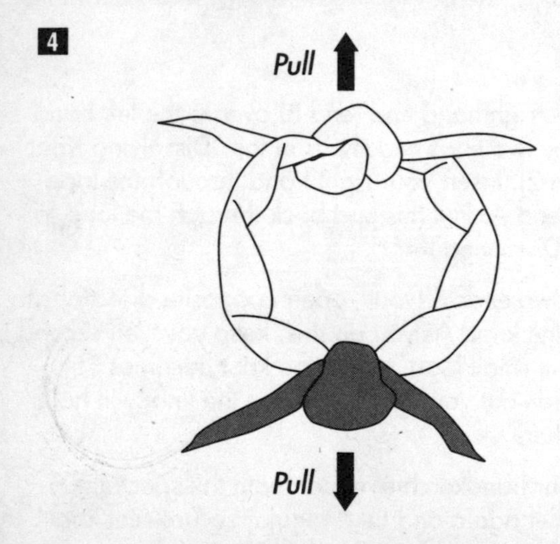

PENCIL THROUGH HANKY

Effect *The magician sticks a pencil through the centre of a borrowed handkerchief without damaging it!*

Requirements *The largest handkerchief you can borrow (a cloth table napkin will do), a pencil 8cm/3in long and a piece of newspaper 30 x 30cm/12 x 12in.*

Preparation *None.*

•••••••••••••••

1 Invite two spectators to assist you. Have them each hold on to two corners of the borrowed handkerchief and stretch it between them so that it is parallel with the floor.

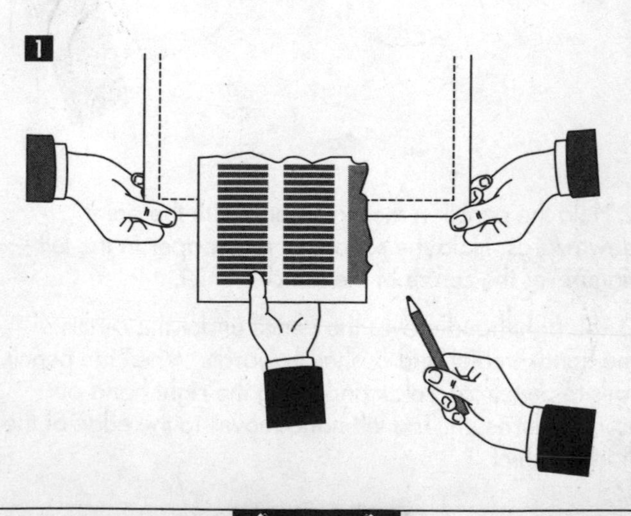

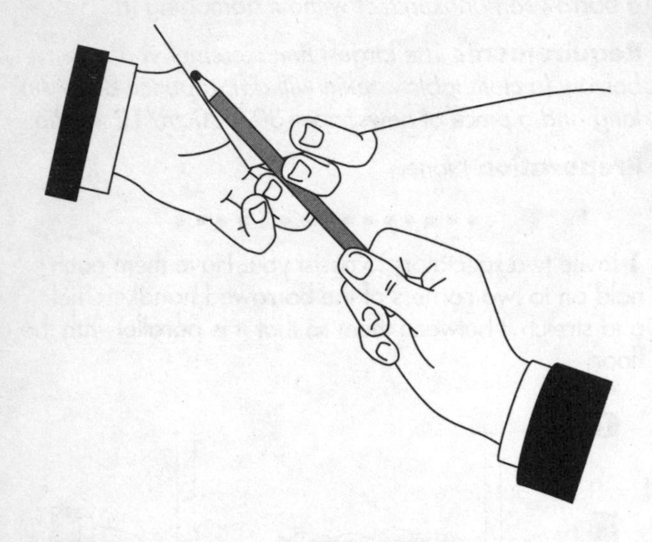

2 Hold the pencil in the right hand with the point downwards. Hold the square of newspaper in the left hand over the centre of the handkerchief.

3 The right hand moves the pencil under the centre of the handkerchief and pushes upwards. When the pencil fails to penetrate, relax and bring the right hand out from underneath. The left hand moves to the edge of the handkerchief.

3

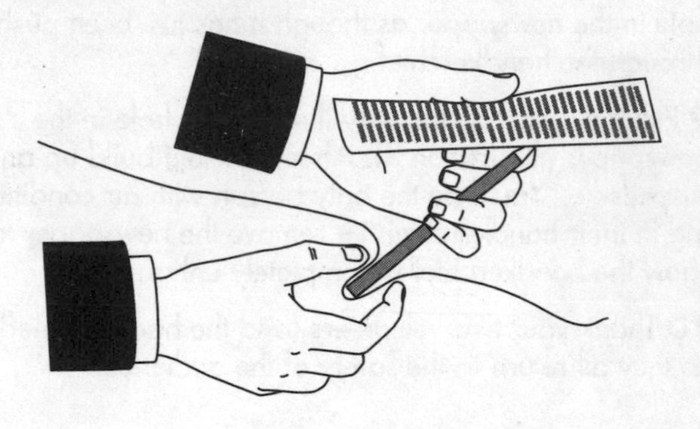

4 Look at the pencil and say, "Of course, the pencil should be pointed end up." Turn the pencil around.

5 As the right hand moves back under the handkerchief you perform the all-important secret move. The left second and third fingers clip the pencil (illustration 2). This action is covered by the newspaper.

6 The right hand does not pause, but continues to move underneath to the centre of the handkerchief as though it still contained the pencil.

7 The left hand moves forward on top of the handkerchief back to the centre.

8 Through the fabric the right hand grips the blunt end of the pencil. With the left hand, push the newspaper down over the pencil (illustration 3). The pencil tears a hole in the newspaper as though it has just been pushed through the handkerchief.

9 Pull the pencil all the way through the hole in the newspaper (illustration 4). After sufficient build-up and suspense – "You'll be the only person with air conditioning in their handkerchief!" – remove the newspaper to show the handkerchief is completely unharmed!

10 Thank your two volunteers (and the handkerchief!) as they all return to the safety of the audience!

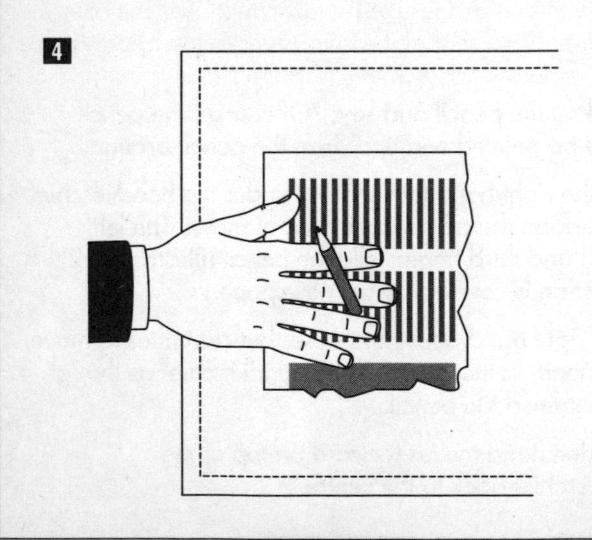

Effect *A coin and a handkerchief are both borrowed from members of the audience. The coin visibly passes through the centre of the handkerchief, leaving it undamaged!*

Requirements *A coin and a handkerchief (both can be borrowed).*

Preparation *None.*

• • • • • • • • • • • • • • • • •

1 Display the coin at the tips of the right thumb and first two fingers so that the audience see one side of the coin. Your left hand drapes the handkerchief over the coin and right hand so that the coin is under the approximate centre of the handkerchief (illustration 1).

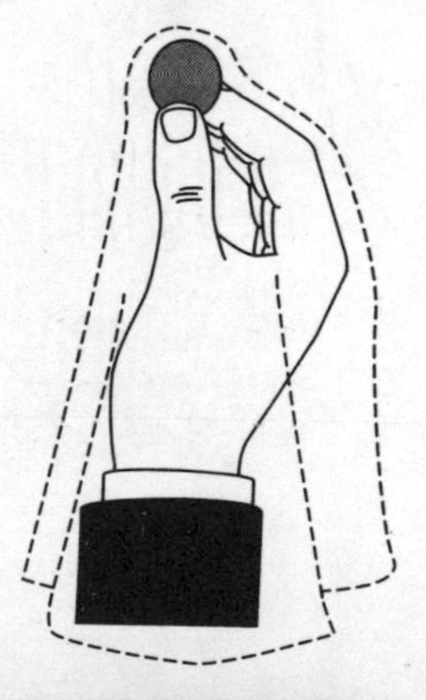

2 As the left hand is adjusting the handkerchief over the coin, your left thumb secretly lifts a bit of cloth behind the coin and folds it behind the right thumb. When you remove your left hand you will have two layers of cloth clipped between your right thumb and the back of the coin (illustration 2), preparing you for the secret move.

3 With your left hand grab the front edge of the handkerchief and lift it back and over the coin. This displays the coin still in position under the centre of the handkerchief. When you cover the coin again your left

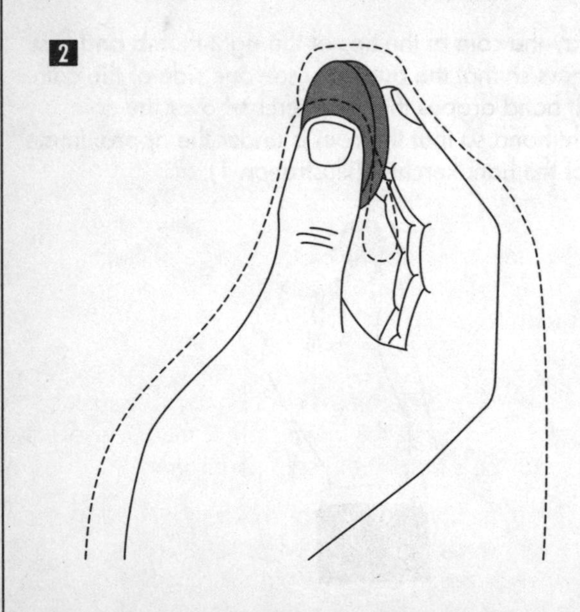

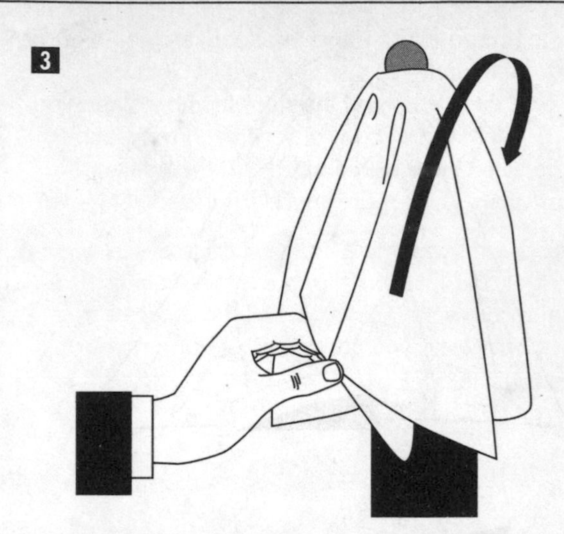

hand takes both edges of the handkerchief over the coin (illustration 3). Now your right thumb is holding the coin outside the handkerchief. The clipped piece of cloth prevents the handkerchief falling away after you have done this (illustration 4).

4 With your left hand, grip the coin from above through the layers of the handkerchief. Your right hand now lets go of the coin and twists the lower part of the handkerchief to reveal the shape of the coin (illustration 5).

5 Slowly push the coin upwards with your right hand, as your left hand takes the edge of the coin – as it magically penetrates through the handkerchief.

4

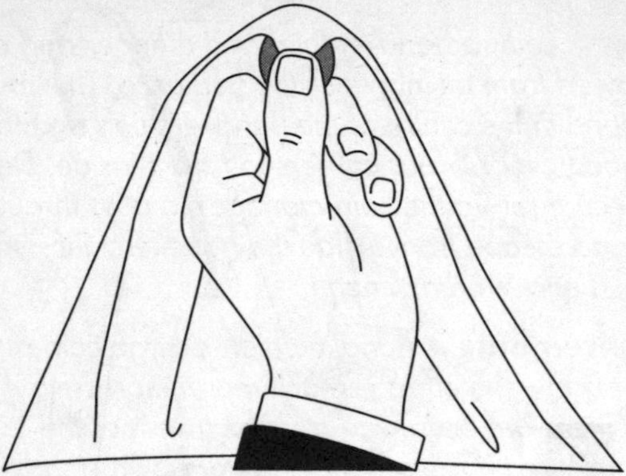

5

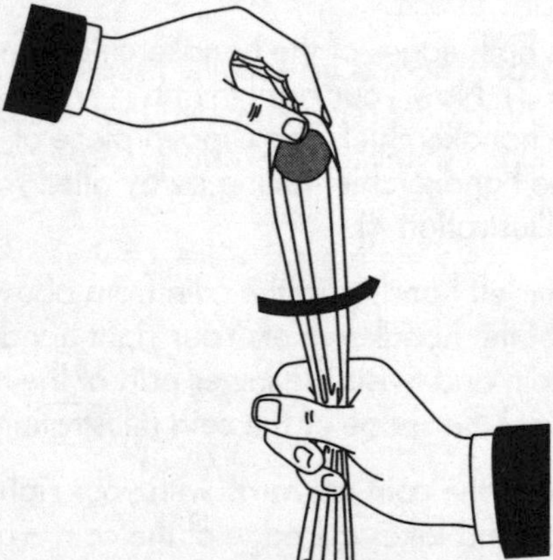

◇ SHRINKING COIN ◇

Effect *A coin, a handkerchief and a finger ring are all borrowed from members of the audience. The coin is wrapped in the centre of the handkerchief, and the ring threaded over all four corners to trap it inside. Despite this secure set-up the coin manages to pass through the ring and escape from inside the handkerchief – much to the audience's amazement!*

Requirements *A handkerchief, a large coin and a finger ring – the effect is much more impressive if all these items are borrowed from members of the audience, but it is worth having your own standing by ready to use if necessary. If you do have to use your own props, have them examined by the audience before you begin the effect.*

Preparation *There is no specific preparation for this effect, but it is highly recommended that you master the "Coin Through Handkerchief" effect before attempting to perform this one.*

•••••••••••••••

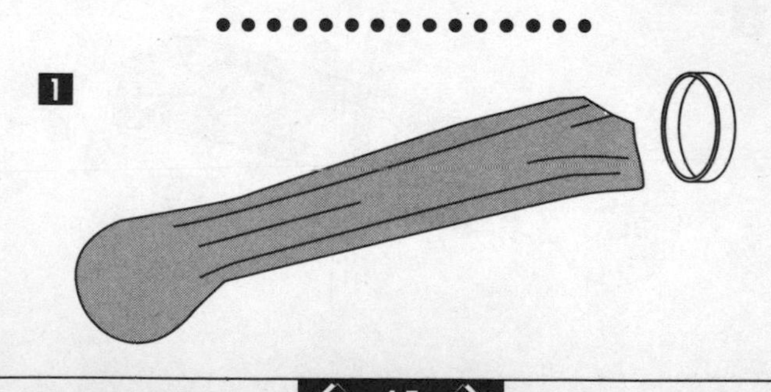

1 Have the handkerchief, coin and finger ring examined by the audience. Then collect them together and invite two members of the audience up to assist you.

2 Display the coin and wrap it in the handkerchief as described in the "Coin Through Handkerchief" effect so that the coin is held outside the handkerchief (illustration 1). Twist the lower part of the handkerchief to reveal the shape of the apparently trapped coin (but do not perform the penetration).

3 Hold the coin through the handkerchief in the left hand so that the coin is resting flat against the left fingers. The "open" side (which would reveal the coin) is resting against the fingertips.

4 Have a spectator thread the finger ring over all four corners of the handkerchief. As they do this hold the coin tightly with the left hand, and with the right hand hold the handkerchief just above the coin to prevent it unwrapping.

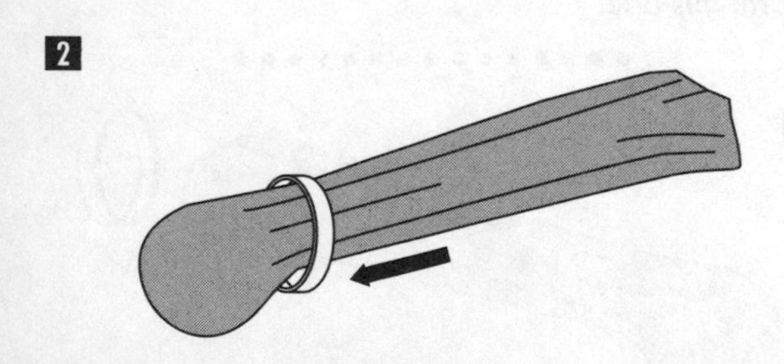

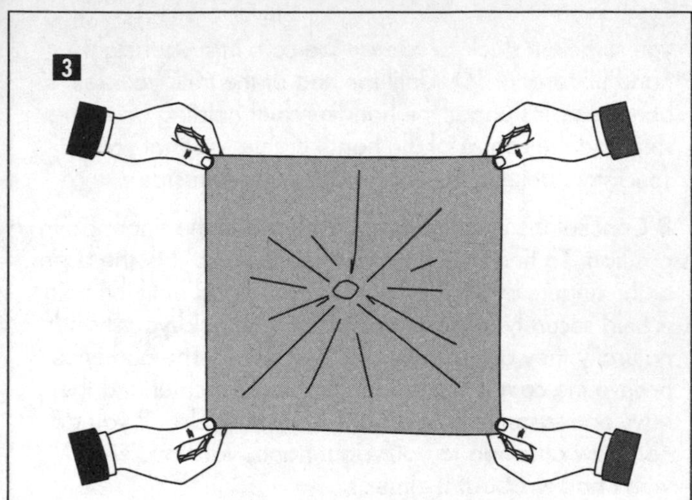

5 Have the spectator slide the ring down the handkerchief until it reaches the coin (illustration 2). The ring will lock the coin in position and prevent the handkerchief unwrapping. You can now ask two spectators to each hold two corners of the handkerchief so that it is parallel with the floor (illustration 3) while you let go of the coin. The coin and ring are both below the handkerchief.

6 Point out the situation to audience – the coin is trapped in the centre of the handkerchief by the ring. It cannot escape as the hole in the middle of the ring is much smaller than the coin.

7 Reach under the handkerchief with both hands. With your left hand slide the ring up the handkerchief to give you sufficient slack to release the coin into your right hand (illustration 4). Until the end of the trick your left hand remains under the handkerchief holding on to the ring and the centre of the handkerchief, so that your spectators believe the coin is still trapped inside.

8 Conceal the coin in your right hand in the finger palm position. To finger palm a coin, simply clip it at the base of the fingers by slightly closing your hand until the coin is held securely in position. (When you hold your hands naturally they are usually slightly closed.) The audience believe the coin is trapped in the handkerchief and they have no reason to suspect it is anywhere else. If you do not draw attention to your right hand, your audience won't bother about it either.

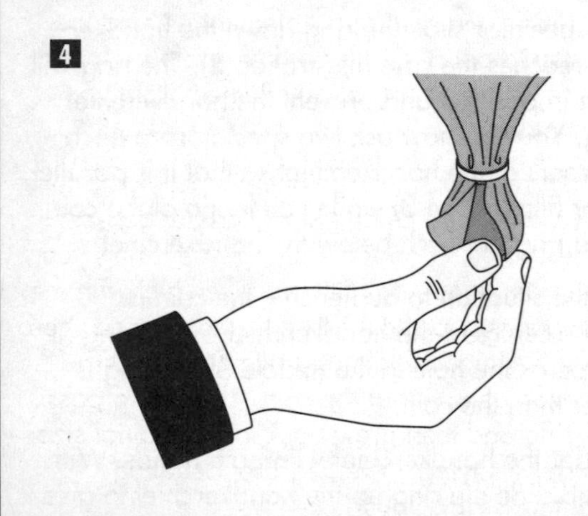

9 Bring your apparently empty right hand over the top of the handkerchief to the middle over the "well" in the centre. Your right hand secretly releases the finger-palmed coin into this well in the handkerchief. Under the handkerchief the left fingers catch the coin and grip it through the fabric.

10 Wave your right hand over the centre in a mystical fashion as though you are performing a "magical pass" over the well. This was your reason for moving your hand to the centre of the handkerchief.

11 Ask the spectators to slowly pull on their corners of the handkerchief. Very slowly with your left hand release the coin. It will appear to rise up out of the centre of the handkerchief as though it is passing through the centre of the ring. This is a very magical moment when done slowly and should get a great round of applause from your audience – and a gasp of amazement from your two "hanky holders".

12 Allow your two assistants to continue pulling on their corners until the handkerchief is stretched flat between them with the coin lying on top in the centre. Bring your left hand out from underneath the handkerchief with the borrowed finger ring to show that it is undamaged. You point out that the impossible must have occurred. The only explanation can be that the coin "shrank" to pass through the ring and then grew back to its original size. You can finish by saying, "I've heard of deflating currency but this is ridiculous!"

COLOUR CHANGES

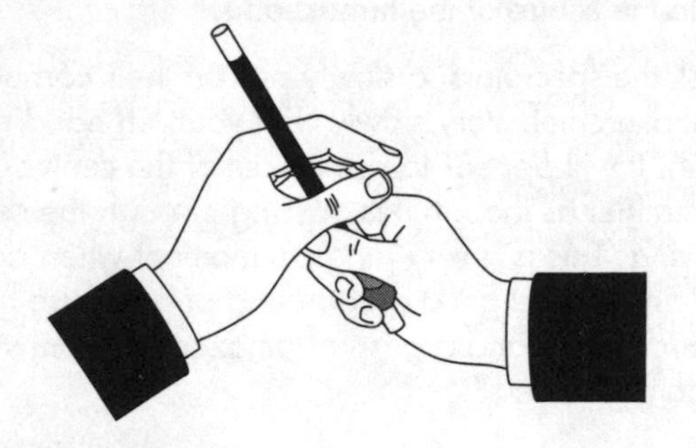

◇ COLOUR CHANGE HANKY ◇

Effect *The magician displays a handkerchief. As the magician's hand is passed over it the handkerchief changes colour.*

Requirements *Two different coloured silk handkerchiefs, a metal ring with diameter 2.5cm/1in and sewing equipment.*

Preparation *Place one handkerchief on top of the other and sew them together just above the centre with a line of stitching about 5cm/2in long. Sew the top corner of the rear handkerchief to the far side of the metal ring. Poke the top corner A of the upper handkerchief through the ring (illustration 1). Fold up the lower corner B of the upper handkerchief and sew it to the near side of the metal ring (illustration 2). Fold the set-up in half lengthwise so that the lower handkerchief covers the folded top handkerchief (illustration 3). Sew the two sides of the outer handkerchief together, ensuring that the inner silk does not bulge out too much, but lies flat.*

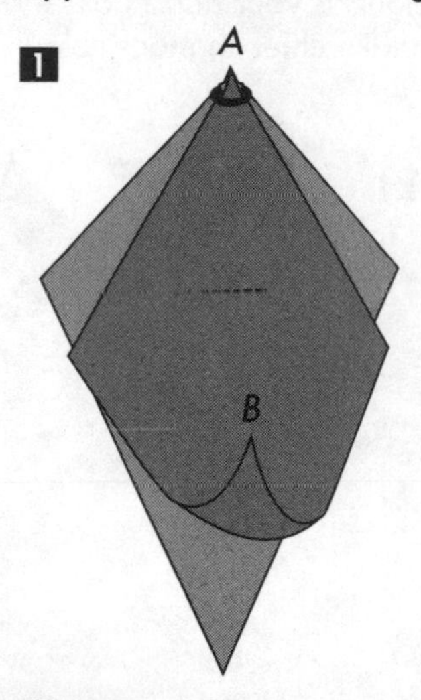

Grasp the tip A of the inner silk through the ring and pull the ring down. This will transpose the handkerchiefs, exposing the inner silk and concealing the outer one. Sew up the sides of the now outer handkerchief to prevent the inner silk from being seen.

• • • • • • • • • • • • • • • •

1 Display the handkerchief to your audience.

2 With the left hand grasp the tip of the handkerchief sticking out of the ring.

3 Pull the ring down over the silk with the right hand. To the audience it appears that the handkerchief changes colour as your hand passes over it (illustration 4). As the handkerchief changes colour, shake it slightly.

2

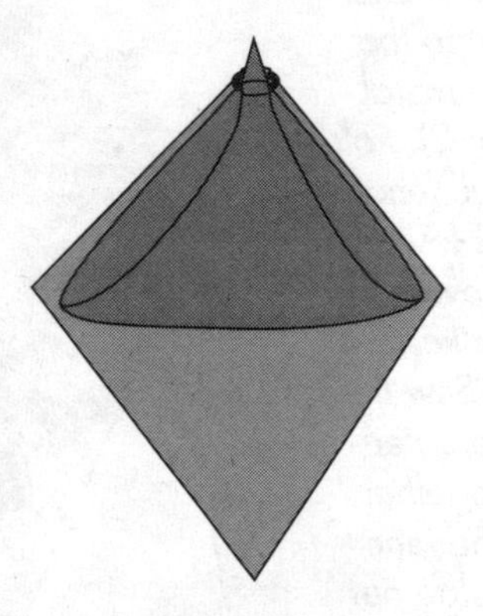

4 You can end the effect there or turn the handkerchief upside down and repeat the process to restore the handkerchief to its original colour.

3

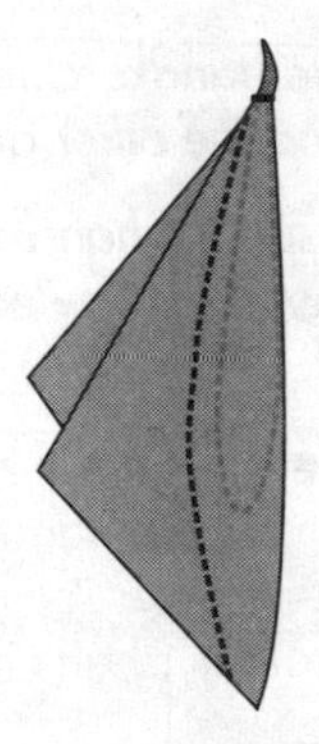

4

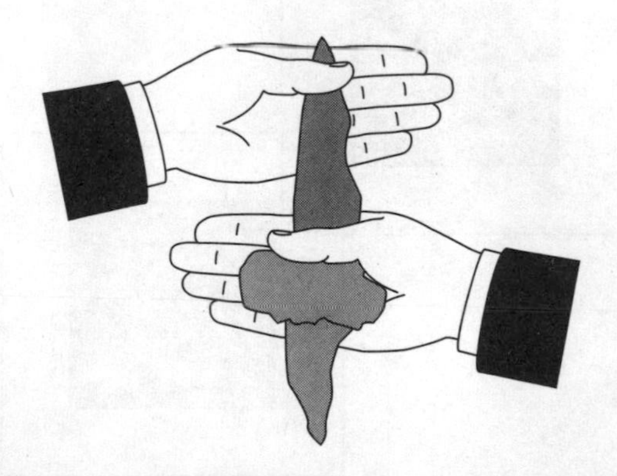

Effect *A red silk handkerchief with white borders is pulled through the hand and changes to a green silk handkerchief with white borders.*

Requirements *A white handkerchief, plus two slightly smaller ones, one red and the other green.*

Preparation *Make a special handkerchief by sewing the two coloured handkerchiefs one each side of the white one (illustration 1).*

•••••••••••••••

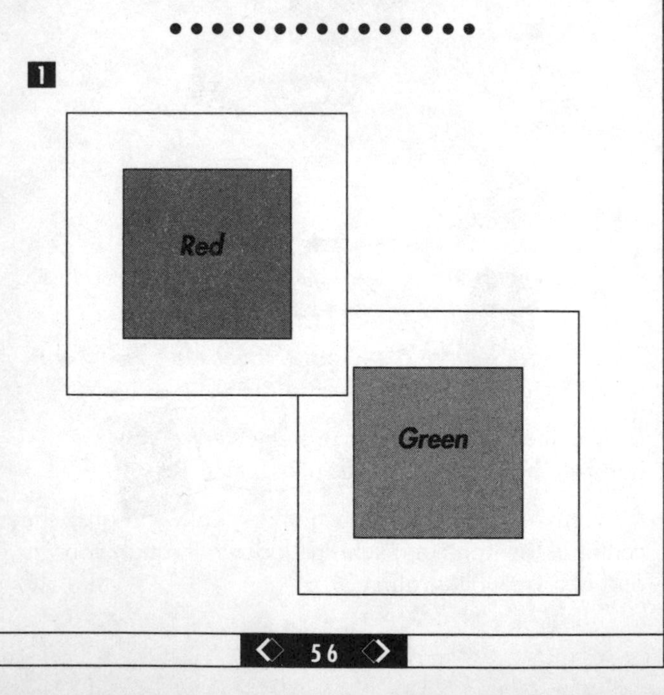

1 Pick up the handkerchief, displaying the red side, and spread it out over your open left hand.

2 Form your left hand into a fist under the cover of the handkerchief.

3 With the right forefinger push the centre of the handkerchief into the left fist (illustration 2).

4 With your right hand reach underneath and grab the centre of the handkerchief. Pull it down through your fist and into view (illustration 3).

5 The handkerchief is now green. Show the green side to the audience, making sure that you keep the red side hidden.

TONY SLYDINI (1901-1991)

Slydini is generally regarded as one of the fathers of modern close-up magic. Like Dai Vernon, he was an inspiration for many magicians to master sleight of hand. He moved to the East coast of America from Italy in his youth and went on to have his own studio in New York for private performances and teaching. Handkerchief magic like the "Dissolving Knot" and "Over the Head" became "real" in his hands.

◇ SILK PRODUCTION AND CHANGE ◇

Effect *After the wave of a magic wand the magician produces a silk handkerchief from his hands, which were empty moments before. Another wave of the wand and the handkerchief changes colour!*

Requirements *A magic wand and two contrasting silk handkerchiefs – say, red and yellow.*

Preparation *Fold the four corners of each handkerchief to the centre. Then roll each one into a tube and wrap them alongside each other around one end of the wand (illustration 1). To perform this as an opener, hold the wand in your right hand, with your hand concealing the handkerchiefs. To perform later, set the wand on your table with other props covering the handkerchiefs.*

• • • • • • • • • • • • • • • •

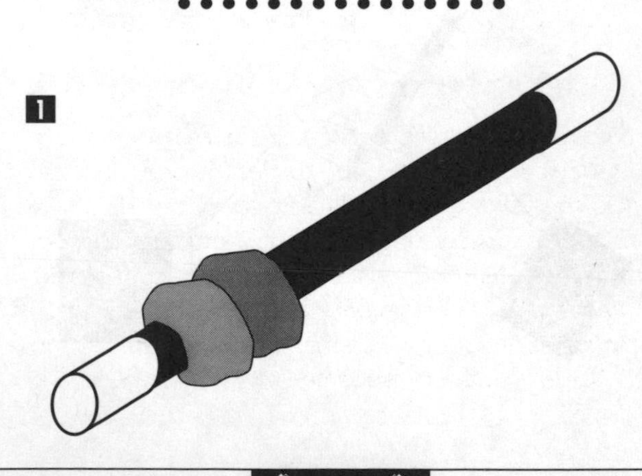

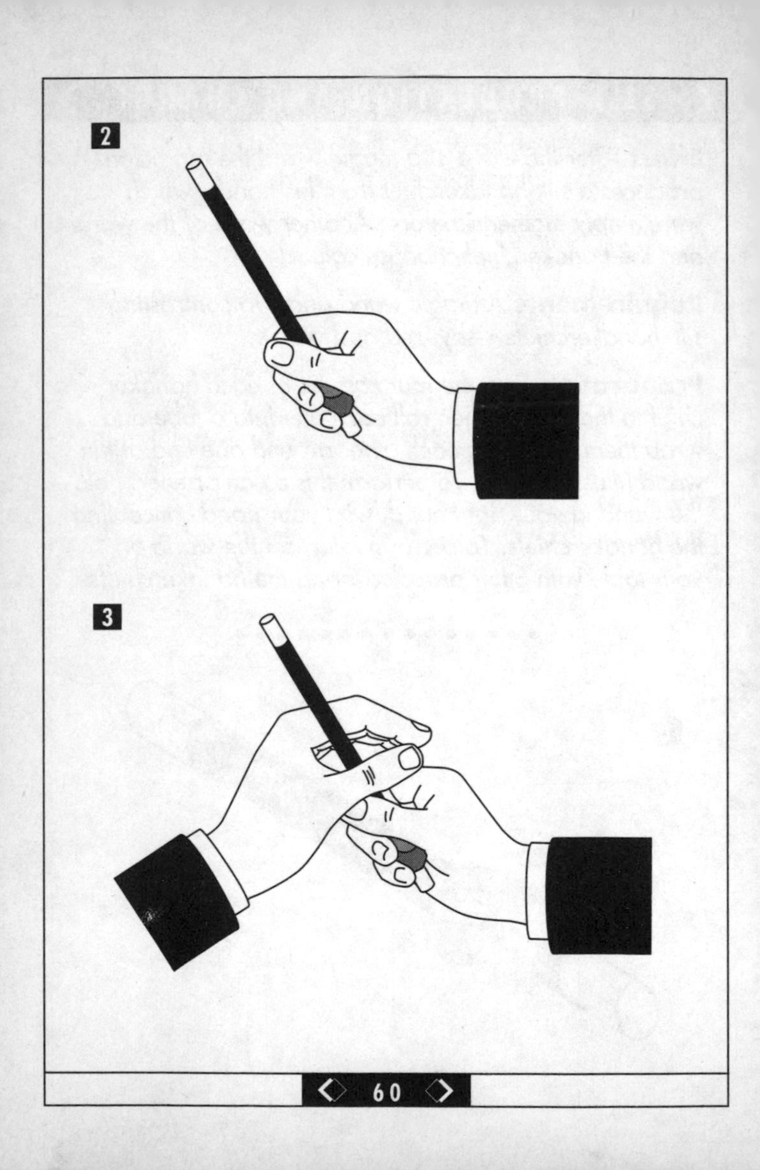
2
3

1 Begin with the wand in the right hand (illustration 2). Tap the empty left hand with the free end of the wand as you say, "My left hand is empty . . ."

2 Slide the left hand up the wand until the two hands meet (illustration 3). The left hand grasps the end of the wand, covering the two handkerchiefs. The wand pivots to the right and the right hand is shown to be empty as you say, ". . . and the right too."

3 The left hand keeps hold of the lower of the two handkerchiefs, as the right hand takes the wand back concealing the other handkerchief on the wand. We will assume the handkerchief in the left hand is red and the one still on the wand is yellow.

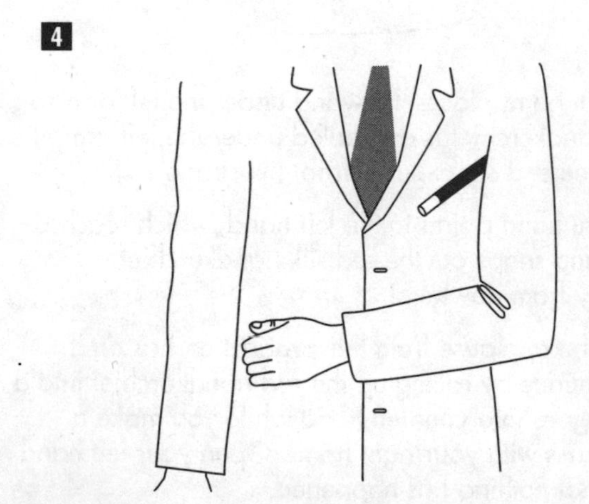

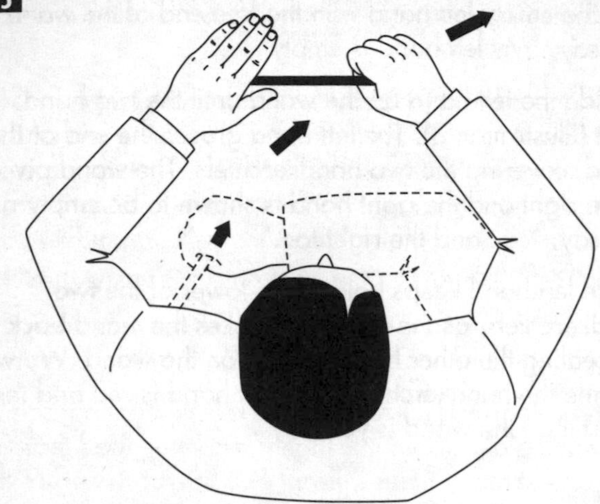

4 The right hand places the wand under the left arm so that the handkerchief is concealed under the left armpit and the free end sticks out in front (illustration 4).

5 The right hand points to the left hand, which reaches forward and snaps out the red silk handkerchief – apparently from nowhere!

6 When the applause from this production has died down, continue by rolling up the red handkerchief into a ball. This goes into your left hand while you make a magical pass with your right hand. Open your left hand to show that nothing has happened.

7 Roll the handkerchief up again, but this time keep it concealed in your right hand while pretending it is your closed left fist.

8 The right hand (holding the red handkerchief concealed) reaches for the free end of the wand and moves it down (illustration 5) behind your left arm (which acts as a screen) and into the left hand which opens briefly to secretly "steal" the yellow handkerchief from the end of the wand. The wand continues moving.

9 Wave the wand over the closed left fist and open it to show that the handkerchief has now changed colour.

When performed correctly this is a very baffling and convincing effect, but it is highly recommended that you rehearse it many times in front of a mirror to ensure that your timing is correct and that in step 8 the yellow handkerchief remains concealed from the audience.

HOUDIN AND HOUDINI

In 1856 Robert Houdin was sent by the French government to Algiers to quell the revolution by proving that French magic was stronger than African magic! On his return he wrote of his adventures in The Memoirs of Robert Houdin. *Nearly 30 years later a young Hungarian boy in America read the book and decided to become a magician. He based his stage name on that of his hero – and became Houdini!*

PRODUCTIONS

◇ THE ORGAN PIPES ◇

Effect *After showing that two tubes are both completely empty, the magician produces silk handkerchiefs and ribbons from inside.*

Requirements *Two tubes about 30cm/12in high and 15cm/6in diameter, which fit one inside the other (it may be easiest to make the tubes to size using stiff paper held together with paper clips), a paper clip, about 15cm/6in of dark thread, elastic bands and your production "load" – ribbons and silk handkerchiefs.*

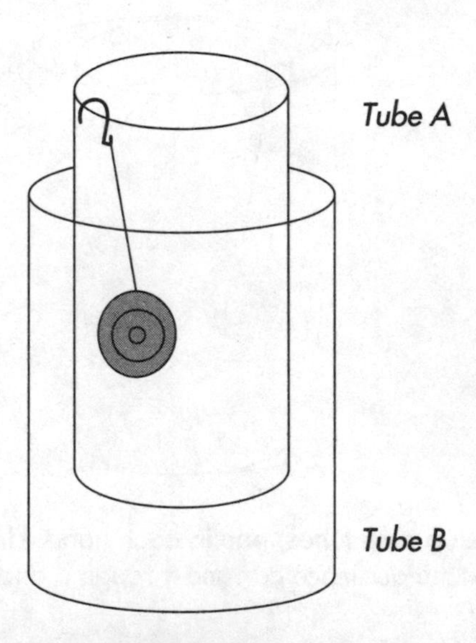

Preparation *Roll up the handkerchiefs and ribbons into a compact bundle and hold it together with the elastic bands. Bend the paper clip into an S-shaped hook. Attach one end of the thread to the hook and the other end to one of the elastic bands. Hook the clip over the top edge of the thinner tube (tube A) with the bundle dangling inside out of sight. We will call the wider of the two tubes tube B.*

Set tubes A and B next to each other on the table.

● ● ● ● ● ● ● ● ● ● ● ● ● ● ● ●

2

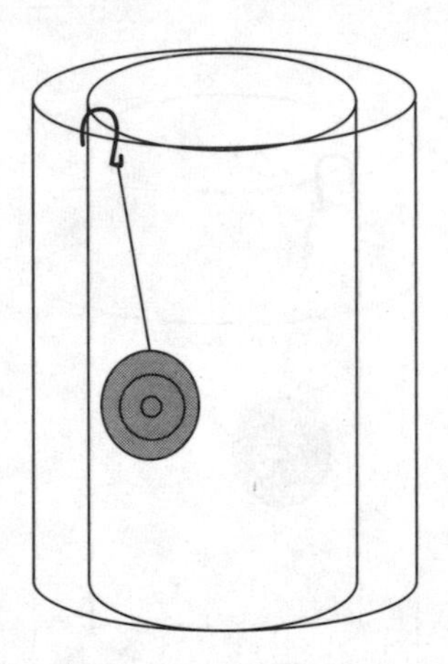

1 Pick up both tubes, one in each hand. Hold up tube B so that the audience can see through it and see that it is empty.

2 Slide tube A into the top of tube B, making sure that the hook clips on to the top of tube B (illustration 2).

3 Allow tube A to slide out of the bottom of tube B. The bundle should remain hanging out of sight inside tube B. You can now hold up tube A to show the audience that it is completely empty.

4 Slide tube A back into tube B from the bottom, so that the bundle is now hanging inside both tubes (illustration 3). Roll up your sleeves and show the audience that your hands are completely empty. Reach inside the tubes and remove the elastic bands from around the

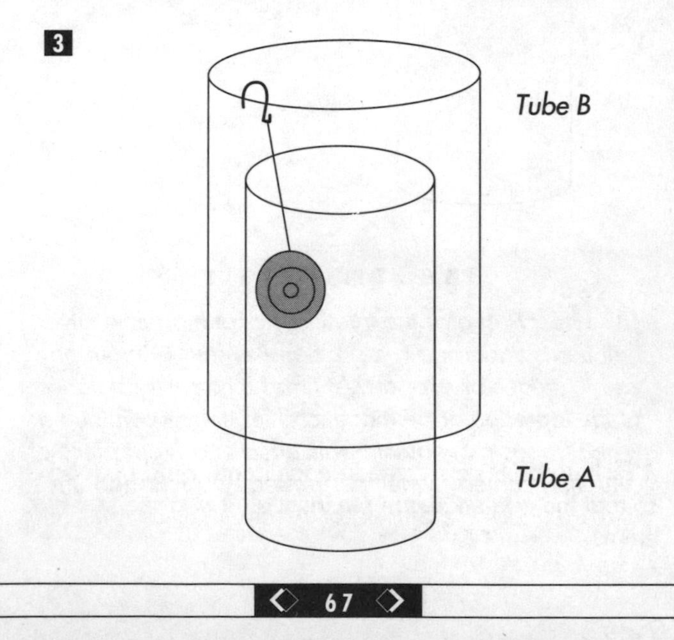

bundle. Dramatically remove the ribbons and handkerchiefs from inside the nested tubes (illustration 4).

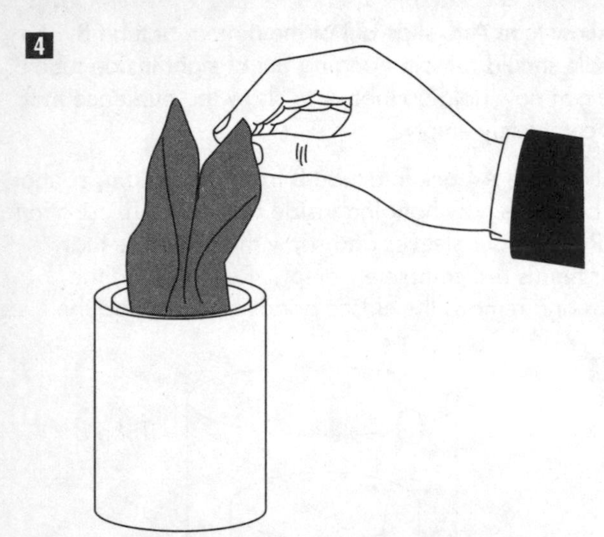

THE ZOMBIE BALL

This effect is one of the true classics of magic. A silver ball floats underneath a silk handkerchief without any visible means of support. At times it comes to balance at the top edge of the handkerchief before continuing its mysterious movements. This effect is a great piece of situation comedy when performed by Ali Bongo, the "Shriek" of Araby.

Effect *This is a startling opening effect. The magician shows both hands empty. After making a grab in the air a silk handkerchief appears in the magician's hands!*

Requirements *A silk handkerchief about 45 x 45cm/18 x 18in.*

Preparation *Spread the handkerchief out flat on a table. Fold the four corners into the middle so that they almost touch (illustrations 1 and 2). Repeat, folding the four new corners into the centre. Continue folding until you have a bundle about 5cm/2in across.*

1

2

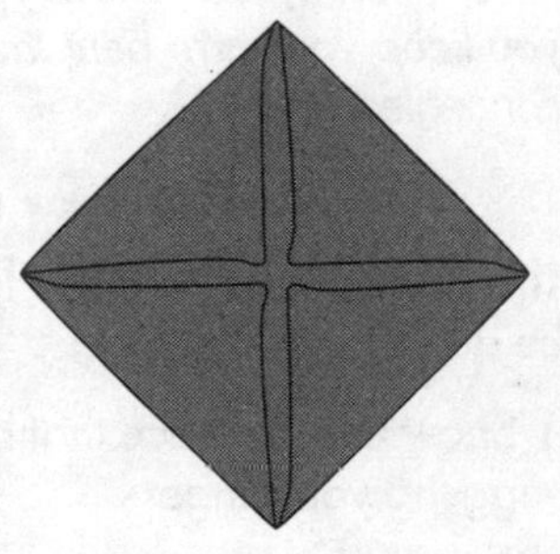

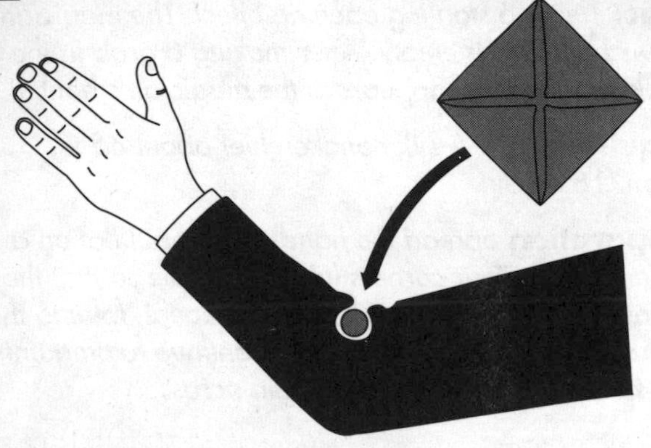

Place the folded handkerchief in the bend of your elbow (illustration 3) just before you begin your performance. If you keep your arm bent the handkerchief will remain concealed.

•••••••••••••••

This effect is over in just a few seconds, but it appears to be quite magical.

1 Show the audience that both your hands are empty by wiggling your fingers.

2 Look upwards. Quickly reach up with both hands and, as you do this, straighten your arms. The handkerchief will be propelled into the air (illustration 4).

3 Catch the handkerchief between your hands. It seems to have appeared in mid-air.

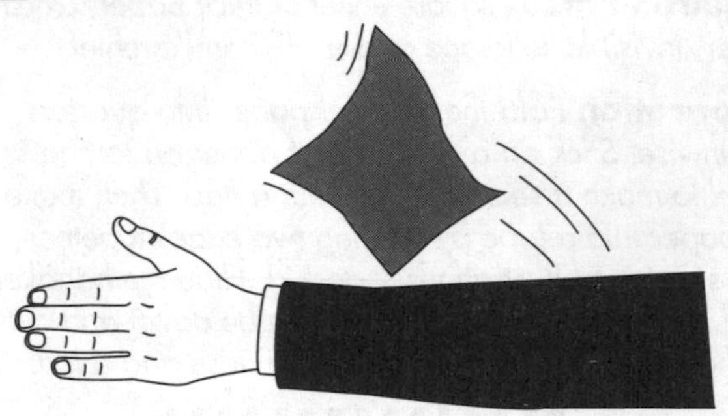

ROBERT HOUDIN (1805-1871)

Robert Houdin was a French watchmaker who became a magician and the talk of Paris with his Soirées Fantastiques at his own specially-built theatre. He revolutionised magic and is credited as being "The Father of Modern Magic". He used his mechanical skills to build many of his effects. In one of the most famous, a lady's handkerchief was borrowed and vanished. Flowers and fruit appeared on a nearby orange tree. One of the oranges opened and two butterflies flew out carrying the borrowed handkerchief, which was then returned to its astonished owner.

◇ AMAZING ARROW ◇

Effect *The magician displays an arrow with a mind of its own – and then produces a handkerchief from inside.*

Requirements *A square sheet of thick paper, extra paper, invisible sellotape and a silk handkerchief.*

Preparation *Fold the piece of paper into quarters lengthwise. Stick an extra piece of paper on to one panel to make a secret pocket with a flap. Then make the paper into a tube by sticking two edges together with sellotape (illustrations 1 and 2). Hide the handkerchief inside the pocket. Flatten the tube down and cut it as shown in illustration 3 to make a nose and a tail.*

•••••••••••••••

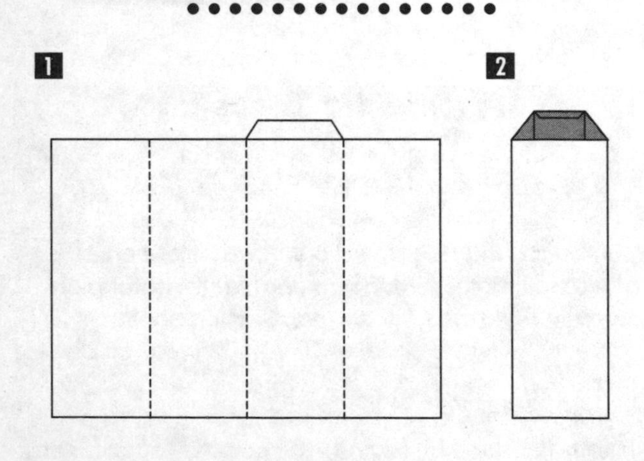

3

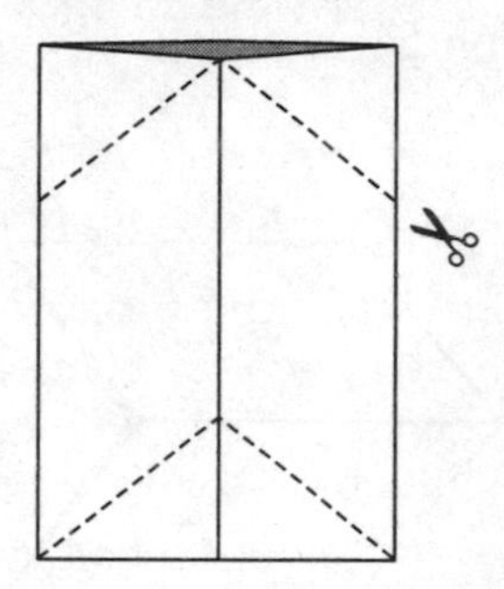

1 Show the arrow pointing to your left and tell your audience that they must never trust arrows as they might be pointing the wrong way.

2 Turn the arrow around so that it is pointing to the right. Say, "See, it is easy to move an arrow. Sometimes it changes direction so quickly it seems like magic!"

3 As you say this you squeeze the two outer edges together so that the tube opens out and folds flat the other way. The arrow is now pointing left again.

4 You can turn the arrow left and right by repeating step 3 as many times as you wish.

5 Finally conclude by saying, "Of course, you can't trust me – I'm a magician. I was just trying to pull the wool over your eyes!" As you say this, reach into the end of the arrow and pull the silk handkerchief out of the secret pocket (illustration 5).

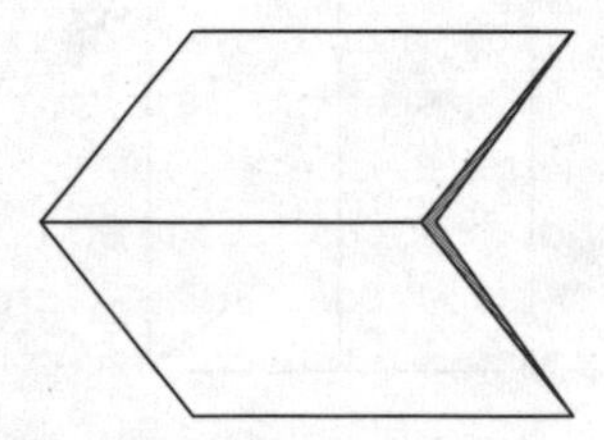

◇ EGGS FROM NOWHERE ◇

Effect *The magician shows the audience an ordinary handkerchief. He folds it in half and an egg rolls out from inside. He tips the egg into a basket. Another egg appears . . . and another . . . and another. This apparently unlimited number of eggs are shaken, one at a time, from the handkerchief into the basket. The magician sets the handkerchief down to one side, reaches into the basket, removes one egg and breaks it into a glass to prove it is real. Walking forward with the basket the magician throws the contents at the audience! To the audience's surprise – and relief – the eggs have been transformed into a basketful of confetti!*

Requirements *An opaque handkerchief 60 x 60cm/24 x 24in, a small basket, a plastic egg, a real egg, a glass, some thread to match the colour of the handkerchief and a supply of confetti.*

Preparation *Attach the plastic egg to one end of a piece of thread about 30cm/12in long. Attach the other end of the thread to the centre of one edge of the handkerchief, so that the egg hangs just below the centre of the handkerchief when the handkerchief is held up (illustration 2). Fill the basket with confetti and hide the real egg inside. Fold the handkerchief and place it next to the basket with the false egg resting on the confetti inside the basket next to the real egg (illustration 1).*

• • • • • • • • • • • • • • •

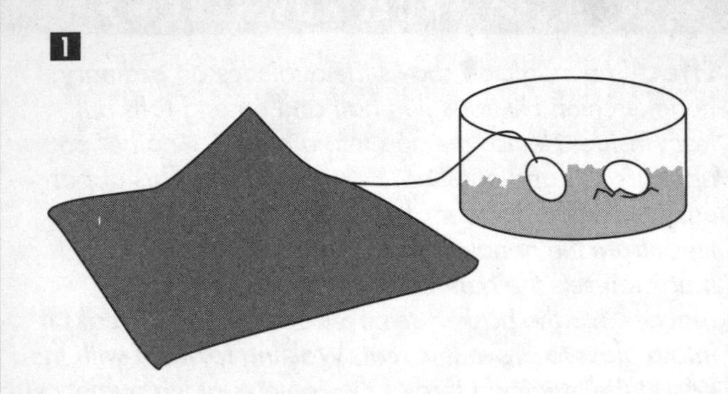

1 Lift up the handkerchief by the edge which does not have the thread attached. The egg will remain hidden in the basket while you show both sides of the handkerchief to the audience. Say, "As you can see, there are no chickens hidden in my handkerchief!" The audience will wonder what you are talking about. They will soon find out . . .

2 Lay the threaded hem of the handkerchief over the top of the basket so that it covers the plastic egg. Show that your hands are empty and roll up your sleeves, saying, "No chickens up my sleeves!"

TOP TIPS FOR TRICKSTERS

Magic with silk handkerchiefs is ideally suited for female magicians because the props involved have a definite "feminine" feel to them.

3 Pick up the handkerchief by the corners of the threaded hem and pull the hem tight between your hands. Lift the handkerchief straight up away from the basket and table. The thread will pull the egg out of the basket and it will dangle concealed behind the handkerchief (illustration 2).

4 Bring the top two corners together in your left hand (illustration 3), concealing the egg in the folds of the handkerchief. Your right hand holds the two lower corners together and moves up to the right until the folded handkerchief is held horizontally.

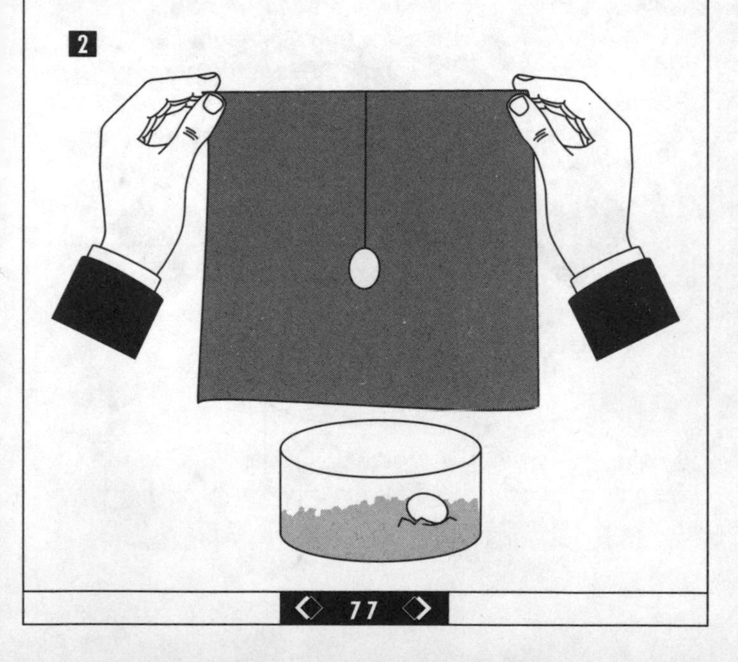

5 Move the handkerchief so that it is to your right of the basket. Lift your right hand slightly and shake the egg out of the handkerchief (illustration 4) so that it falls into the basket and lands on the confetti. Now the audience will understand all this talk of invisible chickens!

6 Rest the handkerchief back on top of the basket. The corners in the right hand go on the table in front of the basket. The right hand moves up to the left hand to take hold of one of the two corners being held in the left hand.

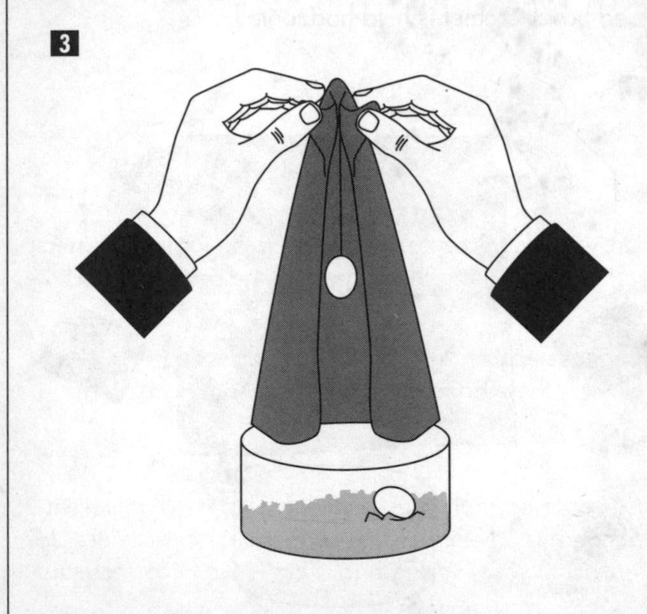

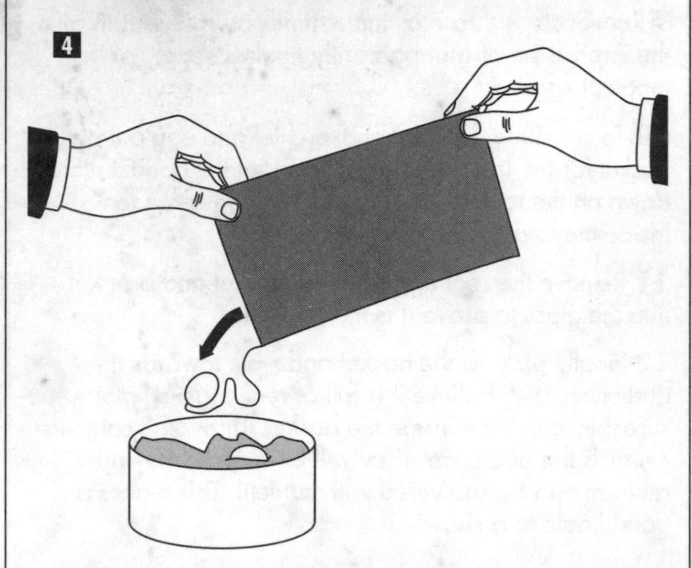

7 Draw your hands apart and raise the top two corners, again secretly lifting the egg out of the basket behind the handkerchief.

8 Repeat steps 4 and 5 to produce a second egg – really it is the second showing of the same one!

TOP TIPS FOR TRICKSTERS

When entertaining children with effects with different coloured handkerchiefs it is a good "bit of business" to get your colours wrong and allow them to correct you.

9 Repeat steps 4 to 7 as many times as you wish to give the impression of an apparently endless supply of magical eggs.

10 To conclude, lift the handkerchief and egg out of the basket for the last time (step 7) and set the handkerchief down on the table, ensuring that the egg is hidden inside the folds of the handkerchief.

11 Remove the real egg from the basket and break it into the glass to prove it is the real thing!

12 Finally pick up the basket and walk towards the audience. They believe it is full of real eggs, so make sure they can't see inside the basket. Throw the contents towards the audience. They will be surprised – and relieved – to be showered with confetti. This makes a good finale to a show!

HARRY BLACKSTONE (1885-1965)

Harry Blackstone toured the theatres of America in the mid 1900s with his spectacular illusion show. One of the highlights of his show was his "Haunted Hanky" effect, in which a borrowed handkerchief apparently became possessed by spirits and began moving and dancing around the stage! This effect is still performed today by his son, Harry Blackstone Jnr, who travels the world with his own illusion show keeping the name Blackstone up in lights.

Coin & Banknote Tricks

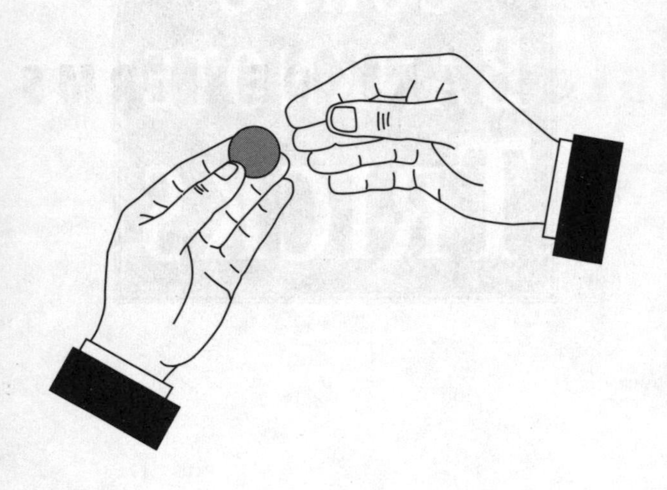

GLOSSARY OF TERMS

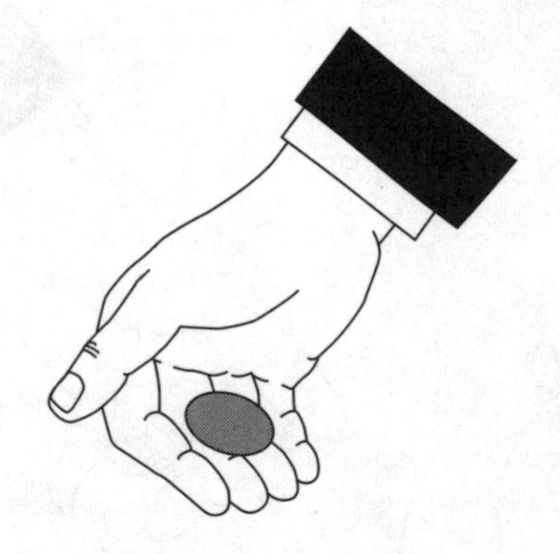

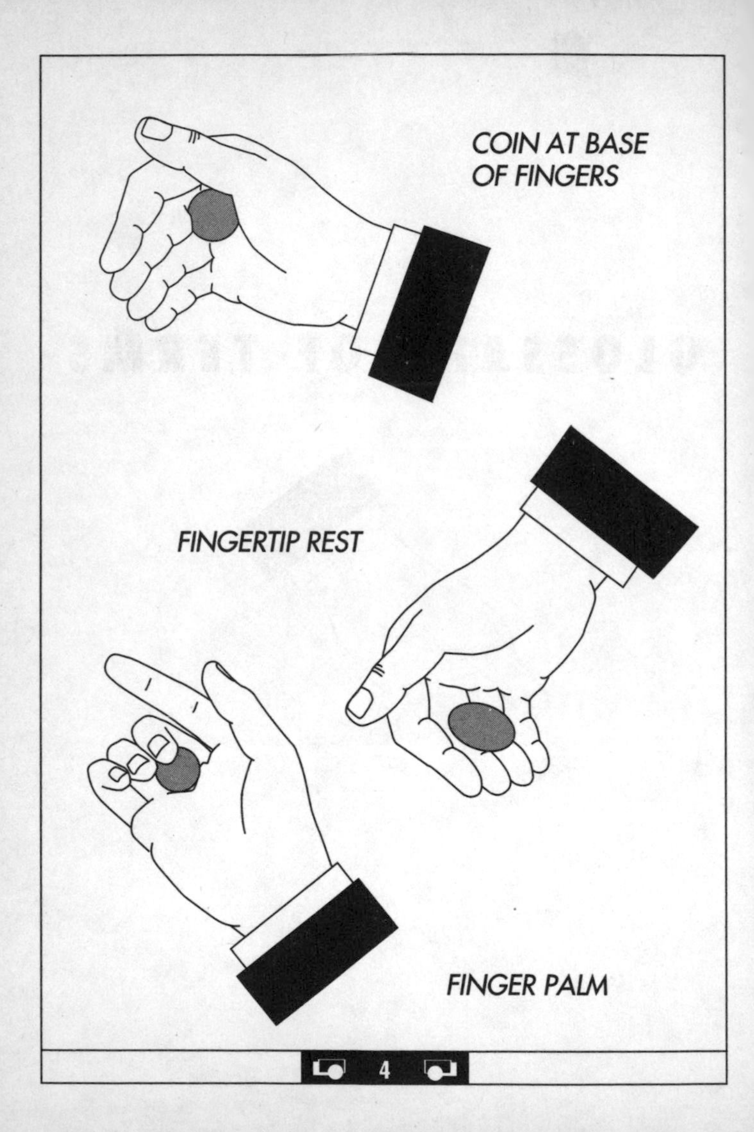
COIN AT BASE
OF FINGERS
FINGERTIP REST
FINGER PALM

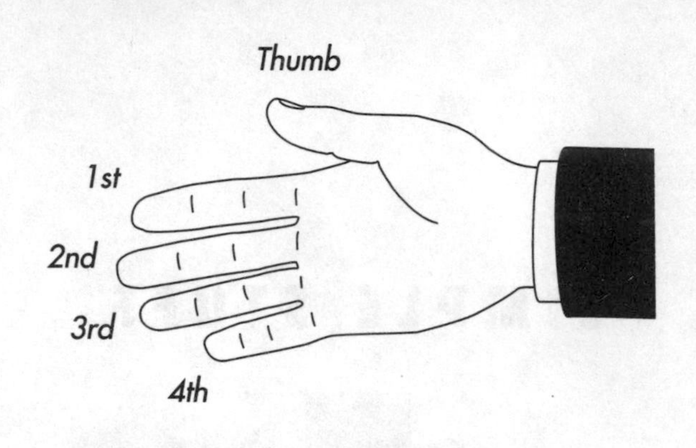

FACE OF BANKNOTE

10

BACK OF BANKNOTE

SIMPLE STUFF

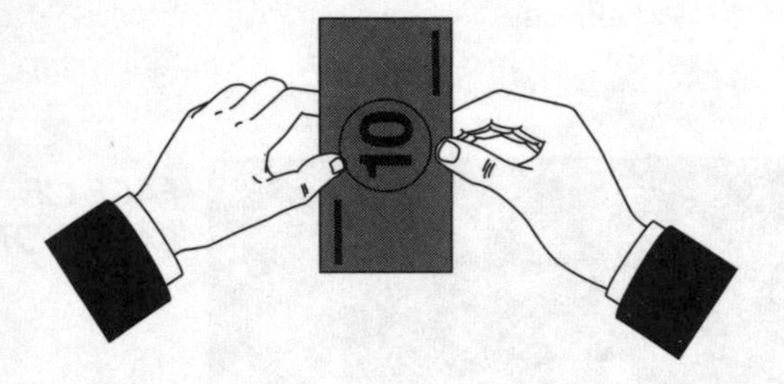

JUMPING COIN

Effect *A coin vanishes from the magician's right hand to appear in the left.*

Requirements *Any two coins.*

Preparation *None.*

• • • • • • • • • • • • • • •

1 Show a coin on the palm of each hand (illustration 1). The coin in the left hand should be below the third and fourth fingers. The one in the right hand should be at the base of the thumb. Hold the hands 30cm/12in apart on a table top.

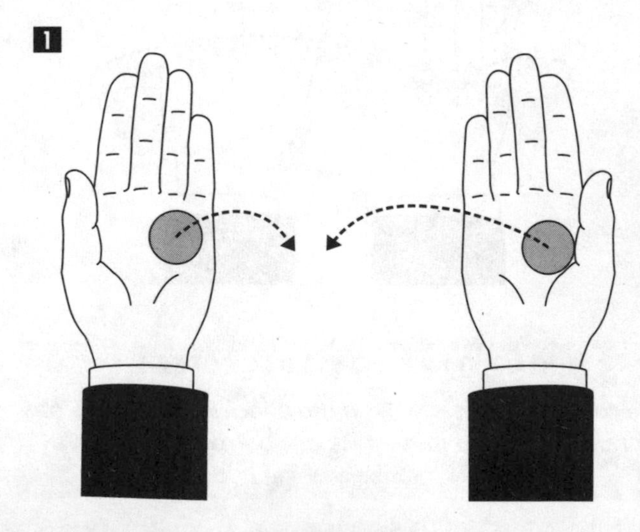

2 At exactly the same time turn both hands over quickly so that the thumbs come close together. As you do this the coin from the right hand will be thrown under the left hand (illustration 2), but to the audience it appears that you have just turned your hands over and there is a coin under each one.

3 Lift your right hand to show that the coin has vanished. Lift the left hand to show that amazingly there are now two coins under it.

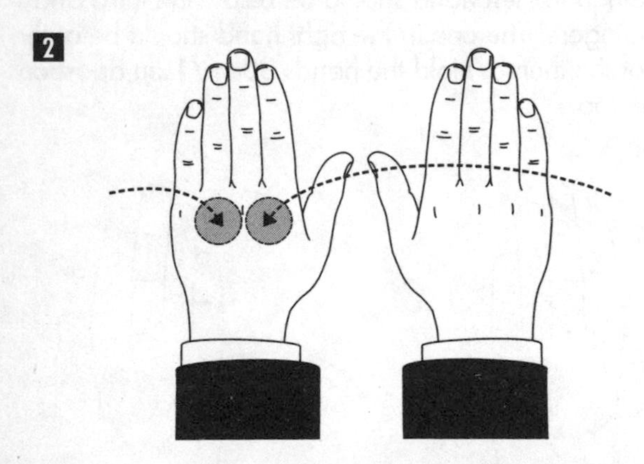

TOP TIPS FOR TRICKSTERS

Money magic is always more effective if the coins or banknotes used in the trick are borrowed from trustworthy members of the audience.

REFLEX TESTER

Effect *This is not a magic trick, but a stunt or "scam" you can try on your friends, using a banknote, to prove that there is no such thing as "easy money". If you use their money perhaps you can make a profit!*

Requirements *Any banknote.*

Preparation *None.*

• • • • • • • • • • • • • • •

1 The right thumb and first finger hold a note vertically at the middle of the right long edge. The open left hand is in position at the middle of the left long edge, but the left hand must not touch the note (illustration 1).

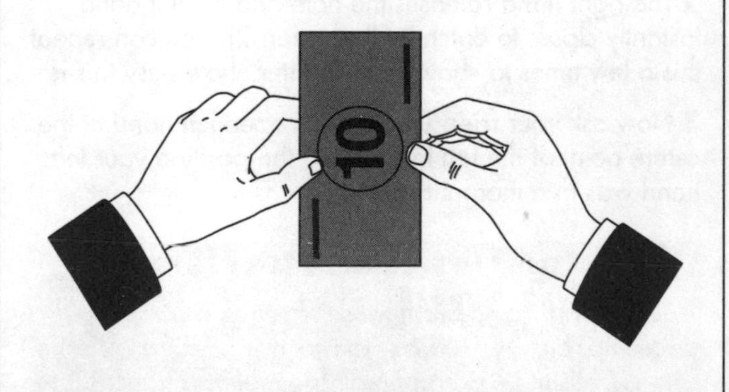

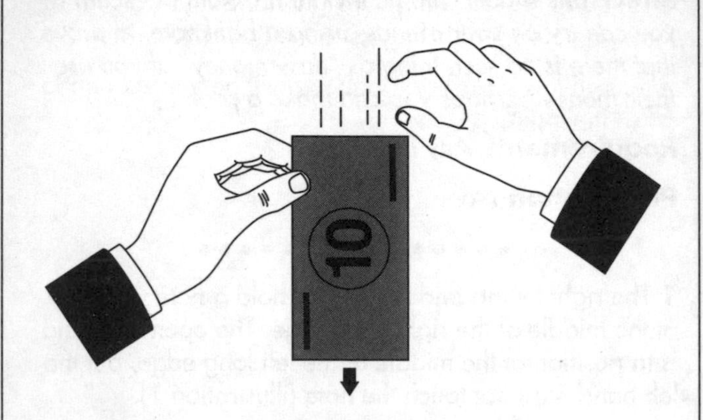

2 The right hand releases the note and the left hand instantly closes to catch it (illustration 2). You can repeat this a few times to show your "punter" how easy this is.

3 Now ask your friend to hold his open left hand at the centre point of the left long side – the position your left hand was in a moment ago.

TOP TIPS FOR TRICKSTERS

Tricks with coins are fine for showing a few people close up, but – with a few exceptions (like the "Miser's Dream") – are not really suitable on stage.

4 Tell them that if they catch the bill they can keep it!

5 Let go of the bill with your right hand and watch it slip through your friend's fingers to the floor (illustration 3).

Although this looks easy, nobody will be fast enough to catch the money.

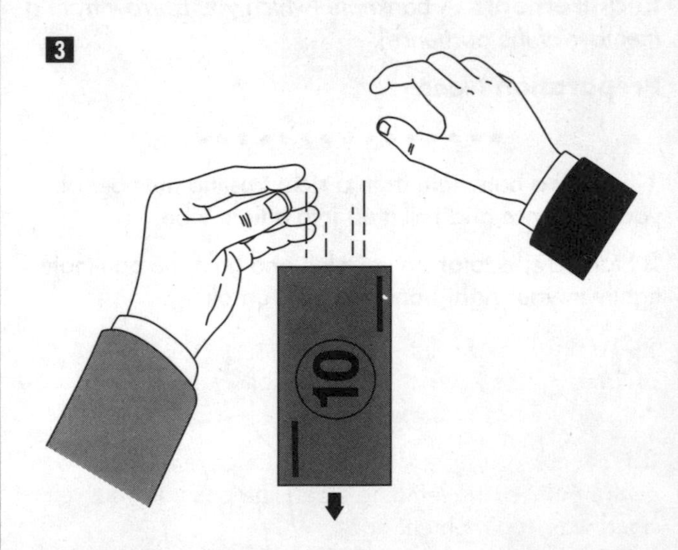

TOP TIPS FOR TRICKSTERS

If you do perform coin productions on a stage it is worth while having the coins silver plated so that they will shine in the stage lights and be easier to see.

VANISHING NOTE

Effect *A banknote is borrowed and rolled up into a tight tube. When it is handed to a member of the audience the note vanishes. It reappears in the magician's pocket.*

Requirements *A banknote (which you borrow from a member of the audience).*

Preparation *None.*

• • • • • • • • • • • • • • •

1 Borrow a banknote from a rich, trusting member of your audience and roll it up into a tight tube.

2 Stand a spectator on your left and hold the banknote tightly in your right hand to stop it unrolling.

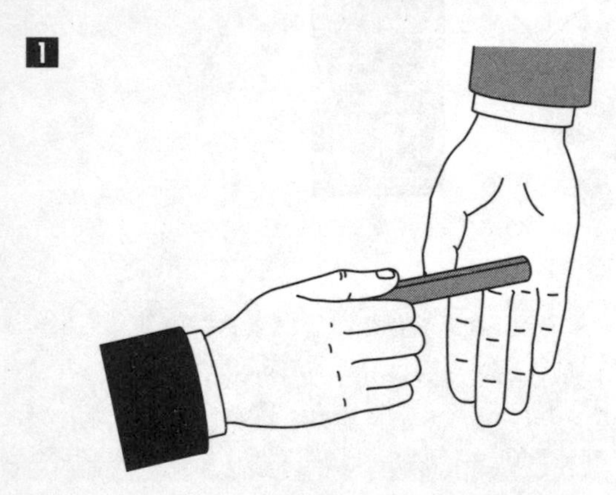

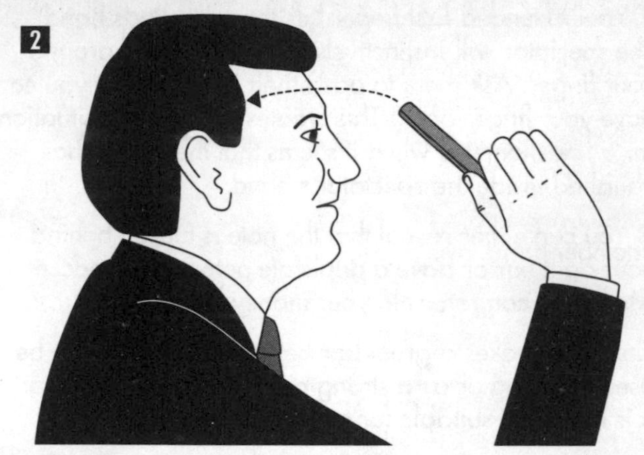

3 Ask the spectator to hold out their right hand palm up. With your left hand hold on to their right wrist.

4 Lift the note up and bring it down to tap the spectator's open hand (illustration 1). Explain that on the count of three the spectator must close their hand around the note.

5 Swing your right hand up in an arc to the right of your face (illustration 2) and back down. Count "one" as the note taps their open hand. Repeat this action and count "two" as you tap their palm again.

6 The next time your hand swings up, you leave the rolled up note tucked behind your ear. The timing must be the same as before – the right hand swings back down as though nothing has happened.

7 Your extended first finger hits the spectator's hand. The spectator will instinctively close their hand around your finger. Ask them to open their hand so that you can have your finger back! This creates an amusing situation for a few moments when it seems that the money has vanished inside the spectator's hand.

8 You can either reveal that the note is tucked behind your right ear or have a duplicate note in your pocket which you can return to your money lender.

The effect makes a great bar bet and stunt, and can be used as a gag or as a strong piece of magic. However, it is not really suitable for a stage presentation.

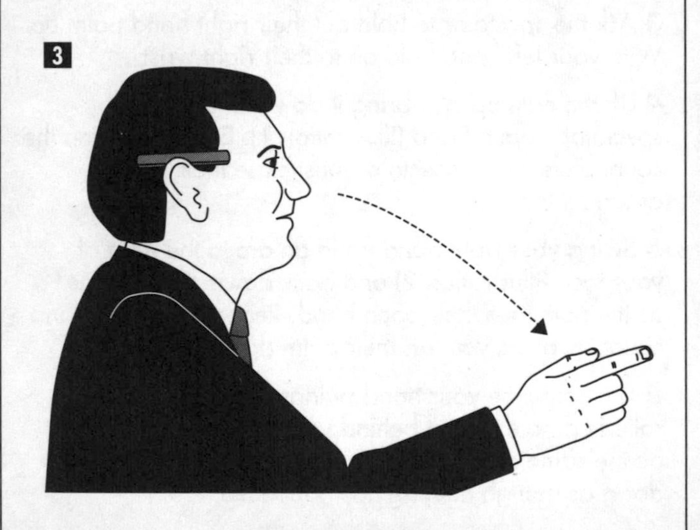

BASIC SLEIGHT-OF-HAND VANISHES

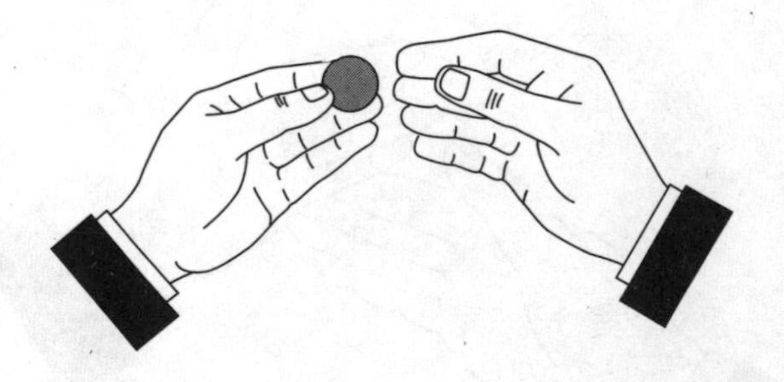

THE FINGER PALM VANISH

Effect *A coin vanishes.*

Requirements *Any coin.*

Preparation *None.*

• • • • • • • • • • • • • • •

1 Display the coin lying at the base of your right fingers.

2 Rest the edge of your right little finger across your left fingers (illustration 1).

1

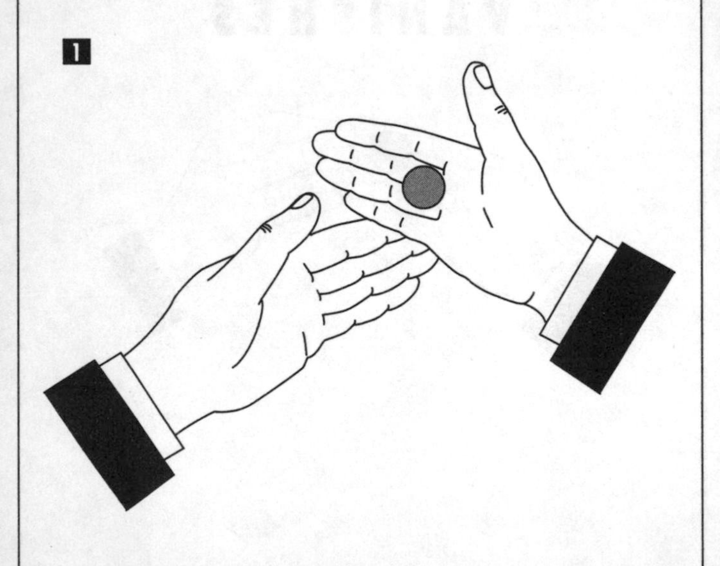

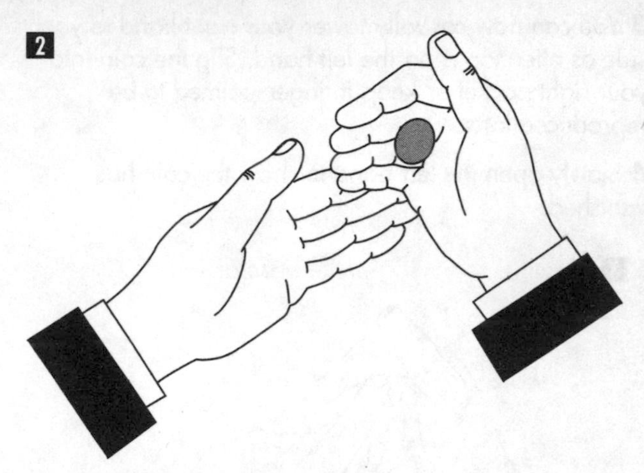

3 Pivot the right hand inward towards you, apparently to tip the coin into your left hand. In fact your right fingers curl inwards to hold the coin securely in the right fingers. This is the finger palm position (illustration 2).

4 Your left hand closes as though it did contain the coin. It moves downwards and turns over, drawing the audience's attention to it. Point with the right hand and move the left hand away to the left (illustration 3).

TOP TIPS FOR TRICKSTERS

If you are performing any coin tricks remember that the audience's attention will be on your hands. Ensure that you give them a good wash before you perform!

5 You can now casually lower your right hand to your side as attention is on the left hand. Slip the coin into your right pocket or keep it finger-palmed to be reproduced later.

6 Slowly open the left hand to show the coin has vanished.

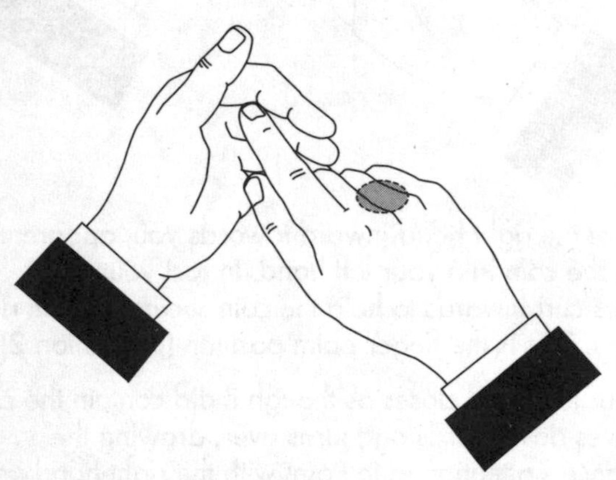

TOP TIPS FOR TRICKSTERS

Before you perform any tricks that will involve the audience concentrating on your hands make sure that you have clean fingernails!

Effect *A coin vanishes.*

Requirements *Any coin.*

Preparation *None.*

• • • • • • • • • • • • • • •

1 Hold the coin horizontally, parallel with the floor, with the tips of your left thumb and fingers. The fingers and thumb should be pointing upwards. Your fingers should be held together so that nobody can see between them.

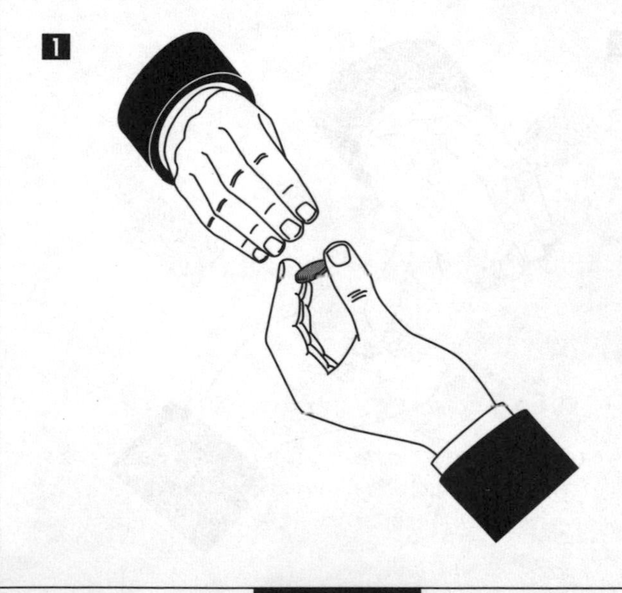

2 Your right hand approaches from behind to apparently pick up the coin (illustration 1). Your right thumb goes under the coin and your right fingers come over the top.

3 As soon as your right fingers cover the coin from view your left thumb releases the coin, allowing it to fall to the base of your left fingers (illustration 2).

4 However, your right hand continues as though it did contain the coin. It clenches into a fist and moves upwards and away to the right (illustration 3). It is important that you watch the right hand move and hold

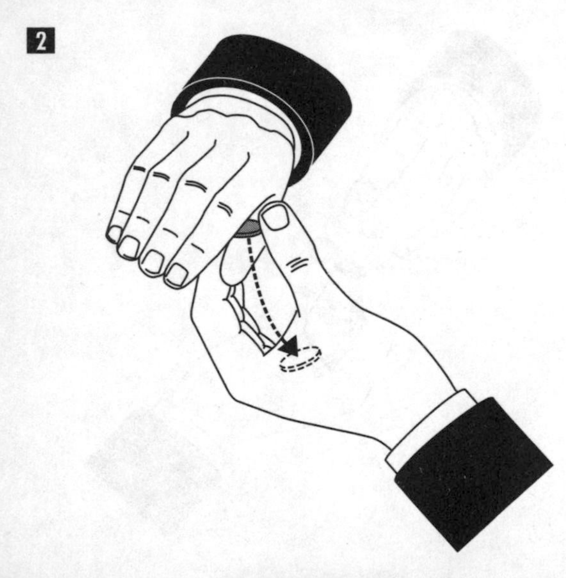

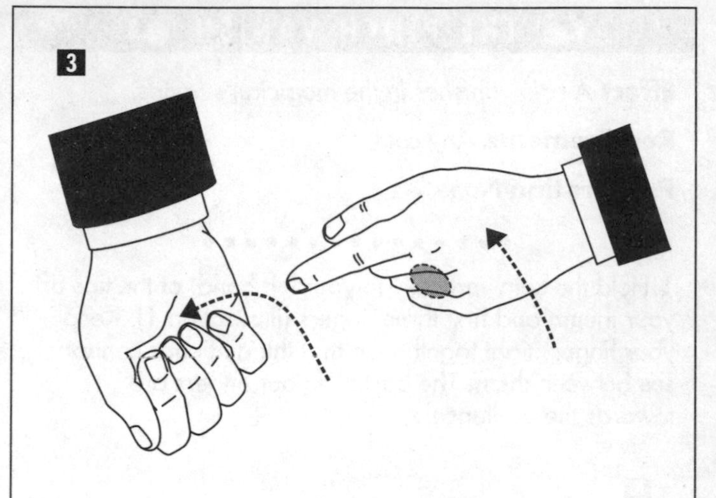

the left hand still. The rules of misdirection to remember here are first, that the audience will watch a moving object, and second, they will look where you look.

5 Close the left hand, clipping the coin at the base of the left fingers (finger palm position).

6 Open your right hand to show that the coin has vanished!

TOP TIPS FOR TRICKSTERS

It is worth while washing your hands before and after you practise as coins can become grubby and dirty very easily.

THE PINCH VANISH

Effect *A coin vanishes in the magician's hands.*

Requirements *Any coin.*

Preparation *None.*

• • • • • • • • • • • • • • •

1 Hold the coin vertically in your left hand, at the tips of your thumb and first three fingers (illustration 1). Keep your fingers tight together so that the audience cannot see between them. The backs of your fingers are towards the audience.

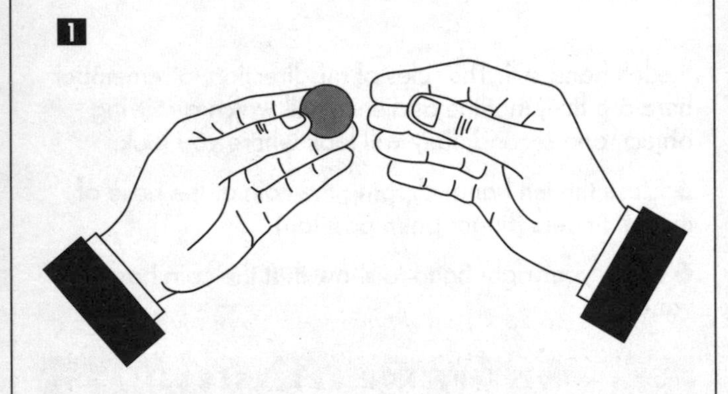

2 The right hand reaches over as though to take the coin from the left hand. The right thumb goes behind the coin and the right fingers cover it at the front.

2

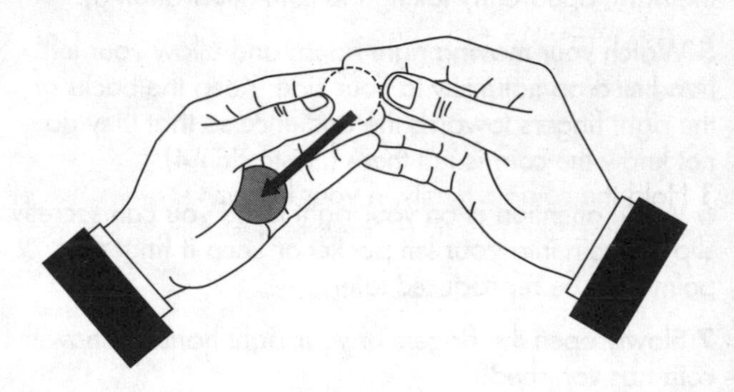

3 As soon as the right fingers completely cover the coin from the audience's view the left thumb releases its hold, and the coin slides down to the base of the left fingers (illustration 2).

DAVID ROTH

This New York coin magician is probably today's acknowledged expert at sleight-of-hand magic with coins. Many of his routines are described in detail in the book, David Roth's Expert Coin Magic, *written, illustrated and published by Richard Kaufman and available from most good magic shops.*

4 The left hand curls slightly to hold the coin in the finger palm position while the right hand moves away to the right, apparently taking the coin (illustration 3).

5 Watch your moving right hand, and allow your left hand to drop naturally to your side. Keep the backs of the right fingers towards the audience so that they do not know the coin is not there (illustration 4).

6 While attention is on your right hand you can secretly slip the coin into your left pocket or keep it finger palmed to be reproduced later.

7 Slowly open the fingers of your right hand to show the coin has vanished!

3

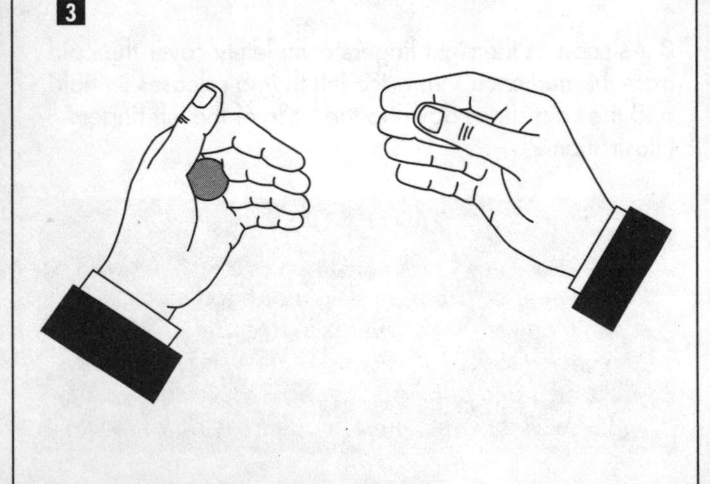

4

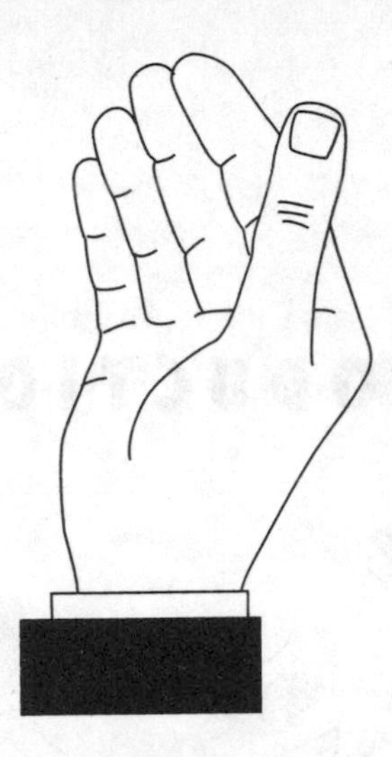

CHUNG LING SOO (1861-1918)

One of the highlights of Chung Ling Soo's spectacular show was the "Dream of Wealth". From mid-air he produced coins, banknotes and a cheque for one million pounds! Although known as the Marvellous Chinese Conjurer, the oriental character was actually a disguise for William E. Robinson who was really born in America! He was fatally wounded on stage during a performance of the famous "Catching a Bullet".

PRODUCTIONS

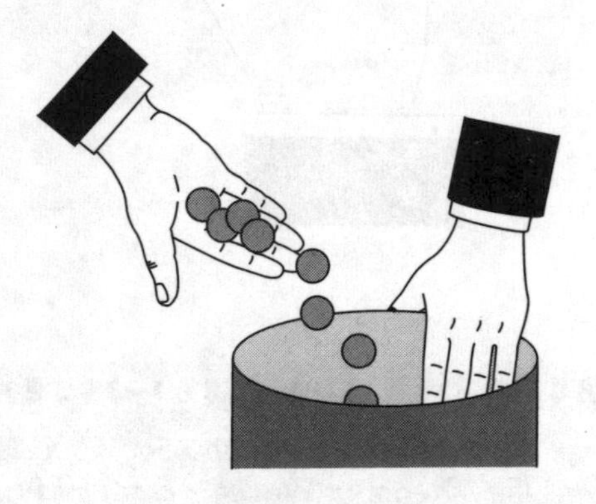

Effect *The magician shows a banknote, folds it into a tube and tips out a genuine coin!*

Requirements *Any banknote and coin.*

Preparation *Place the coin and banknote in your pocket so that they can easily be removed together.*

• • • • • • • • • • • • • • •

1 Reach into your pocket and remove the banknote and coin, ensuring that the coin is kept concealed behind the note. Explain to the audience that this is your private Money Making Machine!

2 Hold up the note with the right hand, holding the hidden coin clipped to the back of the note with the right thumb (illustration 1).

3 Snap the left side of the note with the left fingers. This proves to the audience that the left hand is empty and that nothing is concealed behind the left side of the banknote.

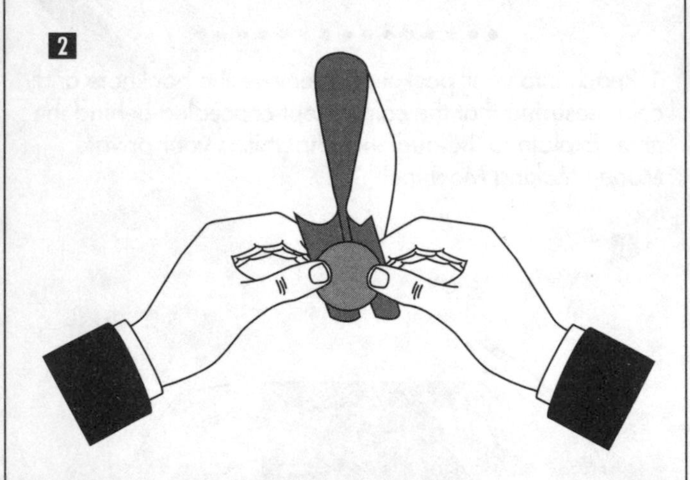

TOP TIPS FOR TRICKSTERS

Gimmicked and fake coins will enable you to do many more tricks – but it is essential to master the basics of sleight-of-hand magic first.

4 Hold the left side of the note in the left hand mirroring the right hand's grip. Bring the two hands together making the note bend as in illustration 2. Secretly transfer the coin from under the right thumb to under the left thumb. Flick the right side of the bill with the right first finger (illustration 3).

PAUL DANIELS (b. 1938)

Paul Daniels is Britain's best known magician, due to his many series of The Paul Daniels Magic Show *on BBC1 and his live performances in theatres around the country. One of his most memorable television performances was the day he made £1,000,000 cash vanish – and reappear! Watching over him on that occasion was newspaper tycoon Robert Maxwell!*

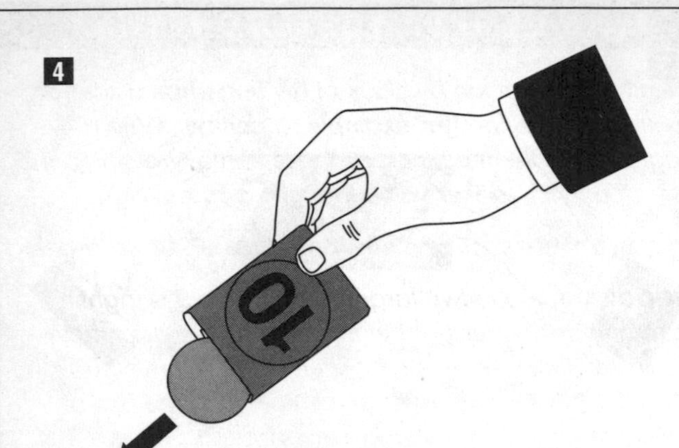

5 Fold the note into a tube, secretly wrapping the concealed coin inside.

6 Tilt the opening in the folded note downwards so that the coin slowly falls out (illustration 4). You have proved that you have made your own Money Making Machine!

FRED KAPS (1926-1980)

This Dutch magician was a master of sleight of hand and manipulation. He was a winner of many famous magical awards – a true World Champion. His act featured the manipulation of banknotes and giant coins, and concluded with the production of an almost endless stream of salt pouring from his fist.

Effect *The magician displays at his fingertips a coin of small denomination (for example, a penny). With a magical pass the magician changes it into two coins, both of a much higher value than the original coin!*

Requirements *Three coins (one small and two large).*

Preparation *The two large coins are held upright near the tips of your right thumb and first finger. They are secretly hidden by the smaller coin which you hold upright and at right angles to them, also at the tips of the right thumb and first finger (illustration 1). Hold this set-up in front of a mirror and you will see that the two*

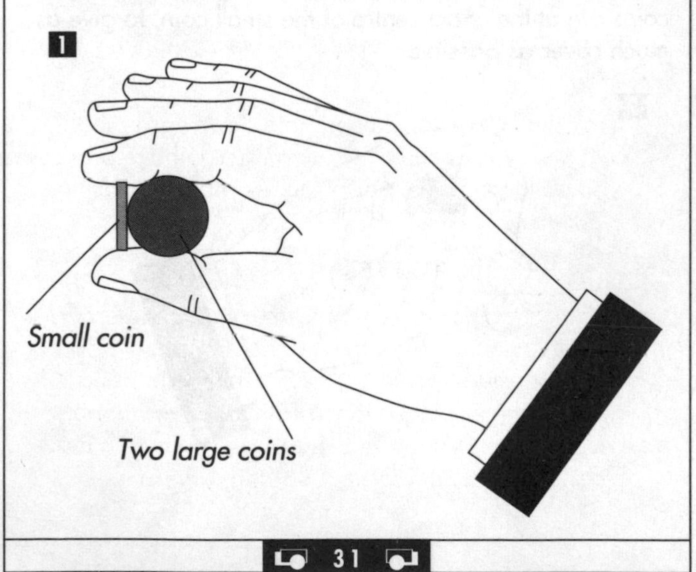

large coins are hidden. Practise the following routine many times in front of a mirror watching it from different angles until you are confident the large coins are completely hidden.

Set up the coins in position and you are ready to begin your performance.

• • • • • • • • • • • • • • •

1 Hold up the right hand to show the small coin face on and at the audience's eye level so that they cannot see the two extra coins (illustration 2). The trick will only work if the coin is held at the height of the audience's line of vision. It is important that the edges of the large coins are at the exact centre of the small coin, to give as much cover as possible.

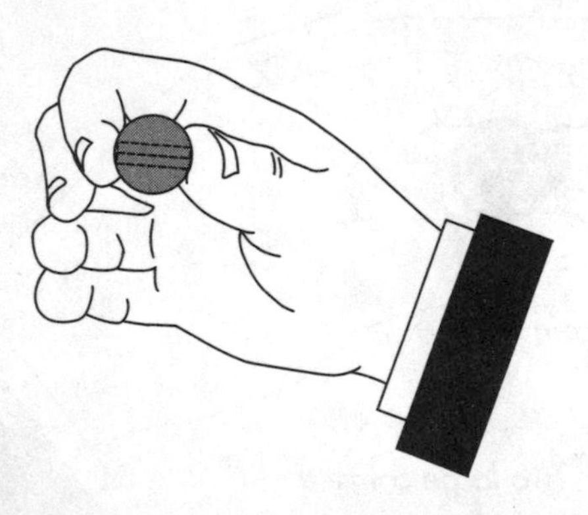

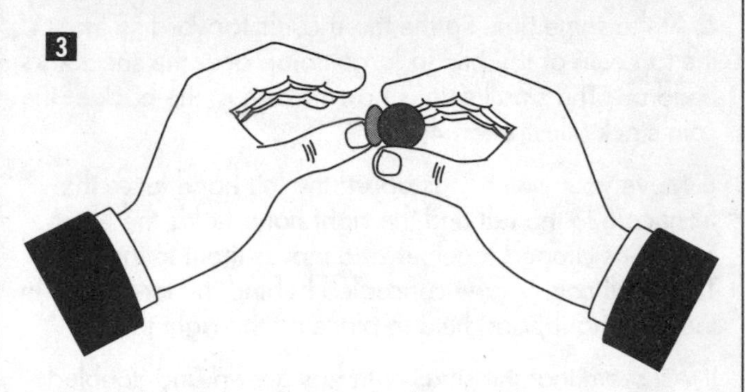

2 The audience have, apparently, seen that your right hand is empty, except for the small coin. Now show both sides of your left hand to prove it is empty.

3 Bring the two hands together with the first fingers and thumbs of both hands pointing towards each other. Again it is essential that the hands stay level with the audience's eye level so they do not see the extra coins.

4 Your left thumb goes beneath the coins, pushing on the bottom edge of the small coin (illustration 3), pivoting it on to the bottom of the two large coins so that all three coins are now in one stack.

TOP TIPS FOR TRICKSTERS

It is a good idea to keep a set of coins especially for performing with. Keep these polished and clean to improve your "professional" image.

5 At the same time tip the three coins forward so that the top coin of the pile (a large coin) faces the spectators head on. The small coin is now hidden at the back of the coin stack (illustration 4).

6 Move your two hands apart; the left hand takes the front coin to the left and the right hand holds the other two coins clipped together and moves them to the right. The small coin is now concealed behind the large coin in the right hand, and held in place by the right thumb.

It will seem that the small coin has grown and doubled in an instant. As you put the coins away be careful not to expose the small hidden coin.

This is a quick visual effect which is ideal for a one-to-one performance, especially when creating extra change at the shop, bank or on the bus!

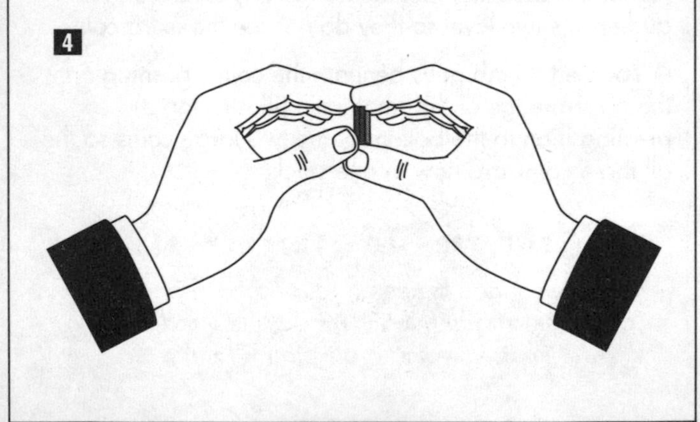

CONTINUOUS COINS

Effect *The magician borrows a handkerchief from a spectator and produces an apparently endless stream of coins from within its folds.*

Requirements *A large cotton handkerchief (preferably borrowed from a member of the audience) and two identical coins – the larger the better.*

Preparation *Place one coin in your left trouser pocket and one in your right trouser pocket. You are all set to produce money from nothing!*

• • • • • • • • • • • • • • •

1

1 Borrow the handkerchief and show it on both sides. Show both your hands are empty so there is no suspicion of you sneaking anything into the handkerchief.

2 Point the fingers and thumb of your right hand upwards with all the tips touching. Your left hand drapes the handkerchief over your right hand so that the pointed fingers are in the centre of the handkerchief.

3 Show your left hand is empty and, with the left hand, grasp the centre of the handkerchief and lift it up. You are going to exchange the positions of your hands so that your left hand is under the handkerchief and your right hand is uncovered. Flip the handkerchief with your right hand and throw it over the left hand. The left hand takes position with the fingers pointing up (illustration 1).

2

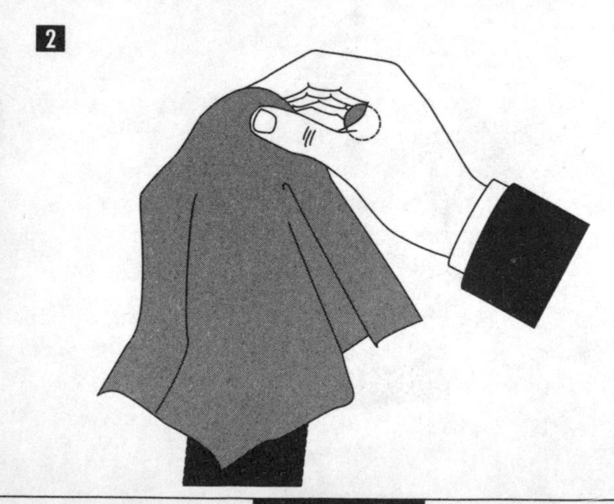

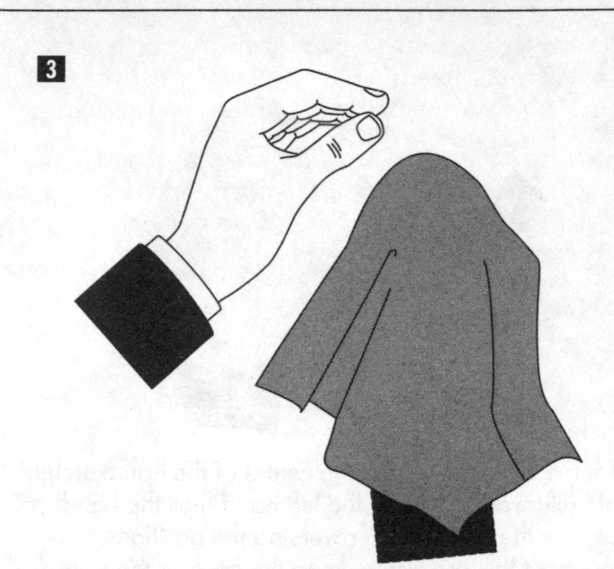

4 You say that you can see something sticking out of the top of the handkerchief, apparently held by the left fingertips. With your right hand you mime taking the object, keeping the back of the hand towards the audience so they cannot see if you have taken anything or not.

5 Place the right hand in your righthand pocket, apparently to dispose of the object. In fact you finger palm the coin in your pocket. The audience's impression should be that you are putting something in your pocket, *not* secretly removing something!

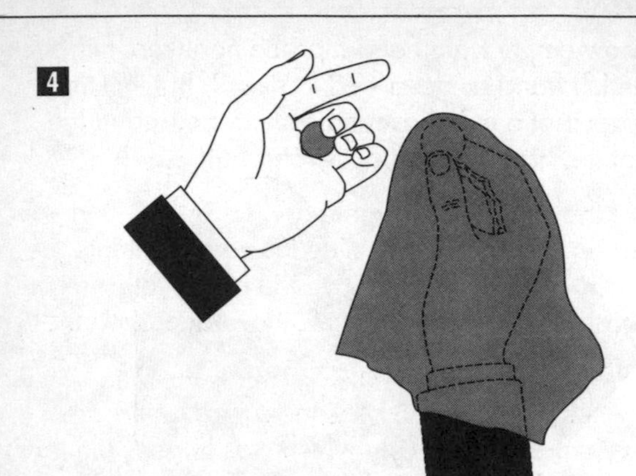

6 Your right hand grasps the centre of the handkerchief again (illustration 2) and the left hand flips the handkerchief over the right hand, reversing the positions. Throughout this procedure keep the back of the right hand towards the audience so that the concealed coin remains hidden.

7 Again pretend there is an object in the centre of the handkerchief and mime taking it with the left hand (illustration 3). Your left hand goes to the left pocket to apparently dispose of the object. In fact it finger palms the coin there and reappears with the coin concealed.

8 The left fingers take hold of the centre of the handkerchief – and, through the material, of the coin in the right hand. The coin in the left hand remains hidden in the finger palm position (illustration 4).

9 The now empty right hand flips the handkerchief back over the left hand as described in step 3. But this time you reveal that a coin has magically appeared in the centre of the handkerchief (illustration 5)!

10 Take the coin in your right hand and place it in your right pocket. In your pocket slide the coin back into the finger palm position and remove the apparently empty right hand. It will appear that you have deposited the coin in your pocket.

11 Now the right hand grasps the centre of the handkerchief – and the coin which was finger palmed in the left hand. The left hand flips over the handkerchief to show another coin has appeared (illustration 6)!

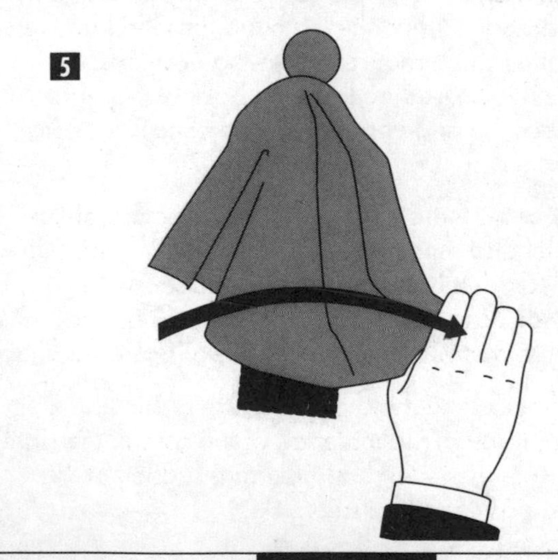

12 The left hand takes the coin and places it in the left pocket where you slide it back into finger palm!

13 By repeating steps 8 through to 12 you can produce an apparently endless stream of coins from within the folds of the handkerchief – just by reproducing the same two coins.

When you think you have profited enough, return the handkerchief to its owner and take your applause.

There is plenty of potential for humour with this effect as you pretend that the owner has got a coin trapped in the folds of their handkerchief. . . and another. . . and another. . . which you keep pocketing until you return the handkerchief!

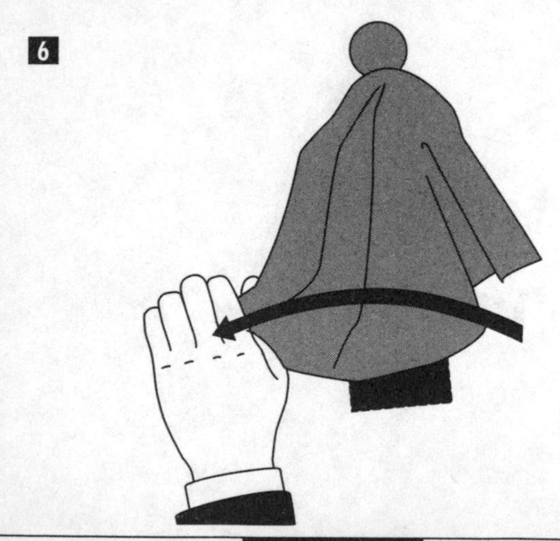

Effect *This is one of the true classics of coin magic, performed by professional magicians all over the world. The magician plucks coins from the air and drops them into a container. In the finale the magician's hands are full of a stream of gleaming coins caught in mid-air.*

Requirements *A special fake coin, a stack of genuine identical coins (about 25), a container (a large tin or a small plastic bucket) and a special holder.*

Preparation *The special coin is made by drilling a hole in a small metal disc the same size as the coins (a blank pet's name tag is ideal for this as it already has*

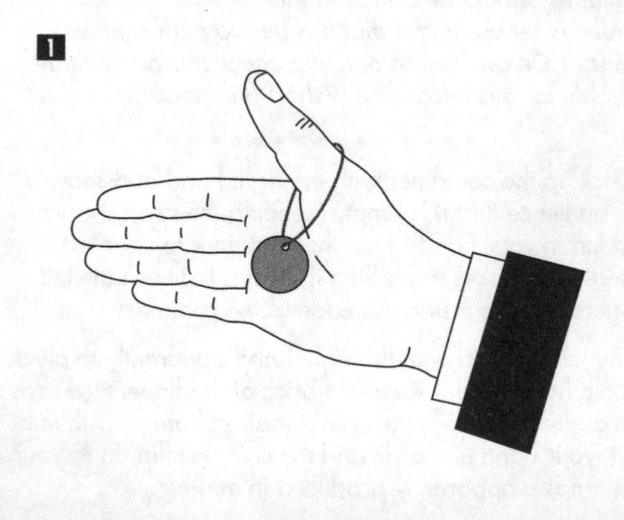

the hole in it). Thread a small loop of cotton through the hole so that it will loop over your thumb (illustration 1).

The special holder is made from an old sock! This will hold the stack of coins that will make your big final production (about 12). To make the holder cut off the toe of the sock and sew around the edge of the hole with elastic (illustration 2). Put half the coins inside the sock – the elastic should prevent them falling out – and safety pin it under your jacket or coat on your right side.

Your final preparation is to loop the thread on the fake coin over your right thumb and stack the remaining coins (about 12) in your closed left hand. The empty container should be on your table.

All this set-up means that it is best to perform the "Miser's Dream" as an opening effect. It is particularly suitable for this because it is short and noisy!.

• • • • • • • • • • • • • • • •

1 Pick up the container with the right hand and show the audience that it is empty (keeping the special coin hidden in your hand). Pass the container to your left hand which takes it, holding the coins between the left fingers and the inside top edge of the container.

2 Reach forward with the right hand apparently to pluck a coin from the air. Keep the back of the fingers towards the audience to hide the coin dangling from your thumb. Jerk your hand upwards and the coin will flip up to your fingertips – apparently produced in mid-air.

2

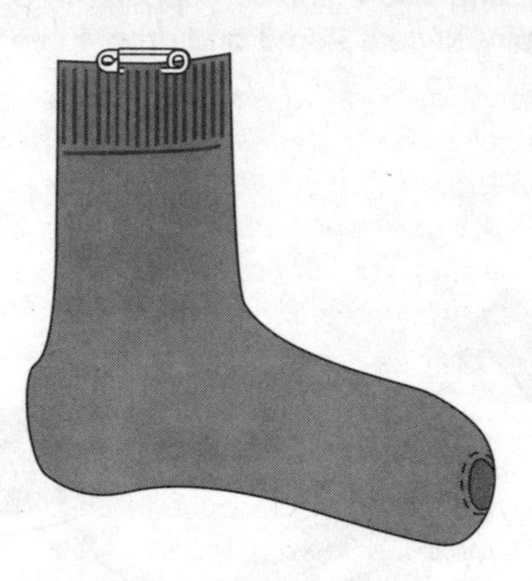

3 Move the right hand to the top of the container and apparently drop the coin inside. What really happens is that you release the coin and it returns to its position dangling around the thumb. At the same time your left fingers allow one coin inside the container to drop to the bottom – the audience will hear it drop. If the timing is right this is very convincing – it seems as though you have just dropped a coin into the container.

TOP TIPS FOR TRICKSTERS

Many fake and gimmicked coins are available from magic shops, dealers and suppliers. You may find a magic shop listed in your local Yellow Pages.

4 By repeating step 2 you can apparently produce another coin! Repeat step 3 and drop it into the container.

TOP TIPS FOR TRICKSTERS

You can have great fun with money magic at any time. When out shopping you can produce the correct change from mid-air or vanish a note as you hand it to the bank cashier!

5 Continue producing coins until all the coins in your left hand have been dropped into the container. You can produce coins from behind your knee, under your armpit or from your audience! It is a very funny situation to apparently produce coins from behind a spectator's ears, or beard and so on.

6 When the last coin has been dropped, allow your right hand to fall naturally to your side as you shake the container noisily and perhaps jokingly ask if anyone would like to contribute to your collection! While the audience's attention is on the container, your right hand reaches under the right side of your jacket and squeezes the coins out of the holder. Any noise made while you're doing this will be covered by you rattling the container in your left hand.

7 Finally place the container on the table or the floor and open your right hand, letting the final big production of coins stream from your hand into the container (illustration 3). The special coin will fall unnoticed among the regular coins.

STREET MAGICIANS

Many magicians began their performing lives "on the street" as buskers, trying to extract money from the passers-by. Ex-street magicians enjoying great success today include Harry Anderson, John Lenahan, Keith Fields, Leo Ward and Penn and Teller.

Effect *This is an alternative way of producing the single coin in your right hand when you are performing the "Miser's Dream". It uses a regular coin.*

Requirements *Any coin.*

Preparation *None.*

• • • • • • • • • • • • • • •

1 The coin begins in the "thumb clip" position (illustration 1). The coin is clipped between the base of the right thumb and the first finger. The coin is hidden from the audience as throughout the routine the back of the right hand faces the audience.

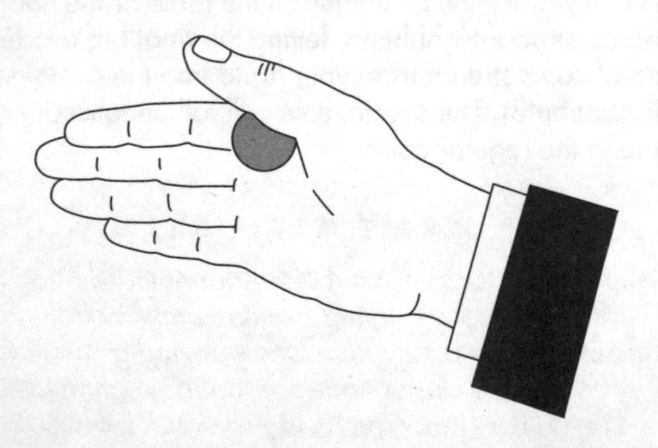

2

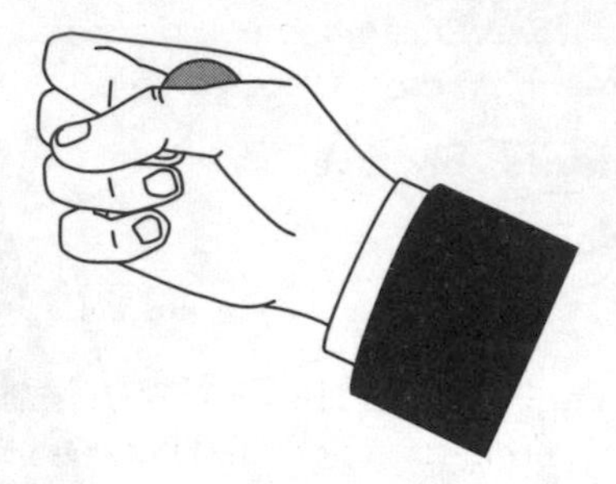

2 The four right fingers all bend inwards (illustration 2). The first finger goes behind the coin and the second finger in front as they clip the coin.

3 To produce the coin the fingers open out again, the first and second fingers bringing the coin into view clipped between them (illustration 3).

TOP TIPS FOR TRICKSTERS

The most important thing in coin magic is to make your hand look natural when it is secretly concealing a coin. If your hand looks tense and cramped it will be noticed. The best advice is to keep a coin "palmed" in your hand all day so that you forget about it – it will help you to act more naturally during a performance.

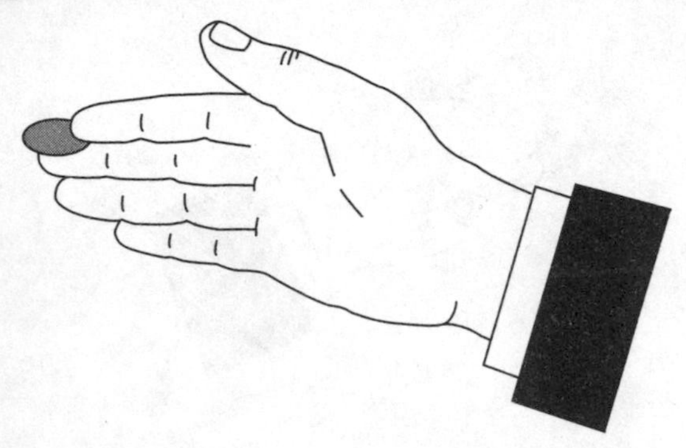

4 To apparently drop the coin into the container simply reverse the procedure. As the right hand moves over to the container, the right fingers close and the right thumb clips the coin again. The right fingers can now be spread and shown to be empty. The coin can then be produced again. . . and again. . . and again.

AL GOSHMAN (1921-1991)

New York magician Al Goshman was one of the first and finest close-up magicians. Until his death he was one of the resident magicians at the Magic Castle in Hollywood. Throughout his act, if you said "please", he would produce a successsion of coins from beneath a salt cellar – each coin bigger than the last.

PENETRATIONS

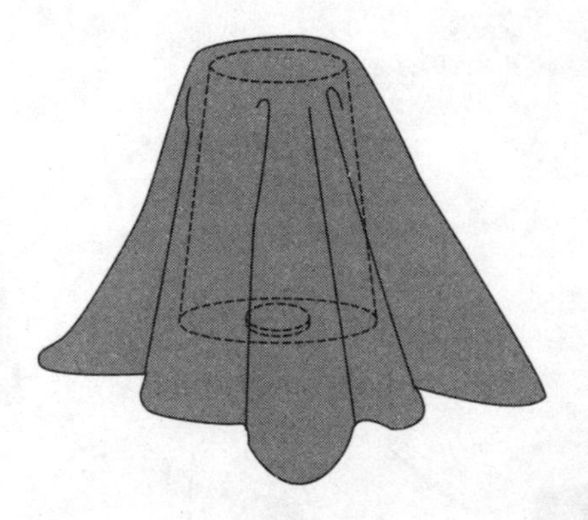

COIN UP THROUGH HAND

Effect *The magician places a coin in the left fist. When he slaps the back of the fist with his right hand the coin appears on top of his fist, having apparently penetrated his hand!*

Requirements *Any coin.*

Preparation *None.*

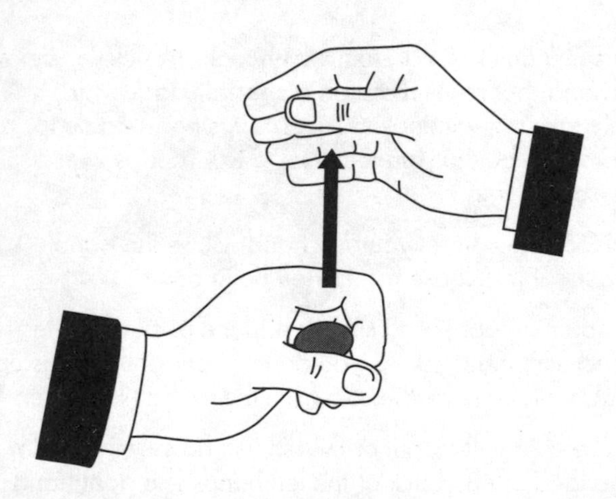

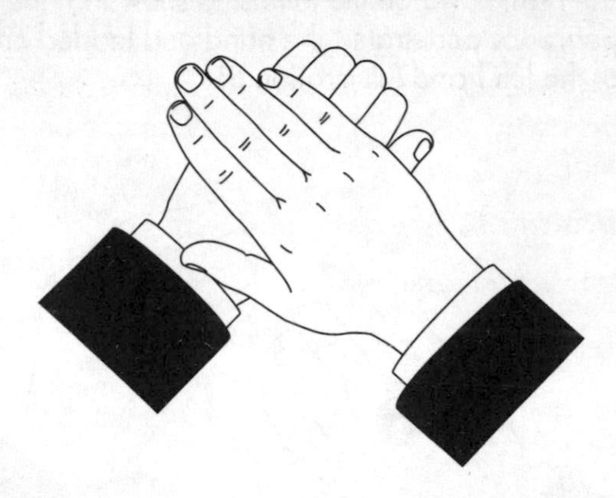

This is a quick visual stunt which looks like clever sleight of hand, but relies more on a special knack which will only take a few minutes to learn. It is not suitable for a big show, but it is fun to do for a few friends with a borrowed coin.

1 Place the coin in your left hand. Close the hand around it in a loose fist, turned palm down.

2 You now appear to simply slap the back of the left hand with the right. As you do this, jerk both hands up slightly and release the coin from the left fist (illustration 1).

3 The coin will fly out of the left fist, hit the right palm and land on the back of the left hand. The right hand then slaps the back of the left, holding the coin in place (illustration 2).

4 Lift the right hand off the left fist to show that the coin has apparently penetrated the hand and landed on the back of the left hand (illustration 3).

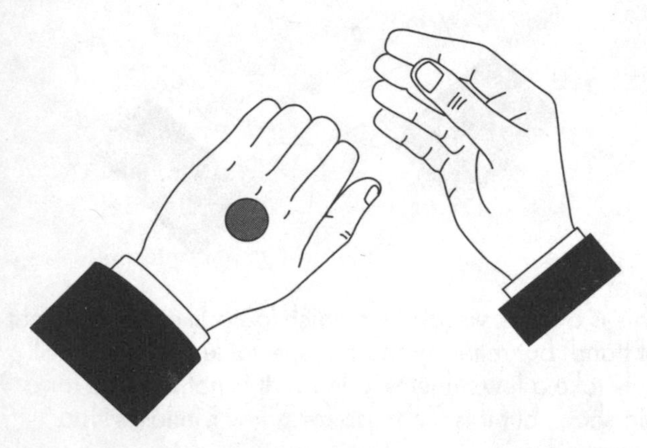

PROFESSOR HOFFMANN (1839-1919)

Professor Hoffmann was the pen-name of Angelo Lewis, a professional barrister and journalist, who was Britain's leading magical author. The first coin tricks to be described in detail appeared in his books. His books are now rarities, sought by magical collectors everywhere. His books included Modern Magic, More Magic, Later Magic *and* Magical Titbits.

Effect *The magician passes a borrowed coin through his right leg!*

Requirements *Any coin (preferably borrowed) and a right leg that is wearing trousers!*

Preparation *None.*

• • • • • • • • • • • • • • •

1 Borrow a coin from a member of your audience. If they wish they can mark it with a pen or crayon.

2 Hold the coin between the right thumb and fingers.

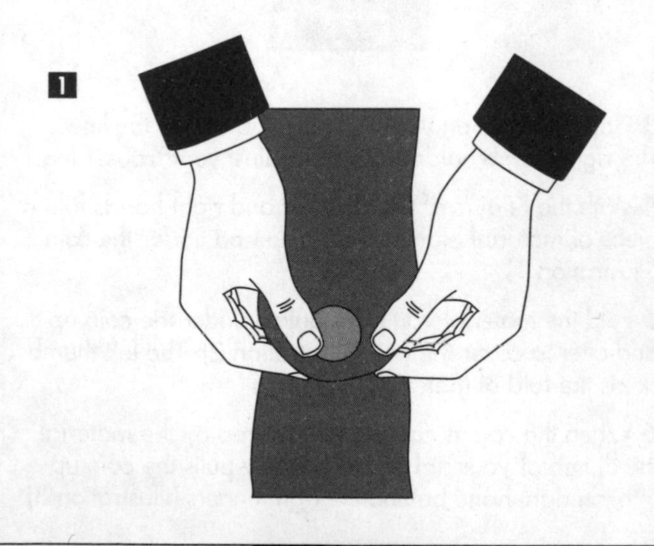

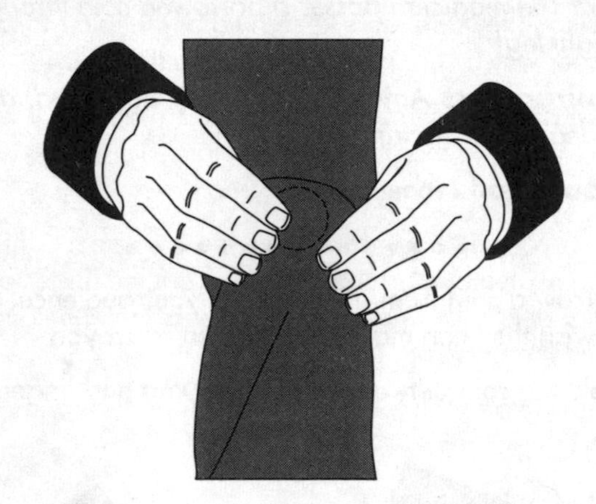

3 Place the coin on your right leg just above the knee. The right thumb holds the coin against your trouser leg.

4 With the fingers of both the left and right hands fold a piece of material of the trousers up and under the coin (illustration 1).

5 Fold the material you have pulled under the coin up and over to cover the coin (illustration 2). The left thumb holds the fold of material in position.

6 When the coin is completely covered by the material the thumb of your right hand secretly pulls the coin up into the right hand behind the right fingers (illustration 3).

7 Your right hand now curls slightly to finger palm the coin. Move your right hand around to the back of the right leg. The left fingers keep hold of the fold of trouser material which is apparently trapping the coin.

8 Release your left hand's grip on the material. It will drop, revealing that the coin has gone. Turn your left hand around to show that it is empty.

9 With your right hand, remove the coin from behind the right knee by pushing the coin from the finger palm position up to the fingertips. It appears that the coin passed through your leg!

This is a great trick for an impromptu performance for just a few people.

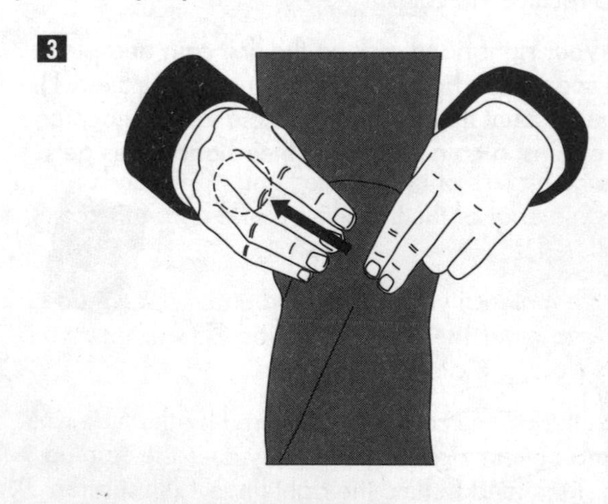

COIN ESCAPE

Effect The magician gives a spectator seven coins to hold. Despite the fact that the spectator holds the coins tightly inside their fist, the magician makes one coin penetrate through the spectator's hand.

Requirements Seven coins of identical value.

Preparation None.

• • • • • • • • • • • • • • •

1 Hold the coins in your cupped left hand and stand facing the spectator who is going to assist you.

2 Ask the spectator to hold out their hand palm up ready to receive the coins.

3 With your right hand pick up the first coin and place it in the spectator's hand counting "one" (illustration 1). Continue to count the next four coins, allowing each one to click against a coin already in their hand – this gets

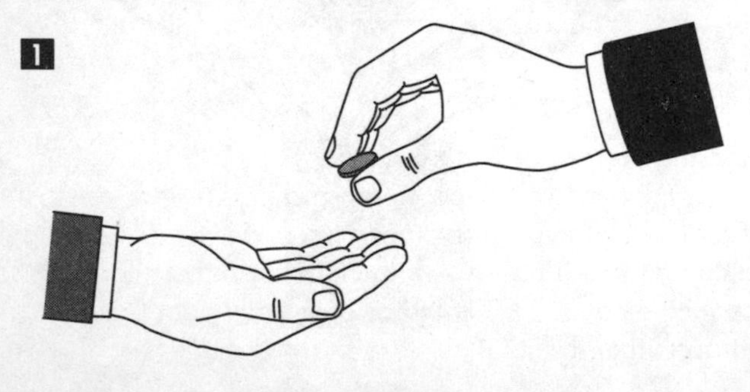

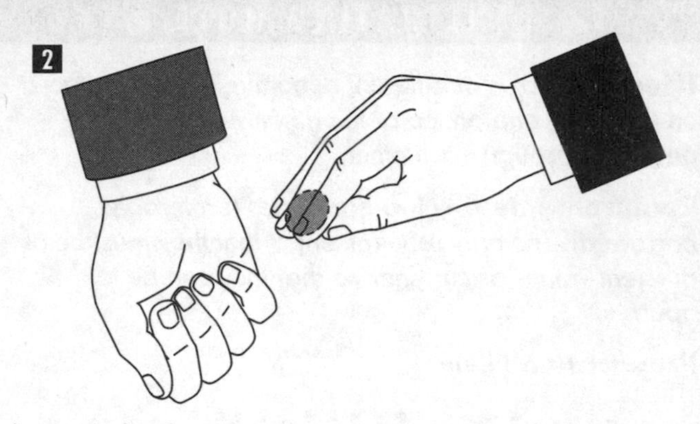

them used to hearing the coin go into their hand. This will allow you to "short change" them in the next step.

4 When you place the sixth coin in the spectator's hand simply click it against a coin already in their hand, but do not let go of it. Keep it gripped between the right thumb and first finger. Make sure that the coin remains concealed by your right fingers.

5 Throw the final coin from your left hand straight into the spectator's right hand. They will snap their fist closed (illustration 2).

6 Bring your right hand underneath their fist, keeping the coin concealed. Slap your hand against the back of their fist. Slide your hand out from underneath revealing a coin in your fingers. Ask them to open their hand and count the coins. One coin has magically penetrated through their hand!

PENETRATING NOTE

Effect *Two notes of different denominations are placed on the table, one on top of the other. Magically they penetrate through each other.*

Requirements *Any two banknotes (preferably borrowed). The only requirement is that they must be of different values or currency so that they can be told apart.*

Preparation *None.*

• • • • • • • • • • • • • • •

1 Lay the two notes on the table to form a V. The point of the V is towards you. The lower note is angled away

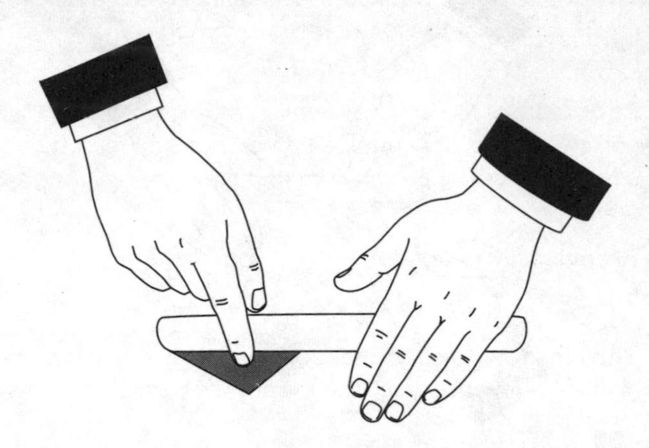

to your left and the upper note angled away to your right. It is important that the note on top is slightly further forward toward the audience. It does not quite meet the edges of the lower note.

2 Make sure the audience is clear which note is on top.

3 Beginning at the point of the V use your two first fingers to start rolling the notes together (illustration 1).

4 Continue rolling until only a small part of a corner of the lower note is visible on the table. When you reach this point stop rolling. More of the upper note will be sticking out as it began slightly further forward.

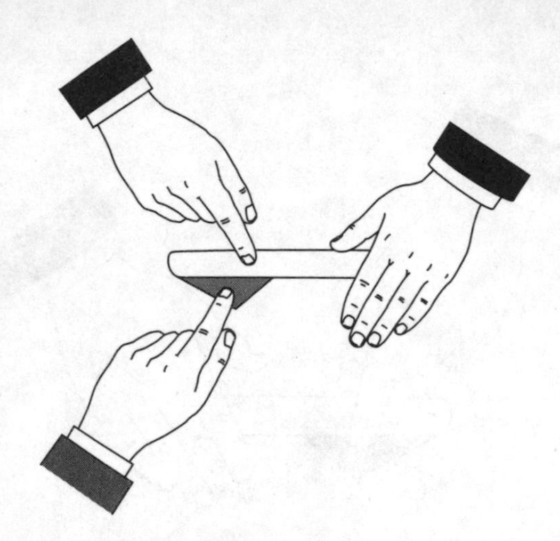

5 Cover the visible corner of the lower note with your left hand. Do this while your right finger points to the corner of the upper note sticking out on the right (illustration 2). Ask a spectator to place a finger on the corner on your right (illustration 3).

6 As they do this, secretly roll the notes forward slightly. Under cover of your left hand, the left corner will flip around the roll – it will go under the rolled up notes and flip back on to the table in its original position. This is the secret move which makes the trick work.

7 Lift your left hand and ask the spectator to place a finger from their other hand on that corner.

8 Point out to the audience that the corners of both notes are now being pinned to the table. Explain this makes any trickery impossible – unknown to them it has already happened!

9 Unroll the notes towards you and show that – incredibly – the two notes have passed through each other. The note that was on top is now below (illustration 4).

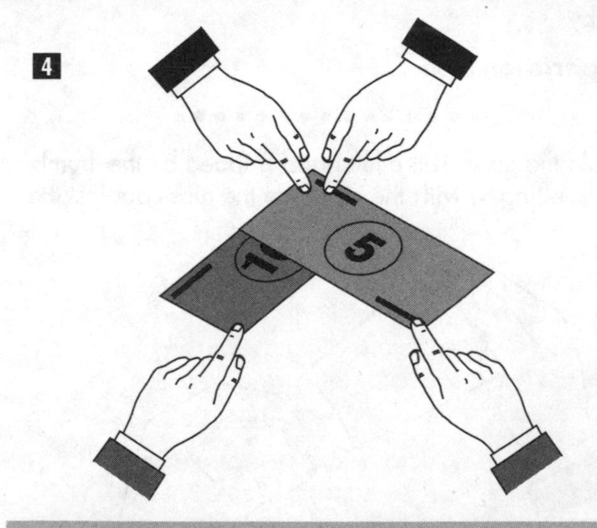

TOP TIPS FOR TRICKSTERS

With a few well practised coin tricks which you can perform with any coins you will always be able to entertain friends any time, any place, anywhere!

Effect A borrowed coin penetrates through the bottom of a glass tumbler, ending up trapped inside.

Requirements Any coin (the heavier the better) and a smooth-sided glass tumbler. It is more effective if these are both borrowed. This is a great trick to do in a bar or at the dinner table with an empty glass that is sitting nearby.

Preparation None.

•••••••••••••••

1 Hold the glass in the left hand gripped by the thumb and little finger, with the mouth of the glass against the

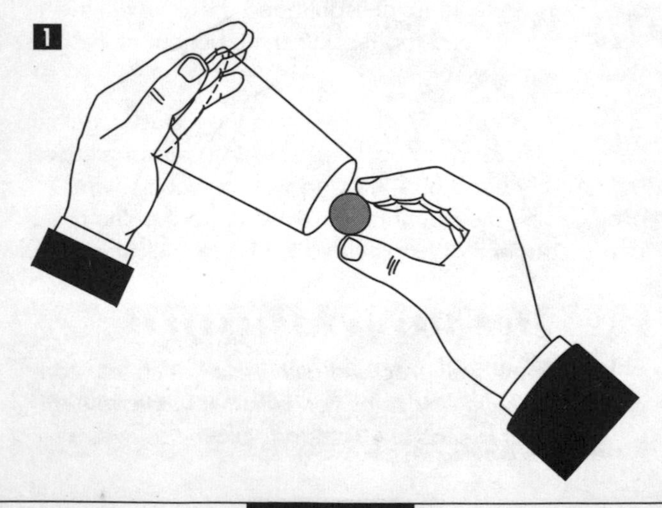

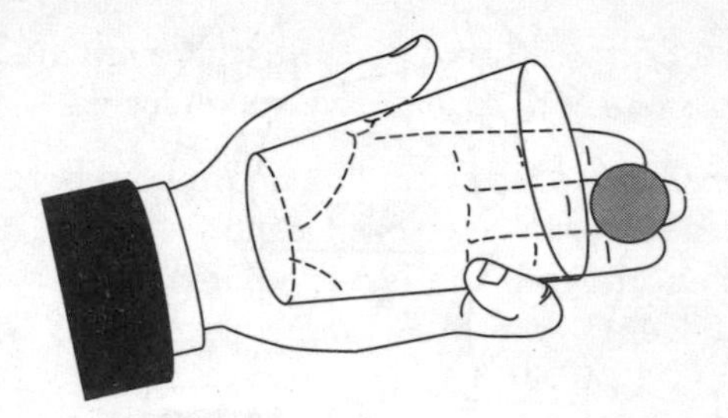

left palm. It is important that the other fingers can be moved without disturbing the grip on the glass.

2 Display the coin in the right hand. Hold it with the right fingertips and tap it against the bottom of the glass (illustration 1).

3 Part the hands and quickly bring them back together. As your hands come back together the coin is released by the right hand and, moving with the momentum provided by the right hand, travels in front of the glass and is caught by the extended left fingers (illustration 2).

TOP TIPS FOR TRICKSTERS

Money magic is not particularly suitable for an audience of young children as they may not be familiar with currency or its value.

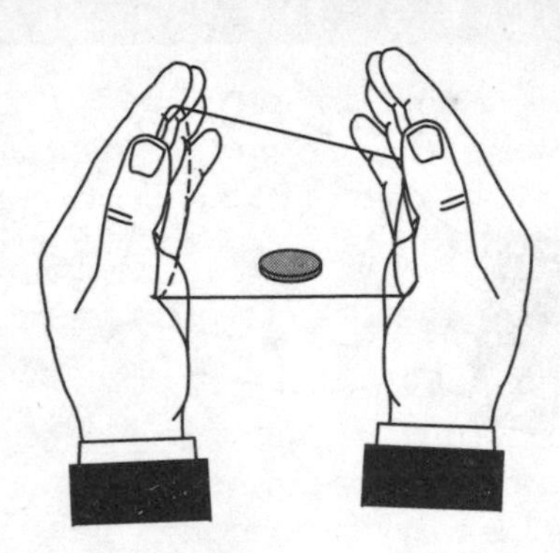

4 As soon as the left hand catches the coin it moves to the left, then jerks back to the right causing the coin to fly inside the glass. At the same time the right hand slaps against the bottom of the glass (illustration 3).

5 Because the coin travels too fast for the eye to follow, it appears to the audience that the coin has visibly penetrated through the bottom of the glass.

PENN AND TELLER

This outrageous American duo have shocked audiences around the world with their "sick tricks" and upset many magicians. They began their performing careers as street entertainers and are now in demand for TV shows and live performances – and have even made their own movie – Penn and Teller Get Killed.

MYSTERY OF THE SEALED BOX

Effect *An empty matchbox is shown and placed in the centre of the table. The magician places a coin under the table. The coin vanishes from under the table and can be heard appearing inside the closed matchbox!*

Requirements *A regular matchbox and two identical coins.*

Preparation *Slide one of the coins between the bottom of the tray and the outer cover. Close the match-box, keeping the coin concealed in its hiding place (illustration 1).*

•••••••••••••••

1

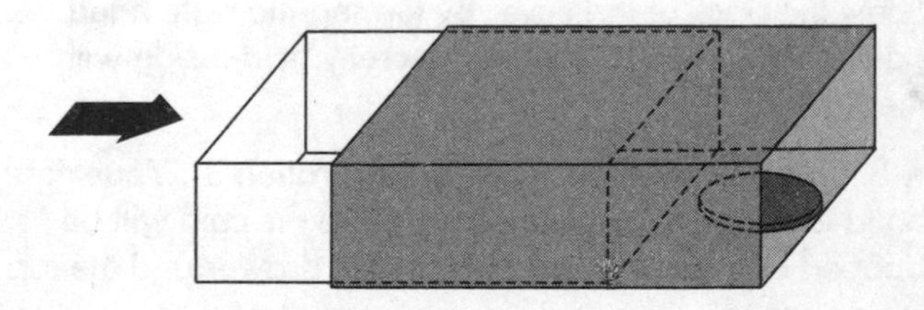

1 Slide out the drawer of the matchbox with the left hand. Hold the outside of the cover with the right hand, palm up.

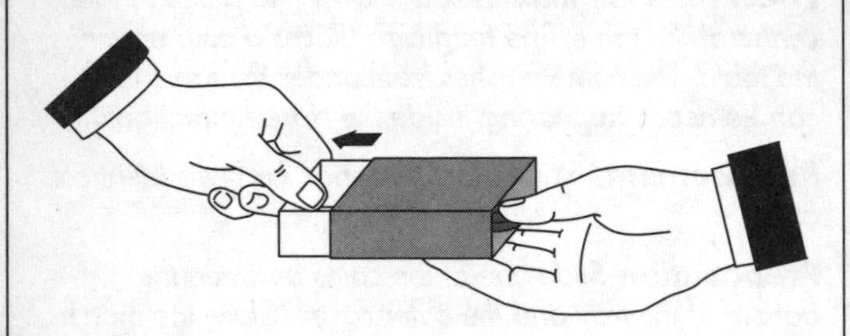

2 As the drawer slides out, move your right thumb inside the cover on top of the concealed coin (illustration 2).

3 Pull the drawer out of the cover and show it is empty. Show the back of the cover by turning the right hand palm down, keeping the coin secretly held inside with the right thumb.

4 Slide the drawer back inside (illustration 3). Your right hand is still palm down and therefore the coin will be trapped between the top edge of the drawer and the top

TOP TIPS FOR TRICKSTERS

Be warned! When people discover you are a magician they may say, "If you're a magician produce some money then!" Now you can!

of the cover (illustration 4). While the drawer is open the coin will stay in this position, but when pushed shut the coin will be heard dropping into the drawer. Place the box with the open drawer on the centre of the table.

5 Take the duplicate coin under the table with your right hand and tap it against the underside of the table. Show that your left hand is empty and lift up the matchbox from the table.

6 Under the table your right hand slides the coin into your sock!

7 The left hand brings the matchbox down on the table and at the same time pushes the drawer closed. The coin can be heard dropping inside the matchbox.

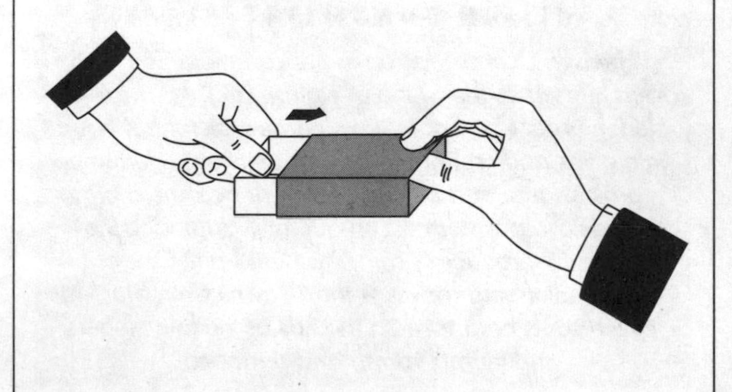

8 Bring out your right hand to show it is empty, and ask someone to open the box to prove that the coin really has arrived inside.

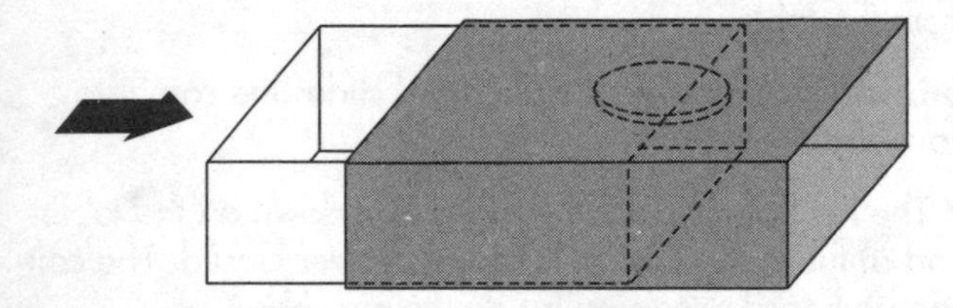

T. NELSON DOWNS (1867-1938)

T. Nelson Downs was an American magician who billed himself as the "King of Koins" (sic). As a railway clerk he spent his spare time learning sleight of hand with coins and creating his own variations. He turned professional and almost overnight became a big vaudeville star with his unique and original act of apparently producing coins from mid-air. One of his most challenging moves is the "Downs Coin Star" in which coins balanced on the tips of the four fingers and thumb vanish and re-appear.

GLASS THROUGH TABLE

Effect The magician covers a coin on the table with a glass. To conceal the coin the glass is covered with a napkin. The magician says that the coin is going to vanish. This doesn't happen, but when a spectator slaps down on the napkin-covered glass it squashes flat! The glass has penetrated through the table!

Requirements A smooth-sided drinking glass, two paper napkins and any coin (this could be borrowed).

Preparation For this effect to work you must be sitting at a table. Prepare by setting the props out in front of you on the table.

• • • • • • • • • • • • • • •

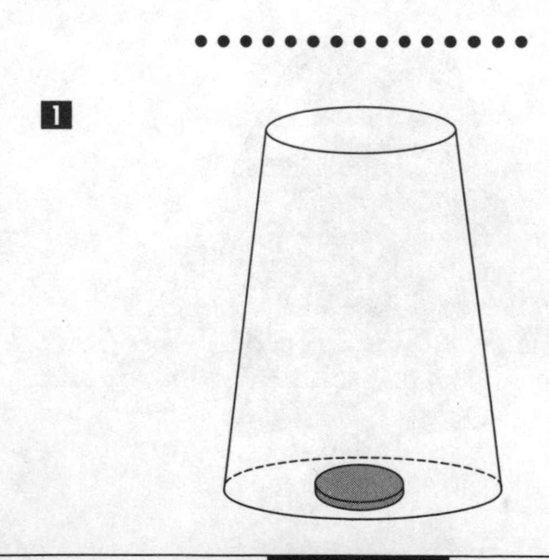

1 Explain to the audience that you are going to attempt to pass a solid object through the table top.

2 Place the coin on the table about 30cm/12in from the rear edge and cover it with the upturned glass, isolating the coin inside (illustration 1).

3 Open out the two napkins and lay them on top of each other covering the glass (illustration 2). Explain to the audience, "The coin must be covered to keep the secret!"

4 Pull the napkins down around the outside of the glass to show its outline and with one hand twist the glass tightly inside the napkins to show its shape more clearly (illustration 3).

2

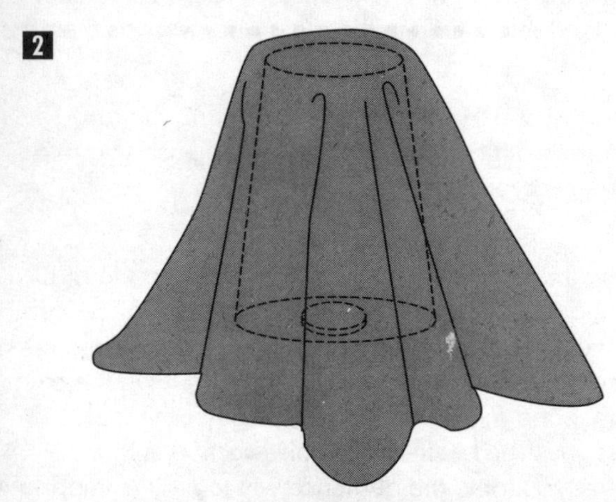

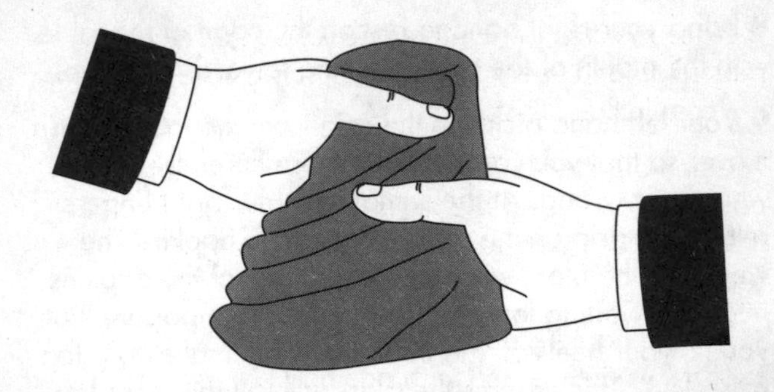

5 Lift the glass and napkins together to show the coin is still on the table. Replace the glass and napkins over the coin.

6 Ask everyone to concentrate on making the coin penetrate through the solid table. If you wish you can even get everyone to hold hands to form a "power circle"!

7 Lift up the glass and napkins together with the right hand and look suprised and disappointed that the coin is still there. Your left hand moves towards the coin to pick it up. While the audience's attention is on the coin, the right hand moves back to the edge of the table nearest you. The basic rule of misdirection is that wherever you look, the audience will look. It is important throughout the next few steps that you keep looking at the coin, not at your right hand.

8 Bring your right hand to rest on the edge of the table with the mouth of the glass pointing towards your lap.

9 Your left hand picks up the coin from the table to turn it over so that you can look at it more carefully to see what went wrong. At the same time your right fingers relax their grip on the glass through the napkin. The weight of the glass will make it slide out of the napkins into your waiting lap (illustration 4)! It is important that you lift your heels off the floor slightly to make your lap a "valley". This ensures the glass will roll into your lap and not on to the floor!

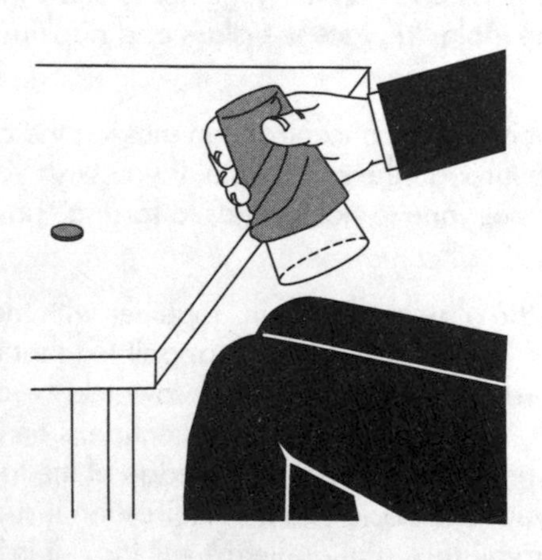

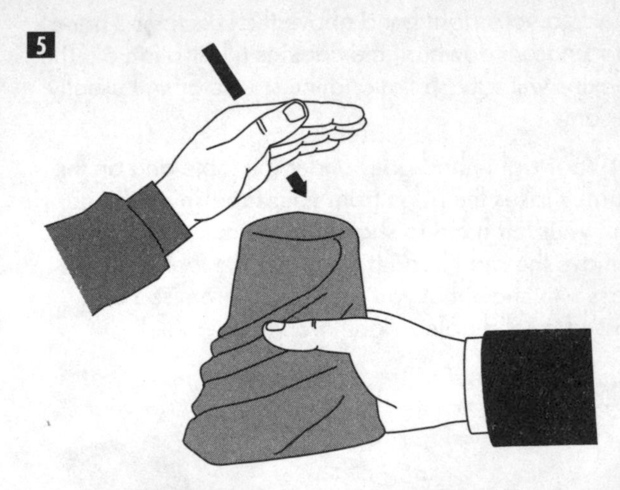

10 Hold the napkins gently in the right hand so that they keep the shape of the glass even though it is no longer there!

11 The left hand places the coin back in the centre of the table and the right hand covers it with the napkins as though they still contained the glass. To the audience it should appear that nothing has changed – the big suprise is coming in a moment!

12 "It didn't work," you say, "because I forgot to get someone to tap the top of the glass." Ask a member of the audience to hold their hand just above the napkins (illustration 5). Try to get someone for this who you think will respond loudly to the surprise.

13 Hold your right hand above the spectator's hand and smash it down on the napkins (illustration 6). The napkins will squash flat and the spectator will usually scream!

14 Your right hand goes under the table and on the journey takes the glass from your lap. Lift up the napkins with your left hand to show that the coin is still there. Remove the right hand from under the table with the glass – to show that you did as you promised and passed a solid object right through the table!

TOP TIPS FOR TRICKSTERS

Even the most famous stage illusionists know a few small coin tricks that they can perform to maintain their reputation when off-stage!

FEATURE ITEMS

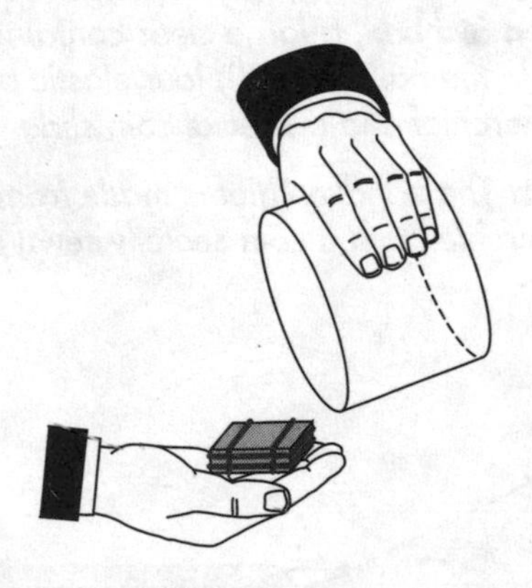

COIN IN THE BALL OF WOOL

Effect *This is in the miracle class, and when well rehearsed will make a great finale to any act or show you are putting on.*

A borrowed coin is marked. It vanishes while held by a member of the audience and appears inside a sealed matchbox which is wrapped in the centre of a ball of wool!

Requirements *A ball of heavy knitting wool, a regular sized matchbox, a large clear container (big enough to hold the ball of wool), four elastic bands, a special handkerchief and a special coin slide.*

Preparation *The handkerchief is made from any cotton handkerchief with a coin secretly sewn into one corner.*

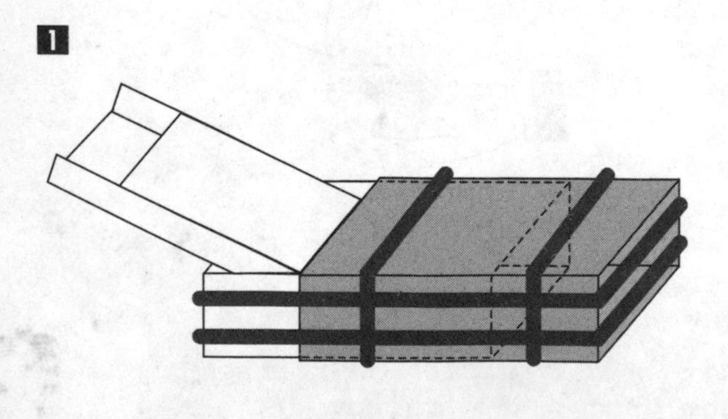

2

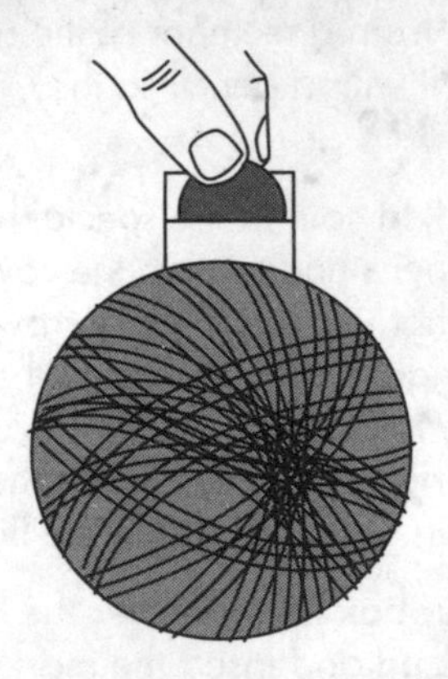

The coin slide is made from any piece of flat metal or cardboard. This is folded into a flat tube so that a coin can be dropped into one end and will slide down and out the other end. This is the secret prop for this effect.

Insert one end of the slide into the open drawer of the empty matchbox and wrap the four elastic bands around the matchbox as in illustration 1. The bands will hold the slide in position and close the box when the slide is removed.

Wrap the wool around the matchbox to form a ball with the matchbox hidden inside. Make sure the wool is not wrapped too tightly otherwise the slide may get stuck when you have to remove it at the crucial moment.

Place the prepared ball of wool out of sight on your table – inside a hat or large box is best.

1 Borrow a coin from a member of the audience and have them mark it with a pencil so they will recognise it in the future.

2 Wrap the marked coin in the special handkerchief. What really happens underneath the cover of the handkerchief is that you keep the borrowed coin finger-palmed in your right hand, and hand the secret sewn-in coin to a member of the audience to hold through the folds of the material. They will believe they are holding the borrowed coin wrapped inside the handkerchief.

3 Reach into your box (or wherever the ball of wool is) with your right hand and insert the marked coin in the coin slide (illustration 2). The coin will slide down into

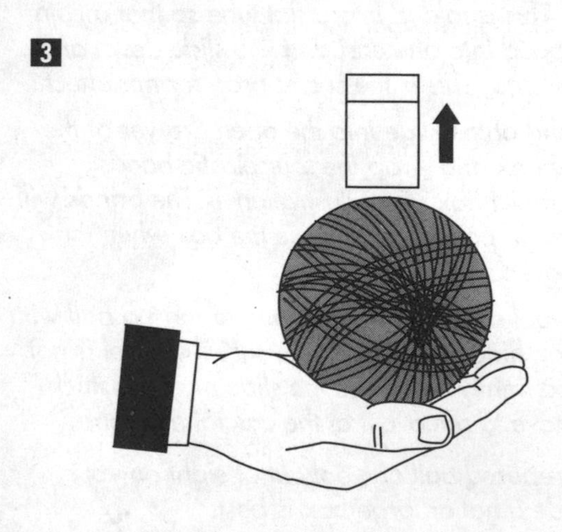

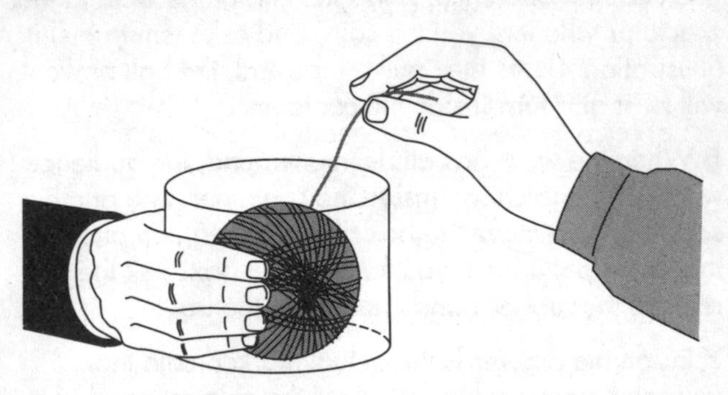

the matchbox wrapped inside the ball of wool. Pull the slide out of the ball of wool, leaving it in the box. Remove the ball of wool and put it in the clear container. Hand this to a spectator to hold.

4 Ask your "hanky holding helper" to stand up, and ask them if they are still holding on to the coin. After they have answered "yes" whip the handkerchief out of their hand and display it on both sides to show that the coin has vanished.

TOP TIPS FOR TRICKSTERS

The most important tip – which has been broken by every coin magician I know – is to be careful not to spend the fake coins you buy!

5 Ask the spectator holding the ball of wool to stand up and face the audience. Hand the end of the wool to the spectator who lent you the coin, and ask them to pull it (illustration 4). As they pull on the end, the ball of wool will twist and turn inside the container.

6 When the wool has all been unwound, the audience will see the matchbox inside the container. Ask another spectator to remove the box (illustration 5). Emphasise that at no point have you touched the box. Ask them to remove the rubber bands and open the box.

7 Inside the drawer is the actual marked coin that vanished moments before! Have the coin returned to its owner for verification and take your applause.

5

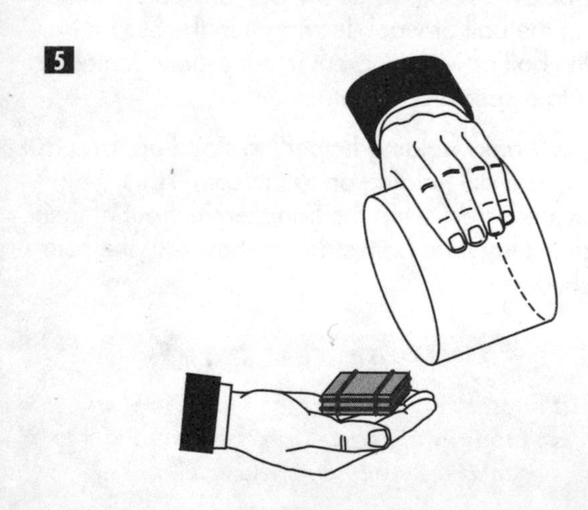